Norma Levine has published two books on Buddhist themes: ***Blessing Power of the Buddhas***, (1st edition Element Books, 1993; Brazilian edition 1997, reprinted in 2009 by Vajra Publications Nepal) and ***A Yearbook of Buddhist Wisdom***, (Quest, USA, Harper Collins UK, 1996, German edition Barthe, 1997).

She has organised pilgrimages to Mt. Kailash in Western Tibet and the hidden land of Pemako in Arunachal Pradesh (NE India), and written for some of the major London newspapers, **The Observer, The Times**, and **The Telegraph.**

She established a web based mail order business, Windhorse Imports in 1986 to provide Buddhist meditation artefacts to a growing community and sold it in 2003.

She has an M. Phil in drama and literature from the University of Toronto and completed a PHD thesis before escaping academic life to live in the book town of Hay-on-Wye on the Welsh borders, famous for its International Literary Festival. She divides her time between the UK and India.

Chronicles of Love and Death

CHRONICLES OF LOVE AND DEATH

My Years with the Lost Spiritual King of Bhutan

Norma Levine

Vajra Publications

Published by
Vajra Publications
Jyatha, Thamel,
P.O. Box 21779, Kathmandu, Nepal
Tel.: 977-1-4220562, Fax: 977-1-4246536
e-mail: bidur_la@mos.com.np
www.vajrabooks.com.np

Distributor
Vajra Books
Kathmandu, Nepal

Cover Photo
Shabdrung Rinpoche, Zanskar 1984, giving blessing

ISBN: 978-9937-506-48-9

Printed in Nepal

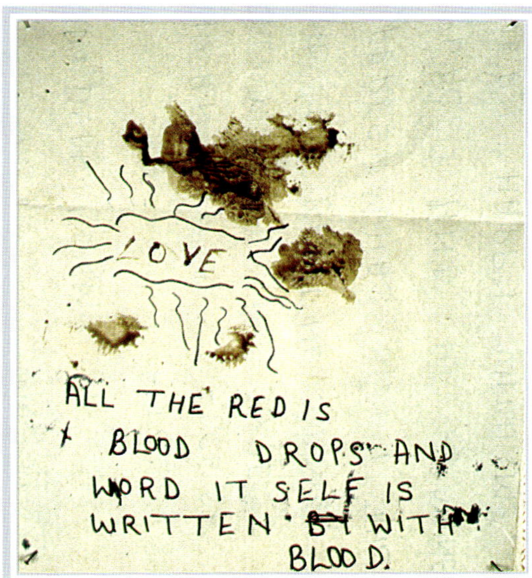

LOVE in blood on letter, 1980

Dedication

*To the Shabdrungs of Bhutan and
the restoration of their lineage*

TABLE OF CONTENTS

This is a true story of a spiritual journey and the incredible but all too human love between a Western woman and a high reincarnate Lama, the spiritual king of Bhutan. It is neither biography nor autobiography. It is a play that arose and disappeared like an illusion; a magical display of comedy and tragedy, history, romance, and transcendence.

Prologue

It was in the Black Mountains where the border between wild mystical Wales and green England divides Hay-on-Wye that my life changed. The ancient mountains worn low with time were spiritually alive in a way I'd never experienced in the virgin wilderness of Canada where I was born. An uncanny light split through the black clouds of the Gospel Pass as though the voice of God was about to roar through. It was 1972. I was in my mid-twenties when I realised we are free to choose the life we live.

That there was a price to pay was not something I could know, not then.

****

In Hay everyone had dropped out of something. I decided to drop out of academic life and not to receive a Phd. in drama. Theatre interested me but the curtain on the stage of my life was pulling open abruptly. It was the time of gypsy wagons and exotic bohemians. The king of the self-styled gypsies was the television playwright, Jeremy Sandford, author of ***Cathy Come Home***, who lived near Hay and travelled the open road in a gypsy caravan. Mark Palmer, whose mother was lady-in-waiting to the Queen, lived in a primitive cottage with his companion, a Somerset gypsy called Morris. It took half an hour for their blackened kettle to boil on the hearth but Roly, my boyfriend, and I enjoyed hanging out with authentic aristocracy. On market day Mark and Morris took the pony and trap to Hay, downed the local cider at The Three Tuns – a hobbit sized pub with yellowing adverts for babycham – and clip clopped back to their Welsh cottage through narrow lanes reeking of honeysuckle and wild rose.

In the mysterious way that things happened at that time, I stumbled upon a twenty-two foot long, two and a half ton showman's wagon made of mahogany with cut glass windows and mirrors, bow fronted cabinets, painted wooden solid rubber wheels, and a chrome plated, coal burning stove parked outside a mews at Swiss Cottage in London, and negotiated to buy it for seven hundred pounds. It had the name of the head showman on the letterbox – Mr Mellors. We transported it as far as the car park in Hay- on- Wye where it stayed while the locals gazed in wonder at it. The hill farmers with four-wheel-drive tractors kicked the hard tires and stared at the level of the storage boxes a few feet above the ground.

After a week of gutteral mutterings and high-pitched vowels, they decided it was sound enough to tow up the steep narrow mountain road to our impossibly romantic parking space on a hillside near a stream backing Hay Common. Mounting the summit of the steepest hill, its weight pulled the tractor backwards and my stately Edwardian dream home crashed into a soft bank, miraculously unhurt. Manouevring it into final position on the sloping hillside, it slanted dangerously without losing balance. Thus the wagon became a legendary landmark just down the road from the standing stones marking the ley lines of the fierce Black Mountains. Winter gales blew the door out of my hands when I went to fetch water from the stream.

My hair was wild and curly and I wrapped myself in a multi-coloured crocheted shawl over Afghani dresses or Victorian velvet blouses and jeans. Roly wore a Moroccan jalaba over a flannel collarless shirt and corduroy breeches held up by suspenders. On weekends we drove the Morris post office van to London where I sold trippy Moroccan glass bead necklaces on the Portobello Road. Roly played electric guitar with a Rastafarian group in South London, and worked occasionally as a carpenter.

We were among the first 'foreigners' to discover the self proclaimed Kingdom of Hay ruled by the eccentric book-king, Richard Booth. The town declared independence on April Fools Day 1977; with a drum roll parade through the streets, of ministers and courtiers, jesters and subjects. In King Richard's court was another April: April Ashley, the first sex change, known unofficially as Offa's Dyke.

King Richard was already a legend. He had married into the Yardley family briefly before buying up the local cinema, fire station, and Hay castle. He wandered around Hay looking befuddled, scratching his head and mumbling with his shirt tails hanging out, as if he had just got out of bed. He was not a businessman but a maverick with a passion for Hay, which beguiled and tantalized him like a woman who had got under his skin. Tales of his escapades were bandied around with wonder and amusement. One day in a Marx Brothers escapade he donned a dog collar and turned up as a vicar at Cheltenham Girls School to release the beautiful local vet's daughter from her sins. All this made great publicity and put Hay on the map but he didn't care about that. He did it because he was King of an eccentric independent kingdom.

Hay had the kind of charm money and planning can't buy. When you walked down the main street and looked into the windows, there was Hawkins the cobbler, Grant the stationer and Maddy the grocer, who delivered to your door and let everyone run up accounts. His florid face beamed with prosperity. Or was that flush due to the sudden increase in young girls, so lovely and free that squeezed past, pressing him against the counter? (Mrs Maddy wore a perpetual look of impending doom). Tony the fishmonger went on holiday to India with Lady Penelope Betjeman to examine erotic Hindu temple architecture. His brother John was a diplomat with a mysterious posting to the Seychelles. With all the ex-foreign office adventurers retired in the area, rumours of spies added an edgy mystique. Nobody was too surprised when Lady Penelope Betjeman drove her pony and trap into town to attend the Catholic mass on Sundays. She adopted a kindred spirit, called Mike the Meadow, because he lived in a bender on a meadow near Hay Common with his horse Taliesin and dog, Vajra. In perfect attunement with the times, they belonged to the same social stratum.

On market day you could see the hill farmers from the Black Mountains in corduroy breeches and heavy boots clustering on street corners, a woodbine tucked behind an ear. There was nothing the hill farmers wouldn't do for you and most of the time they did it for next to nothing. Tom Morgan lived with his sister Mary, no toilet, no electricity; Arthur Hope lived alone, kept his eggs in a drawer, and went to church every Sunday; Ted Greenow lived with his mother, Granny Greenow, in the garret of New Forest Farm, home of Viv Phillips, roadie for Traffic. People still talk of the times when Stevie Winwood, lead singer of Traffic, used to walk into the Blue Boar pub, and play piano as the mood took him.

Crossing the Wye from Clyro, you could see the perfect positioning of Hay Castle right in the centre of town with the streets and shops radiating towards it. With the Black Mountains protecting it from behind and the river snaking in front, Hay looked like a miniature Avalon, an enchanted kingdom under the spell of Welsh dragons and benevolent witches, hidden from all but those who had the fortune to be there at the right time. I was bewitched.

The Great Eastern Trucking Company on Broad St. opposite the clock tower had a big sun painted on a truck unloading outside the door. Inside were Afghani dresses, embroidered waistcoats, quilted jackets with dragons emblazoned on the back and, on a few shelves in the back room, jars of tahini, crunchy organic peanut butter, and packages of Jordan's organic flour. Bob and Monica, who had lived in Afghanistan, were the owners. Bob, who looked like an outlaw who had temporarily misplaced his rifle, pulled the women while Monica sold dresses.

Monica and Bob separated; and I took over the lease to start a natural food shop. I convinced Mr Evans, Barclays Bank manager, it was the right time for this daring enterprise, and he agreed to a two hundred pound overdraft. I drove the Morris van to Community Supplies in Camden Town and loaded it with sacks of brown rice, lentils, and boxes of dried apricots, dates and prunes. I opened the sacks and left them on the floor with scoops inside, impelling my small clientele of lifestyle pioneers to serve themselves – and don't forget to recycle your paper bags and jars!

Every weekday and Saturday, you could find me behind a massive glass topped mahogany counter bought from John Grant, the stationer, who was so startled that anyone should wish to buy his colossal Edwardian bygone that he let it go if for fifteen pounds. Behind me in neat rows were large glass sweet jars of herbs and exotic spices – vanilla pods, cinnamon sticks, liquorice sticks and a jar of mysterious sticky red Japanese plums – which no one was courageous enough to try, until Rosamonde bought a generous portion for her aunt's tea party. She watched their faces pinch horribly as they spat out the salty sour mess into their napkins. Macrobiotics swear by umeboshi plums, I assured her.

Mr Hitchcock, the grocer down the road, sold me a family heirloom, a biscuit counter with Carrs Biscuits written on the glass doors. I convinced the local baker to experiment with granary flour. Roly built shelves, and painted a sign 'Country Stores' that swung in the wind outside the shop. Freaky Pete painted the large windows with Beans Grains, Herbs Spices, Honey Oil, Seeds Nuts in an artistic curve. (Every summer passing tourists came in to ask what honey oil was.) I placed hanging baskets of asparagus and spider plants to create a feeling of natural abundance. On Radio 4 Women's Hour there was a program about the benefits of whole food and soon Country Stores was on the list for market day. I became known as Norma the Health.

The scope of the clientele was as various as Hay itself: farmers, gentry, alternative life-stylers, bookish eccentrics and tourists during the season. They were all careful not to handle the food, which was out in the open. One fateful day I caught sight of Kurt parking his powerful new Range Rover and striding across the road with his young companion; and I suppressed an urge to run into the back room, pull the curtains and lock the door.

Dressed in denim overalls and checked cap covering black wavy hair around a ruddy square jawed face, Kurt, an American, adopted the manner of a country squire. He fingered the box of dates and stuffed two into his gaping mouth. He chewed and grinned with devilish impudence before he drawled in a dramatically low voiced transatlantic accent, 'how are you'. His delivery turned it into an ironic statement, to which no answer was possible or required. As always, he was on an important mission and had no time to waste. He wanted Roly to come to the Wenallt (his farm) for an important assignment. He left a note with the words CONFIDENTIAL and URGENT in red letters underscored three times on the sealed envelope and strode out munching a handful of walnuts.

Kurt was married to a Scottish heiress called Maggie, quite beautiful in a queenly way, with long reddish hair, long legs and spaced out eyes as if she were seeing the world for the first time. Too much money and too much dope, I thought to myself dragging a half-hundred weight sack across the wooden floor. Maggie and I enjoyed a relationship of candidly expressed female competition. 'You're the only woman I was ever jealous of,' she would confide years later. 'You were beautifully dressed like a perfect little doll in your dainty Victorian petticoats. You looked like you'd never get your hands dirty; while I was stuck with babies and big milky breasts.'

Their improbable story went like this: Kurt was hitch-hiking through Scotland when he got picked up by Chogyam Trungpa, a young Tibetan Buddhist reincarnate Lama graduated from Oxford, who would later become a renowned teacher in the US. Trungpa took him to Samye Ling, a Tibetan Buddhist Centre on the Scottish borders, where he was guru to a growing number of 60's spiritual seekers. Among the many celebrities and hippies whom the brilliant Trungpa magnetised was Maggie Russell, the daughter of a wealthy Scottish businessman. Trungpa, who was fascinated by the British Raj, spotted the aristocrat in Maggie – whom he dubbed Queen of the Hippies – and asked her to marry him. She consented, although secretly she thought he was too little and rather weird. Kurt had his own designs on Maggie, and invited her to the Dylan concert at the Isle of Wight. They returned to Samye Ling to announce their engagement. On hearing the news, Trungpa went into a brief retreat and when he came out he consented to marry them.

With Maggie's money they bought a sixty acre hill farm in the Black Mountains for an undreamt of price. 'Ten thousand quid', the farmers muttered in wonder as they drank their pints at the Swan on market day. It was the highest price anyone had paid for hill land in Hay history; **and**, they nodded knowingly, houses were just bricks and mortar, not worth a penny more.

So the squire and his lady lived on Maggie's Farm keeping goats and bee-hives, selling cheese and honey, renting the land for sheep grazing to Arthur Hope and having babies. When Maggie finally awoke to the alarming reality of her marriage, the strident opening line of Dylan's song, 'I ain't gonna work on Maggie's Farm no more', from the fateful Isle of Wight concert, started to implode like an omen. It came crashing through the collective unconscious pointing straight at her for making the mistake of marrying Kurt, whom Trungpa called 'the black moon of Chicago'; instead of Trungpa himself, poet and warrior. She came to feel Maggie's Farm was her personally tailored prison, her karma for not recognising the most extraordinary Buddhist teacher of our generation.

Now Buddhism entered our lives.

To transcend their domestic confusion they turned Maggie's Farm into a Buddhist Centre. The Wenallt was renamed Karma Naro and given in trust to the Karmapa, said to be the greatest enlightened master of East Tibet. It was the omniscient Karmapa who foresaw the Chinese invasion and escaped to Sikkim in 1959 with his sacred treasures, amongst them, the legendary Black Hat, the very sight of which was said to liberate beings from intense suffering within seven lifetimes. In 1976 Kurt and Maggie's connection with Trungpa and Tibetan Buddhism re-emerged as a momentous event for us: an acceptance from the 16th Karmapa to come to Hay-on-Wye during his tour of the UK. The letter that Kurt placed on my glass-topped counter informed, commanded, instructed and cajoled Roly into building a throne for the glorious Karmapa.

Roly's throne was a labour of love, French polished panels, with steps leading up to its richly decorated summit: massive front and back cushions covered in sumptuous regal gold brocade. The throne took up about half the space of an impossibly small shrine room whose walls were already covered in sacred representations of deities on scrolls: some were black and bared their fangs while treading on human corpses, others were in blissful sexual union; some were pure and white radiating compassion and loving kindness.

For most people, "Tibetan Buddhism is a fabulously exotic construct, as remote and strange a religious tradition as any in the world, ineffably far away."[1] But to me these images were telling the unadorned truth about the raw energy of human emotions.

Another painting, the Wheel of Life, which I'd dismissed in fashionable hippie hallways as pretentious décor, now compelled me to have a closer look. A massive black, ferocious demon was holding a wheel divided into six sections in his gruesome fangs. 'That's Yama, the Lord

---

1 Peter Popham, The Independent, May 15, 2007

of Death,' drawled Kurt relishing his role as guide. 'He's holding the six realms of existence.' He pointed to the hells where small figures reminiscent of Hieronymous Bosch paintings were being tortured by heat and cold; then to the 'hungry ghosts' who were starving because their necks were too tight for any food to go down; and the animals who had to kill each other for survival. At the top of the wheel were indolent gods indulging in sensual pleasures like Hollywood superstars, encroached upon by titans who were fighting to break into paradise. In the centre was the human realm with people doing what people do: fighting, having sex, bargaining, being busy. 'It's all samsara', sighed Kurt dramatically, 'the world of delusion.'

At the hub of the wheel were a rooster, a pig and a snake frenziedly chasing each other. 'They represent passion, ignorance and aggression, the forces that drive samsara,' said Kurt. There were twelve figures on the rim of the wheel, each, he explained, interacting in a psychological chain reaction to drive us inexorably in an assembly line through perception, contact, craving, grasping and so on, to sickness, old age, death, and then rebirth repeating, perhaps at a different section on the wheel, the same obsessive patterns. I felt I was looking at a graphic depiction of the world, a psychological mappa mundi. Up and down endlessly on the wheel, like a game of snakes and ladders. For the first time I understood the meaning of life: it was to break through the chain reaction, to be liberated like the buddhas sitting serenely outside the wheel.

An immense powerful dragon with supernatural light coming through its body, which Trungpa had painted from a vision at a cave in Bhutan, occupied almost the entire wall on the other side of the shrine room.

Now picture a long maroon bus with Tibetan monks inside wending its way carefully through the narrow lanes towards a Welsh farmhouse near Hay. We watched as a middle-aged, broadly built man with receding hairline descended regally from the gold brocaded front seat, helped by his attendants. He paused for a long moment to look around at the dishevelled group holding white offering scarves and reciting his mantra, 'Karmapa Chenno'; then upwards towards the hills to the skyline; and smiled at the universe with every cell in his body. Thick clouds of juniper smoke filled the air as an offering to the great 16th Gyalwang Karmapa. An attendent carried a black silk hat-box containing the Black Hat.

In a frenzied briefing before Karmapa's arrival, Kurt told us the Hat was presented to the 5th Karmapa by the Emperor Yung Lo (circa 1405) who saw a non-material form of the crown above the Karmapa's head – said to be woven from the hair of one hundred thousand dakinis (enlightened female buddhas)- and had a material replica made. The Hat was a spiritual crown marking Karmapa as the Buddha of Activity for the Dark Age. So the spiritual King came to town – and just like that my life started to go in another direction, on every level.

Karmapa occupied the throne completely. He had a spiritual dignity that made it his rightful seat, just as the lion proclaims his natural dominion. His eyes seemed to cover all directions and dimensions: the people crammed together bursting out the doorway into the sitting room, the house, the Black Mountains right out through space and time. One of his eyes was noticeably smaller than the other and seemed to move independently.

I looked at this man who seemed to see everything. His body seemed unlike flesh and blood. He was as pure as the elements: wind, water, earth, air and space. (A photograph taken of him a few years later would show a blur of multicoloured lights instead of a solid body.) His expression changed constantly like clouds shifting across the sky. Sometimes he smiled with delight like a child; sometimes he stared wrathfully black as thunder. The force of his presence alone brought a hushed silence to Karma Naro. It felt like the tiny room had turned into a cathedral-like space. A muffled sob came from behind me; I turned round to look at Maggie, her face wet with tears.

A monk wearing a yellow fringed hat shaped like a half moon prostrated three times while the assembly started to chant a liturgy. The ritual master was piling rice onto a gold plate and offering it up to Karmapa. Two monks blew long Tibetan horns in a haunting wail so loud and long it startled thought patterns, blowing them away like clouds. The sound went beyond words into primordial memory. The Karmapa slowly opened the Black Hat-box, took the black heavy silk crown in his hand inspecting it with his gaze, and put it on his head holding it down with one hand, elbow up forming a salute. With the other hand he fingered a crystal rosary moving it deftly, twirling the beads around three times. The horns continued while he gazed with eyes that seemed to dissolve the fiction of time and the boundaries of space.

Time was standing still. There was a feeling of expansion, everything stretching like elastic; a sense of openness as if nothing were fixed or substantial. It was the experience of 'the world in a grain of sand …infinity in the palm of your hand and eternity in an hour."[2] Compassion was a presence you could almost touch.

The horns stopped, the rosary stilled. Karmapa removed the Black Hat and put it carefully back into the box. People got to their feet unsteadily and formed a queue holding white offering scarves and envelopes with offerings

---

2 Blake:Auguries of Innocence

while the monks chanted the mantra Karmapa Chenno: Karmapa know me. With lowered heads we went to the throne to receive a red cord with a knot in it that we tied around our necks. Karmapa looked at every person and truly seemed to know each one.

The experience of being fully complete, of oneness, in the eternal present was mystical: Karmapa showed it to us so powerfully that it was hard to miss. 'Words are liars,' said Karmapa in the final line of a commentary on ultimate wisdom.

Our close friend Graham looked dazed and for once, lost for words. A highly literate man who gobbled up everything from Shakespeare to Carlos Castaneda, Tolkein and Mervyn Peake, he had done peyote and macrobiotics in equal measure. He was shaking his head in wonder. Mike the Meadow, towards the end of the queue, was holding up his dog to receive Karmapa's blessing. Arthur Hope held his hat in his hand as if he were in church and went humbly before Karmapa like an angelic choirboy.

In the afternoon, Kurt informed us, there was to be an empowerment of Karma Pakshi, the second Karmapa, and I was invited to attend. It involved a commitment to the Buddhist path. In my heart I knew I was a Buddhist, but what did all these ceremonies mean?

'What is an empowerment? And who is Karma Pakshi? And why should I go?' I asked Jamgon Kongtrul, the young incarnate Lama accompanying the Karmapa. 'You don't need to understand it,' he replied beaming with great compassion. 'Just go.' He smiled so sweetly I felt I was with my original family at last: my tribe, people I could trust to the core. So I went.

Karmapa was on the throne this time wearing a ceremonial brocade hat. He recited a Tibetan text and suddenly he seemed to transform into another Karmapa, a yogi from another life. As he got down from his throne I looked down at his bare feet and then up to a skullcup in his hand. He took a long handled silver spoon and poured a small amount of liquid into our cupped hands; and as he moved from one to the other of us – there were only about seven people in the room – he was dancing joyfully like a wild yogi drunk on the nectar of liberation.

Before he left Karma Naro, Karmapa went up the mountain to the highest point of the land and buried a ritual dagger to empower it. He prophesied there would be a flourishing community one day in the future and claimed Karma Naro in the Black Mountains as his last 'black' acquisition. Nobody knew exactly what that meant, except that it was good.

The impact of the Karmapa was difficult to measure because it is impossible to pinpoint exactly what causes events to happen. But in the aftermath what happened was this: Kurt and Maggie's marriage fell apart. Kurt came out of the closet; Maggie went back to Trungpa. Arthur Hope would never forget 'that Tibetan man'. I became a serious Buddhist practitioner, as did Graham. However alien the meditations were to a Western mindset – prostrations to the great masters, rounds of mantras in Sanskrit and complicated visualisations – I plunged into it enthusiastically. Roly was determined to go to the East and find Karmapa at his monastery in Sikkim.

Two years later, in 1978, Roly and I went overland to India. We booked tickets on an express bus going to Athens, determined not to stop overnight after Istanbul until we got to Afghanistan. The plan was to meet Graham in Kabul.

With music from loudspeakers blaring day and night, we bumped along passing Venice until we got to Athens, where we boarded another bus to Istanbul stopping for one day to gaze in wonder at the Blue Mosque and get lost in the famous bazaar. As we passed through an eerily deserted town in Iran we were told that the Shah was fighting for supremacy and there had been a massacre of local people. He was deposed a year later

After nine days and nights we arrived in Kandahar and breathed a sigh of relief feeling safe for the first time. The fields were green, the poppies were in bloom and the people were gentle, generous and welcoming. We ate wholesome food, smoked the hubble-bubble, rested for a few days and moved onto Kabul, a primitive, bustling town with an economy boosted by the hippie culture. Mountain people walked proudly to market leading their donkeys, saddlebags loaded up with handmade carpets, silver jewellery, and apricots. At the Green Hotel on Chicken Street, we met Graham, as planned. To celebrate, we went to an opium parlour where I sampled a small quantity of opium and instantly slipped from my chair onto the floor.

In Jelalabad we sat in the famous rose gardens amidst the heady perfumes making a major decision: to move diagonally northwest to see the ancient massive stone Buddhas at Bamiyan and Band-y-Amir or to continue our progress eastwards over the Khyber Pass into Pakistan. We decided to go directly to Pakistan. Halfway between Jelalabad and the border, the bus driver picked up emergency news on the radio: the Russians were bombing Kabul. It was the last time anyone would be able to make the overland journey to India. The East was crashing behind us like a house on fire.

It was night as we stumbled exhausted off the bus in Lahore. A horse pulling a cart piled high with boxes fell in its tracks while a sweating wild-eyed man in soiled Pakistani pyjamas clubbed it. In the chaos of my screams, a hustler grabbed Graham's arm and took us to the 'best and cheapest' hotel, the Ringo Guesthouse. He arranged a free massage; Graham hung up his money belt, fell asleep and discovered when he awoke that his money had mysteriously vanished. The hotel management promptly proposed a rescue package. They would make a special pair of shoes. Graham would wear the shoes across the border into India, go to an address in Delhi, take off the shoes and receive his payment. Can't say fairer than that, said the manager benignly. We took a bus to the border and unnoticed, walked the line between Pakistan and India, before continuing by train to Amritsar.

Graham's mind had been working constantly since the incident. He would not deliver the shoes to the address in Delhi. We would go straight to Dharamsala, and in the peaceful Buddhist environment of the Dalai Lama it would come to him – the next step in clearing his karmic account sheet of mind-bending drugs.

Mr Nawrojee, the stationer at the bus stand in the town square, had been in McLeod Ganj during the British Raj. His Edwardian glass topped counters filled with yellowing newspapers were strangely reminiscent of Country Stores. Mrs Nawrojee floated in and out trailing swirls of saree silk, her face covered in ghostly white powder. A Mem Sahib sensing the decline of her species, she lived in the shadows between the sun's rays.

Mr Nawrojee directed us up the hill to Balcony House, a rustic wooden structure on two floors, which he would rent for a very modest amount per week. Within days Graham had figured out a strategy. His adventure, comically narrated with literary allusions, was a crowd pleaser. His spellbound audience agreed to smoke just one joint each, and let the rest go up in flames. On an astrologically auspicious day the ritual bonfire of the vanities took place and Graham was re-born. He bought a primus stove, an apple pie tin, an oven and some paper plates and set about making apple pies to sell in the bazaar every day. As the fame of apple pie man spread throughout the hill station, each day was a sell-out.

After a month, the pleasures of breakfast at Last Chance Café – where the astrologers gathered to discuss impending disasters while the freaks smoked chillums – were wearing thin. We had come to India to find Karmapa, not to hang out aimlessly with the hippie scene; but none of us had enough money to get to Sikkim at the far northeastern corner of India. And there had been no reply to our letters addressed to His Holiness Karmapa at Rumtek Monastery.

Just as I was beginning to make plans to return, a reply to my letter arrived from the abbot of Samye Ling Buddhist Centre in Scotland.. The letter advised me to go and see Tai Situ Rinpoche, the heart-son or intimate disciple of the Karmapa, and gave me his address near Bir in the Kangra Valley three hours bus ride from Dharamsala.

In the life-stories of the Tibetan masters there are accounts of meeting the guru, the arduous journeys to get there, how the very name of the guru makes one's hair stand up on end. I thought they were exaggerations. But I could feel my scalp tingling at the name Tai Situ Rinpoche, and I felt a crazy burst of excitement. I literally jumped on the next bus and reached Bir as the monsoon rains were gathering for the evening downpour.

In the morning I followed a village boy who took me on the long forest road to Sherabling. Vultures as large as farmyard geese took off from the treetops overhead and landed with a thud. I could hear the sound of jackals in the distance. Rhododendrons were dotted into the pine trees, flashing pinpricks of red long past their season. At mid-day we arrived.

Tai Situ was sitting on a modest sized cushion quite close to the ground opposite an old man who seemed to be his guardian, in a building that was in a construction site. He was very young and beautiful with wide-spaced eyes and smooth light gold skin. His gold silk shirt and monk's robes looked somehow stylish. He beckoned to me. We talked for hours like old friends who had not seen each other for years, until I felt I had known him all my life and he was closer to me than my mother. The words we spoke were just ordinary words and the conversation, though intimate, was the kind of exchange one has with best friends. But such limitless love and joy radiated from him, it filled my heart with happiness. At that moment Tai Situ appeared as a beloved saviour, someone whose very presence could charge my mind with enlightened power and lift me up forever. I fell into spiritual love, the most powerful emotion there is.

I took out a Buddha statue I had bought in Delhi and asked him to bless it. He opened up the bottom, filled it with special substances, sealed it, and performed a small ceremony empowering it, he said, with the essence of the Buddha. A month later on an extremely dangerous bus journey from Kashmir to Ladakh, the statue, wrapped in a cloth inside my handbag, mysteriously disappeared. Strangely, the cloth remained. I could not imagine how it had been removed and stolen; but when I returned to Sherabling later that summer and narrated the extreme dangers of the journey, Tai Situ explained it had dematerialised, and that was 'good, very good'. The empowered Buddha statue, it seemed, had saved our lives, its materiality consumed in the process. However alien to everything I'd known, this resonated deeply inside me. I wanted to learn more and realised beyond doubt that Tai Situ was my Guru.

Graham and Roly arrived and also forged a strong connection with Tai Situ. We were part of a growing community of Westerners who were magnetised by his expansiveness, his curiosity about Western culture, his loving-kindness. Tai Situ wrote lyrics, which Graham put to music and sang in a post Dylan twang at picnics with the Tibetan monks. Songs with titles like Cosmic Mandala, Street Buddha and Little Boy from Tibet.

We thought of Tai Situ as our precious spiritual brother. He gave us the best rooms in the centre of the courtyard complex, within the inner sanctum of the monastery. In the late afternoon, he came into the courtyard and threw a frisbee with the young monks. At Diwali, the festival of lights marking the Hindu New Year, he lit fireworks, each explosion bursting flowers into the black autumn sky. In the early morning we saw him walk the path that led to the cement toilet and shower cubicles in a white towelling robe, his face luminous as a full moon.

It felt like we had walked into a magic circle ruled by a benevolent king; and words like confusion, frustration, loneliness, anxiety and illness had been banished forever from the realm.

I was in Tai Situ's shrine room one autumn evening. As the chanting of the monks and the shrill music of Tibetan trumpets proclaimed the mystical hour before sunset, I asked my Guru to explain tantric sexual union, an esoteric practice involving the physical union of male and female partners in meditation.

'There are three mudras or seals', he said. I understood this to mean there were three ways to engage with the practice of tantric union. 'There is karmamudra,' he said, 'which is union with a woman. There is samayamudra, which is union with a dakini. And then there is mahamudra, the great gesture.' He looked at me intently and held my attention with his gaze of great loving-kindness.

'I understand the first two unions, but how does mahamudra fit into it?' I asked.

He seemed to be waiting for the question. 'It is like this,' he said. I saw him enter a zone of intense high energy, like an eagle gathering the totality of its power into itself before plummeting hundreds of feet to pick up a small object from the ground. At the same time, I felt my energy moving upwards until we seemed to meet in open space. His expression was naked, his eyes moist. In that gap it felt like both of us had dissolved the personal level. We gazed at each other wordless, profoundly still for minutes. I watched the play of light in his face, the movement of sensuality in his mouth, the expression of spontaneity in his whole being. It was mahamudra, the great gesture. This meeting of minds changed my life.

A few days before I was due to leave India, Tai Situ gave me a simple piece of paper for my birthday with four lines drawn on it. He explained what it meant.

'The four great rivers – birth, old age, sickness and death.'

'That's pretty basic stuff,' I said.

'Yes,' he replied, 'that's what deluded existence is.'

Later I found the poem that went with it:

Four great rivers
Taking away your freedom
Who realizes is free
And plays in the garden
Flourishing in all dimensions.

The experience of non-solidity, of lightness arising from the meeting of minds lasted for two months after I returned to Hay-on-Wye. My shop, my home, my partnership with Roly (who remained in India) was in upheaval. None of it affected me emotionally, as if it were happening to someone else. I sorted things out, made plans to renovate the showman's wagon, sell it and sell the shop. By the end of the summer I had sold the showman's wagon and the lease on the shop for enough money to buy a modest house in Hay. I had no hesitation in sacrificing all normal security and moving to India. All I wanted was to receive the precious teachings that could liberate in one lifetime.

I ordered champagne and invited thirty friends to a celebratory dinner at a new club in Hay. In front of a fireplace with flamboyant owner Ellie on piano, we drank champagne and dined on mussels and guinea fowl. By midnight the decade long party in Hay was over. It was November 1979.

My yearning for transcendence had become more intense over the year. Nothing could diminish my longing for the ideal of sacred love that had been awakened at the core of my being. The meeting of minds with Tai Situ had demonstrated pure non-physical union. But there was also, as he pointed out, physical union called karmamudra, expressed in the embrace of male and female buddhas: the union of compassion and wisdom, bliss and emptiness. Their eyes met in a gaze that was filled with rapture. They were lovers who had drunk the elixir of eternal wisdom and were saturated with bliss.

That was what I was seeking – the secret method that transformed passion into compassion and wisdom, the alchemy of enlightenment. Sacred love.

Act One

"Making mistake after mistake I walk the unmistaken path."
(Khenpo Tsultrim Gyamtso)

CHAPTER 1

THE MARRIAGE PROPOSAL

Mandi, Himachal Pradesh, India 1980

Shabdrung Ngawang Jigmai, the exiled spiritual king of Bhutan, looked at himself in the mirror on the veranda of Bijai Palace, the crumbling remains of what had once been the Dalai Lama's temporary residence. I watched him, invisible for a moment, before climbing the stairs to the veranda.

It was a late autumn afternoon in Northern India with a hint of impending darkness, but I could see him tying and untying a blue scarf around his large head, inspecting every part of his reflection. He was wearing a tight, ill-fitting jacket, which hugged his massive chest and hips struggling to reach his short, heavy thighs. His face was broad with a prominent nose, full sensuous lips and fearless mocking eyes. He touched his moustache, an as yet undefined accessory, which seemed to preoccupy and bemuse him. His body, like a tightly packed container, rested on two small delicate feet. Whirling around abruptly, he stretched out his hand to greet me. 'Aha, why did you take so long?'

The question seemed to come from someone who was neither man nor boy, but a force field of magnetic male energy. I was taken aback. There had been no prior contact, no arrangement, or plan.

I grasped the outstretched hand in front of me feeling its warmth, the broad smoothness of the young firm palm. He pressed my hand vigorously until the rings on my fingers scrunched together. A strange feeling passed through my mind: this was someone new in his body but old in his mind.

'I am Jigmai', he said without hesitation.

'It means fearless,' I replied.

'No. That is Jig-me. My name is Jig-mai. It means indestructible'.

'Just Jigmai?' Graham asked.

'Well, you see', he said pointing to his makeshift turban, 'sometimes I am Man Singh. But you can call me Jigmai. It's good enough for now. No formality.'

We entered the house, passing a small room where four men were sitting on narrow cots playing cards and smoking beadies – rough tobacco rolled up in a leaf. The guards looked carefully at Graham's tangled untrimmed beard. He was wearing Pakistani pyjamas, held up by a string gathered at his waistline, a loose long sleeved collarless shirt and heavy leather sandals. And then they stared at me, in body hugging stretchy trousers and sporty velour top that shamelessly revealed hips and thighs, my long hair faultlessly layered. I had no idea of the sexual signals my Western clothing was giving out. We entered a moderately sized cement room furnished with solid, second-hand institutional furniture and sat on a chintz-covered sofa. A young Himachal boy with rosy cheeks and dark curious eyes brought tea. Jigmai was sitting in a comfortable upholstered chair.

We introduced ourselves and said that we had heard about him from Chloe, an English woman living high in the mountains above Mandi. She told us he wanted intelligent company. He had a deep resonant laugh, which resounded like a clap of thunder. Two of the beadie-smoking bodyguards said something to him in Hindi. 'I must go now.' He excused himself hastily. 'Guruji is waiting. Take dinner with me tonight. I'll meet you at the Raj Mahal at 8 pm.'

The Raj Mahal, considered the best hotel in Mandi, was situated in the centre of town within a walled garden. We sat near a bougainvillaea hedge, inhaling the scent of jasmine and magnolia, while waiters scuttled around our table. 'Namaste Maharaj', 'Namaste Prince,' they greeted Jigmai. A few passersby – could have been school friends – called him Man Singh.

'One – no, two pecks of whisky on the rocks,' he commanded.

'Will you join me? I don't think you are a nun are you?' he said, his eyes taking in my lip gloss, my long thick chestnut hair and the gold hoops in my ears. I felt his gaze spread over my body. The muscles in the pit of my stomach quickened with excitement. 'I'll join you in a whisky, but I'll have it neat, no ice.'

'And Mr Cottrell?'

'Just a lassi, thanks' said Graham firmly. 'I've taken vows, no intoxicants.' He rescued his tattered cotton shawl from the ground and threw one end over his shoulder.

'Your diet is very strict, Mr Cottrell. I suppose you are Milarepa.' Jigmai looked at the large wooden rosary beads hanging prominently on Graham's chest and laughed uproariously downing his whisky in one go. The ice crackled as he banged his empty glass emphatically on the table, summoning the waiter. 'Hanji, one more, no, two more pecks.'

'Now tell me' he said, emboldened by the alcohol. 'You are foreigners, but you are Buddhist. How does a foreigner become a Buddhist?'

'We met Karmapa in Wales', said Graham. He performed the Black Hat ceremony in a room big enough for about ten people. I was reading Don Juan,' he explained to Jigmai, 'a series of books about a Mexican shaman who advocates the use of hallucinogenic mushrooms to reach higher consciousness. But when I met Karmapa, it all changed. I'd had no experience of anything like it – he was a Buddha.'

'I was studying drama', I said, 'researching a doctoral thesis on an English playwright.

'I also went for BA in literature,' Jigmai interrupted excitedly, 'at Mandi College'. "All the world is stage," he quoted. 'What do you think?' He riveted his gaze on me.

I hesitated a moment and then quoted from *The Tempest*. "We are such stuff as dreams are made on, and our little life is rounded with a sleep."

He looked impressed. 'You will have to teach me.' His eyes sparkled momentarily.

'Actually, a lot of Shakespeare is very Buddhist,' said Graham.

'We wanted to see Karmapa again', Graham continued, 'so we journeyed overland to India to go to his monastery in Sikkim. Through a series of accidents too intricate to explain at this very moment, we ended up in Dharamsala and found our way to Sherabling, the monastery of Tai Situ, Karmapa's heart son. He is also extraordinary, very young and friendly. He is supposed to reincarnate as the future Buddha, Maitreya, I am sure you would like him; in fact, you should meet him' he added. 'He made us feel we belonged there, so we stayed.'

'I went back to Wales,' I continued, 'sold everything and came to live in India. I want to practice the dharma, to receive the precious teachings from my Guru.'

'It's far more strange that we are sitting here talking to the real king of Bhutan. All our karmas have converged in this moment,' said Graham, leaning back in his chair like an Oxford don amazed at the birth of a new thought. His large rimless spectacles seemed to hum with intellectual speculation. He looked at Jigmai earnestly 'Did you ever meet the Karmapa?'

'I was recognised by the 16th Karmapa,' Jigmai replied quietly. 'I don't remember how it happened, it was not formal, but later I found out he had said, 'He is the one.' Actually, they tried to make him recognize a false Shabdrung but he refused. "He is the rightful one," he said, "I cannot recognize another." Please keep this secret', Jigmai requested.

He swallowed the rest of his whisky, a tight concentration appearing around his eyes. 'Ngawang Namgyal, the first Shabdrung of Bhutan, was a very great spiritual master; he created the kingdom of Bhutan. He was an artist, an administrator, a politician, and a great meditator. But not just meditator', Jigmai paused. 'A mahasiddha. How do you call someone like that?' he asked Graham. 'There is a name in English.'

'Accomplished yogi. Man with miraculous powers', he added.

'No, a combination, someone who is many things,' Jigmai explained.

Ah yes,' said Graham as coolly as a contestant in Brain of Britain, 'a renaissance man.'

'Yes, that's it, Jigmai replied triumphantly. 'He defended Bhutan from Tibet – the invasions of the 5th Dalai Lama. He just sat in his cave and called on the protectors to help. The protectors are very strong in my lineage.'

But you know', Jigmai looked at us with utter candour, 'the bare facts,' … he looked playful, 'the harsh reality' –

the phrase appealed to him; he hesitated, looking for another.

'The unadorned truth', Graham suggested, 'the bottom line,'

'The nitty gritty,' I added.

'The naked truth,' Jigmai said, exultant at hitting the right words, 'is that I am here now, sitting with you at the Raj Mahal in Mandi, the incarnation of Shabdrung Ngawang Namgyal, and I have nothing. Not even this body is mine.'

He talked as we drank, the night enclosing us like a blanket. For centuries the remote Himalayan kingdom of Bhutan was ruled by a succession of reincarnate spiritual kings, enlightened beings known as the Shabdrungs. In 1907 a powerful warlord of the most dominant secular tribe wrested control away from them and established a hereditary monarchy. The Shabdrung of the day was murdered in 1931, a silken scarf shoved down his throat. Since then, in order to maintain their control, the rulers of Bhutan had murdered the Shabdrung reincarnate when he was still a child. In 1957 Jigmai was born. He was now twenty-four, the longest a Shabdrung had lived for fifty years.

'I heard the story about the first murder in 1931,' I told him. 'It's terrible. How could they be Buddhist and still murder the great spiritual king?' I asked.

'Yes, one later incarnation was killed also,' he replied casually.

'That's how the hereditary kingship began?'

'Ummmm. Yeah.' The alcohol now coursing visibly through his blood, he bellowed his laughter. But it was chilling, more like a war cry.

Pondering this extraordinary story of being reborn, each time to be murdered, I found myself asking a question, which astonished even me. ’Why could you not just stay away longer instead of coming back into all this mess? I mean, not come right back, stay out of the body for a while?’ I asked.

He smiled gently at my ignorance. ‘It doesn’t work that way.’

He jiggled the ice in his glass and downed the whisky like an actor in a B movie. ‘When I was four years old my uncle took me out of Bhutan and gave me to the Indian government for safe keeping. It was during the border war with China. I walked for many days – I still remember it – my feet were swollen and blistered. Sometimes they carried me; sometimes I rode on a horse. After some time, we crossed the border into Arunachal Pradesh, to Tawang Monastery.’ He stopped to recapture a memory. ‘I remember chasing the chickens.’ He picked up a bottle of ketchup from the table as if to launch it at an invader and laughed victoriously. ‘Bloody chicken!’

Graham joined in the laughter. ‘It sounds like you were very naughty.’

‘Yes, the Lamas tried to teach me but I refused to study.’ His eyes narrowed, becoming cold and fierce. ‘These bloody Lamas, they know how to prostrate and offer white scarves, but they’re playing politics.’ He looked at us registering the effect of his words. We were plainly out of our depth. ‘My family is the blood line of Chengage Khan’, he proclaimed triumphantly.

‘You mean Genghis Khan?’ Graham said.

‘Yes, Chengage Khan’ **and**, he added with relish, ‘Drukpa Kunley. You know Drukpa Kunley?’

Drukpa Kunley was a famous Bhutanese yogi, who is said to have left marks on the rocks in Bhutan using his penis like a wand. We were on familiar ground once again, the miraculous legends of outrageous Buddhist saints. I marvelled at the bloodline of Genghis Khan and Drukpa Kunley! Then, a moment of sexual curiosity: did he inherit the ability of his yogic predecessor?

'I stayed in Tawang', Jigmai continued, 'until I was nine. Then the Indian government brought me to Himachal Pradesh, to Tso Pema. Many people heard about me and came for blessing. But I was under strict protection of the Indian Government. They didn't want me killed again.'

'You mean if China tried to annex Bhutan like India did to Sikkim, they were holding the rightful king?' asked Graham.

'Well played, Mr Cottrell.'

'So you're a pawn in the game.' Graham concluded.

'How did the people react to all this? 'I asked perplexed at the cover-up.

'All of Bhutan is with me', Jigmai said emphatically. The people want their king back.'

'Did you have your monks around you?' I asked, looking for domestic details to flesh out this epic tragedy.

'Not really,' he drawled ironically, 'just Guruji. But he's crazy.'

'Did you have anyone to play with?' I probed.

'Just the ants on the windowsill,' he mumbled. I used to make piles of sand and stones for them to climb and watch them carry it away, each tiny piece. To kill the time,' he said in a barely audible murmur. He seemed to be retreating into a world of his own, but it was only momentary. He changed persona abruptly.

'I decided I didn't want to be a monk. I wanted to learn English and go to university. Shakespeare. Aaarggh.' He fell on the table as if struck from behind. "Et tu, Brute!" The best play, what do you think? Julius Caesar. Isn't it?' he said enjoying the role.

'The unkindest cut of all', I added on cue.

'So that is how I came to Mandi Town.' He sat up and concluded his narrative decisively. 'Come on, Mr Cottrell.' He waved his hand regally in the air as if he commanded an entire country. 'Let's en-**joy**!'

I heard a clink on the ground and looked down. My earring had dropped from my ear creating a split in the earlobe. I touched my torn ear in disbelief. Jigmai picked up the earring. holding it out to me. Now you will always remember this meeting;' he remarked with concern, 'Your ear will remind you. I think it will never heal.'

He walked us to our hotel. 'Write to me,' he instructed as we thanked him for the meal. I nodded. 'When are you coming back?' he inquired. There was a pause, a moment of silence in which we both sensed the bleakness of his exile.

'I'm going to Delhi tomorrow. I'll buy some English books for you,' Graham said on sudden impulse. 'Then I'll come back to Mandi and teach you English Literature.'

'Oho thank you. 'Will you teach me Oxford English, Mr Cottrell'?' he teased.

We laughed, shook hands and parted. I watched him disappear into the night, a short, sturdy but somehow elegant young man in a hastily improvised modern costume. A character in search of an author, I thought, but the time was out of joint. We could hear him singing the refrain of a Hindi love song, which resonated in the still night, the notes drawn out, boldly exaggerated.

****

You had to be tough to live at Sherabling, a Tibetan monastery in the foothills of the Himalayas in NW India, built on a ridge of land with two other ridges on either side. The ridges were covered in wounded pine trees, the branches lopped for fuel, the trunks gouged for resin. In the winter, leopards came down from the mountains and snatched small dogs and calves. In the summer, as it now was, the heat brought out the reptile population. Gigantic lizards, like small dinosaurs, came out to sun themselves on the rocks. Long fat muscular snakes slithered hastily out of sight at the sound of approaching footsteps behind the thin exhausted trees. At night jackals prowled the forests, shrieking their relentless grief. The water supply dried up and one by one the small group of Western devotees all got amoebic dysentery.

Somehow none of this mattered, such was our fervour to serve our Guru. In that initial intoxicated stage of devotion, Tai Situ Rinpoche was a Buddha, whose pure love melted our hearts and saturated Sherabling in light rays. It seemed simple enough. We would build houses, receive the teachings, do retreats and attain enlightenment. I thought it might take up to ten years.

But the honeymoon was nearing its end when I came to live at Sherabling.The 16th Karmapa, from his sick bed in Delhi, issued instructions to his heart son, Tai Situ, that the time had come to introduce some muscle into our spiritual training, that love and light alone were not going to purify our karma or accumulate the necessary merit.

Overnight our sun king disowned his vision. From favoured children we were now just hippies, bearing all the dirt and shame of our disruptive culture. Steadfastness, loyalty, respect, devotion, tradition were the virtues that counted now. Silently the aspiring yogis and yoginis crept back to their retreat cells to bang their knees in endless prostrations and clack their beads in rounds of mantra.

We had to learn the importance of distance in the guru disciple relationship, the subtle distinction between intimacy, which is vital for the meeting of minds; and familiarity, which makes the relationship disrespectful and worldly. There is a Tibetan saying: the guru is like a fire. If you sit too close you get burned; if you are too far away you don't get the heat. We had to find an appropriate distance and let go of expectations to become pliable, bending like a reed in the wind.

During this cultural inter-regnum, Graham left for Mandi with a rucksack filled with titles by Carlos Castaneda, and RD Laing, to spend two weeks initiating Jigmai into Western thought. A week later he was back at Sherabling. 'It's impossible', he reported. 'The Superintendent of Police came around every day and asked me questions for several hours. His mad minder, an old monk called Guruji kept throwing tantrums and arguing with Jigmai in Tibetan. I didn't understand any of it but I knew he wanted me out of there. And worst of all, Jigmai was impossible to teach. He just wasn't interested in learning. We drank together, played cards, and killed time. However,' he said in the tone used for objective reportage, 'he did ask several times about you. He wanted to know what you were like. I said you were a serious Buddhist practitioner, that you'd sold your business and home in Wales to come and learn the dharma, that you had studied for a doctorate, and I said, no, you were not interested in men.' He looked at me owlishly from under his spectacles, waiting for a response.

I did a Guru Yoga retreat during the summer monsoon – reciting prayers of devotion to the guru. When I came out three months later, gigantic flowers had sprung out of the parched sandy soil, the withered grass had revived green and vigorous, and streams gushed over boulders. I walked in wonder in this Rousseauesque landscape, the doors of perception cleansed, the blessing of the Guru pulsing bliss into wisdom-mind.

When I finished the retreat I went to Tai Situ's room and prostrated full length three times in front of his throne. But now I saw a new side of him. 'What do you want?' he asked. 'I would like to do the Vajra Yogini practice', I replied sincerely. The red dancing Vajra Yogini, with blazing hair and ecstatic eyes was the main archetype, from the vast pantheon of Tibetan deities, who magnetised me. She was the essence of liberated female sexual energy. The 'yidam,' or archetype-guide, is said to bring about miraculous powers quickly. 'If you want to be a great yogini,' Tai Situ replied, 'you have to purify negative karmas.'

He set us all on a regime of fasting, praying and silence for six months doing the practice of the compassionate thousand armed Chenresig, called Nyung Nyes. As in all spiritual disciplines, self-denial and austerity has its place in Buddhism. It was not self-mortification to drive out original sin, as in Christianity, but the fast track to clearing latent seeds of the five poisons – ignorance, passion, anger, pride and jealousy – before they sprout into full blown actions that propel us into rebirth in the lower realms. Then, the idea is, you can recognise your original nature, which is pure from the beginning, like a buddha. Graham and I went into retreat together to help each other through the ritual. By that time we both had chronic amoebic infections.

It was during one of the breaks in this austere ritual, in late December, that Jigmai turned up out of the blue, as unexpected as snowdrops in winter. We were waiting to see Situ Rinpoche, when a jeep pulled up directly below the window of the monastery. The unshaven Indian driver was casually dressed in army fatigues, smoking a beadie. Two other similarly dressed bodyguards with low-slung rifles were sitting in the back seat. Jigmai stepped out from the front of the jeep. He was wearing a perfectly tailored

English dark blue wool suit and black shiny shoes. A checked trilby, perched at an angle on his head added an improbably sporty touch. He carried an umbrella as an improvised walking stick, which resonated on the cement floor as he disappeared from view down the corridor leading into the dining room at the rear of the monastery.

I was ushered into the room to see Tai Situ. The walls were hung with precious paintings of the mahamudra lineage of enlightened masters. A golden throne covered in gold brocade cushions was placed carefully to the right of the window looking out onto the courtyard. The curtains were pulled back to let in the winter sun. To the side of the throne was a shrine with silver offering bowls and a large butter lamp burning brightly. The throne rested on a thick Chinese carpet embossed with a green and white snow lion. Rinpoche, whose skin was unusually white like Chinese nobility, sat on the throne like an emperor. His shoulders were covered in a soft wool golden shawl. The air seemed permeated with gold dust.

'Rinpoche, before we begin, I just have to tell you something.' I began. 'You know the spiritual king of Bhutan, the one who lives in Mandi? I don't know what his proper name is but we call him Jigmai – he has just turned up in a jeep with a couple of bodyguards.'

A monk walked into the room suddenly and whispered to Rinpoche in Tibetan. 'He says that Shabdrung Ngawang Namgyal is downstairs in the restaurant,' replied Rinpoche. 'He is very great; he is like the Dalai Lama.'

'Do you mean he is as enlightened as the Dalai Lama? Or that he has the same status?' I asked with amazement.

'I don't know what his spiritual realization is, but he is very great, his lineage is very great. He is the King of Bhutan like the Dalai Lama is the King of Tibet. You have met him?'

'Yes,' I said, 'some months ago in Mandi. We had dinner at the Raj Mahal. He's very strange, not like a traditional Lama, not like a Lama at all. He's very powerful, but not in the usual peaceful way. He's like a warrior.'

'Why has he come here?' asked Tai Situ.

'I don't know, but I'd like to go downstairs and see him' I replied.

Jigmai was sitting in a corner of the dining room when Graham and I walked in. There was a current of unrest, a flurry of whispering and furtive gazing as the monks dashed in and out in a tailspin, unsure what to do with their unexpected VIP guest.

'Ha Ha Mr Cottrell and Miss Lee Vine,' he addressed us. 'It is very good to see you. You have changed,' he said looking at Graham's clean-shaven face and spotless Jimi Hendrix t- shirt and jeans. 'And you too', he said looking at my face. 'You are thinner.'

'But look', I said glancing at the monks hovering nearby, listening with interest, 'we're in a retreat house very near here, let's go and have tea. It's very basic but at least we can enjoy your company. Today we're not fasting or silent, so you've arrived at a perfect time.'

We escorted him gingerly along a narrow forest path skirting a stream, his shoes causing him to slip a few times, and entered a shady glen where the retreat house was located. It was a primitive arrangement with an outdoor kitchen under the grey slates of an overhanging roof, a bucket of water, a basin, and a primus stove for cooking. Inside the house there was one small dark room with a table and bench, and a wood burning stove. The floors were mud polished with cow dung in the local style. Up the narrow stairs was the shrine room where we prayed during the day, and slept on our wooden prostration boards at night.

We sat our honoured guest on a cushioned bench downstairs next to a window, and knelt on a straw mat at his feet. 'How did you come to be at Sherabling?' I asked. 'Actually I didn't know this was Sherabling', he replied. 'I was in Bir and inquired where was Tashi Jong. I was directed on this road. It was my great surprise to find this is Sherabling.' I lit the primus stove to make tea.

'Was it very difficult to get out of Mandi?' Graham asked.

'I had to seek permission from the S.P (the superintendent of police). He lifted his hand to his ear as if picking up a phone and acted out the part with gusto.

'Hello S.P. This is V.I.P.' I wish to go out of station for a few days.'

'Then please you send your B.G. (body guard) to come here, obtain the forms and fill them out.'

He put his hand down to replace the receiver.

He picked up his hand again to answer the phone.

'Hello, hello Guruji, this is the D.C. The S.P. has informed me that you wish to request permission to go out of station. Then please be informed that your papers have been sent with your B.G.'

He replaced the phone.

Again he picked up his hand to answer the phone. 'Hello V.I.P. This is S.P. Have you received your papers? Then please come here to HQ before going out of station?'

'Why should I go to HQ? You come to me at B.P.' (Bijai Palace).

'Respected Sir, we are obliged to send three B.G.'s with you. Please understand it is for your protection and to comply with R. and R.' (rules and regulations)

'Goodbye S.P.'

'Goodbye VIP'.

We laughed, clapped our hands and whistled.

'More tea?' I lifted the brown teapot.

He looked up suddenly and our eyes met for a moment. I recognised the pain of loneliness momentarily relieved. 'It's good to be among friends, what do you think?' he asked.

We were distracted by rustling in the bushes beside the stream, the sound of footsteps and a thump at the door. The Khenpo – Tai Situ's abbot – entered, a man in his late fifties with grey hair standing up on end, dishevelled maroon robes and the imperturbable smile I was beginning to recognise, on the faces of the most advanced monks. His face lit up with delight and recognition when he saw Jigmai. Apparently he had known him when he was a child at Tso Pema. He pressed his sweating palms together and bowed in respect. Jigmai stiffened into his formal role. There was an exchange in Tibetan. The Khenpo bowed many times and pressed his palms firmly together. He was imploring, Jigmai was adamant. Finally the Khenpo retreated and shuffled out the door, heading towards the monastery.

'What happened?' we asked Jigmai.

'Situ Rinpoche requested to meet me, but I said no.'

Graham and I looked at each other with concern. This was an unprecedented turn of events. 'Please Jigmai,' we begged, please go and meet him. It makes it very awkward for us.'

The Khenpo returned, this time bearing a large white silk offering scarf. He made three full- length prostrations on the mud floor to Jigmai, his robes emitting dust each time he stood up. At the third prostration, he placed the scarf across Jigmai's hefty thighs and pleaded with him. Hands folded, he looked reverentially at the disinterested object of his devotion and begged him in impeccable, honorific Tibetan to take tea with His Eminence the Tai

Situ Rinpoche. 'No,' said Jigmai succinctly. 'I am taking tea with my friends here.' He dismissed the Khenpo.

Eccentric as he appeared, the Khenpo was Tai Situ's most significant envoy. Graham and I were paralysed by this breach of protocol. 'Look Jigmai,' Graham said, 'I am very honoured you are here in our house having tea with us, but we cannot offer you tea when our Guru has invited you. It would be shameful for us to do so. We are his disciples, we are in his mandala; we have to observe the protocol.'

'You have to understand,' I continued, 'he is our Guru. Please have tea with him, then come back here and have dinner with us. It's only four o'clock. There's plenty of time.'

Jigmai looked as reluctant as a child coerced into school. 'The Tibetans will gossip, they will think we are barbarians with no shame,' said Graham imploringly. 'We may even have to leave the monastery.' Jigmai appeared not to be listening.

To our amazement the Khenpo arrived a third time, bringing two monks with him. He repeated the ceremony and, with a final prompt from us, Jigmai left escorted by the monks.

'This is an historical moment,' said Graham with relief. 'We have brought together the Tai Situ and the Shabdrung for the first time in their lives. It will be written up in their life stories. I wonder what they're going to say to each other.'

Ten minutes later, while we were still marveling at our place in history, Jigmai returned. 'Did you see Tai Situ?' we asked in disbelief. We had been expecting the two rinpoches to talk well into the evening. 'Yes. He met me at the door and offered a scarf. His attendant – he is Bhutanese – and an old man both prostrated and offered me scarves. Then

Rinpoche placed me on a throne.'
What level was it at? I wondered. Tibetan protocol was very exact with regard to height of seats.
'Slightly higher than his own.' he continued as if reading my mind. 'Then some monks brought tea. He invited me to dinner but I said no, I was meeting some friends here.' He laughed scornfully, pleased with his defiance of hierarchy and propriety. 'It is better not to talk too much the first time. Was I right?' he asked with feigned innocence. His expression showed a complex mixture of defiance, pride, playfulness, and humour.
'What did you talk about?' I asked.
'I asked him what his hobby is. He said he was building a monastery, that he didn't have time for a hobby.'
'That was it?'
'Yes. He invited me to come back and said he would make formal arrangements for me. I thanked him and left. I do not think I will be staying at his monastery, but possibly quite near it,' he concluded, fixing me with an intense gaze.

It was dusk. The horns, drums and chanting from the evening prayers sounded clearly from the monastery; but Jigmai was listening to Bob Dylan and Ry Cooder on my new stereo cassette. We put on Slow Train Coming. When 'You Gotta Serve Someone' came on, Jigmai turned up the volume, his interest totally engaged.

> You may be a state trooper, you might be a young Turk,
> You may be the head of some big TV network,
> You may be rich or poor, you might be blind or lame,
> You may be living in another country, under another name
> But you're gonna have to serve somebody.
> Yes indeed,
> You're gonna have to serve somebody.
> Well it may be the devil or it may be the Lord
> But you're gonna have to serve somebody.

I saw his eyes widen with recognition at the line "Living in another country, under another name".

The music of the new world blocked out the sounds of his ancient past. He was thrilled, his eyes closed in thought-free rapture, an ironic smile on his face. His eyes opened wide to observe me while I served dinner, following each movement as I walked in and out of the primitive mud walled room bathed in candlelight. I felt the sudden disorientating presence of desire, unnervingly naked without the adornment of love. An hour later, after we had eaten every morsel of cauliflower cheese and potatoes, I brought out Graham's surprise birthday cake lit with thirty-two candles. We cheered as he blew out the lights. Jigmai's face was glowing with contentment. 'If I had this kind of cooking every day I would become very healthy.' He looked like a child who had suddenly found the nurture he needed to grow. My heart reached out to embrace his.

At eleven o'clock the Indian bodyguard knocked on the door for the third time. 'Guruji, we are cold and hungry outside.' Jigmai picked up his hat and clasped my hand. 'Thank you. We had nice time and good food. I will send my jeep tomorrow to pick you up at 3 pm. You will come and have tea with me at the Tourist Lodge in Bir. Then I will go back to Mandi Town, by the grace of God.' He laughed broadly, showing a mouth packed with white teeth; the long, pointed canines protruded, competing to dominate his youthful mischievous grin.

****

We waited in the long grass by the side of the road at a little distance from Sherabling. 'Beauty and the Beast,' Graham remarked sardonically as we walked down the forest road together. I was wearing my best 1930's silk tea dress, with espadrille sandals laced up the calves and a wide-brimmed straw hat. There were so few occasions to wear a dress at Sherabling that I took advantage of this opportunity to feel feminine and pretty. And besides, I was going to tea with a high Lama. He carried the precious stereo player and a selection of cassettes. Little currents of warm air fanned us as we turned to face the sun. The landscape seemed to hang in timelessness, the white peaks of the Dhauladaur mountain range dazzling like a vision, its stillness echoing birdsong.

A rickety jeep pulled up with one very sullen, unshaven driver. We bounced in the back seat for five miles along a pot-holed forest track. Overhead, parakeets flew in graceful formation from the surrounding pine groves, mocking our slow bumpy progress. The rhododendrons were just beginning to burst into passionate red flower.

Half an hour later, we pulled up at a large house with a veranda, bearing the unmistakable mark of colonial dilapidation. Jigmai greeted us at the top of the steps and ushered us into the cold, dark institutional guest room. The wooden floors creaked and sagged, the high ceilings reaching beyond human habitation with small birds on the rafters darting excitedly to and fro. A chowkidar wearing a scarf tied around his head and dun coloured salwar kameez, brought tea in a large stainless steel teapot of the kind once used by British Rail. He poured the dark brown liquid into white, heavy institutional cups. We turned on the music, but the electricity was down. With a loud bellow, Jigmai summoned the chowkidar, instructing him to fetch batteries from the bazaar.

Graham picked up the Hindi movie magazine displayed prominently on the table. 'Do you read this?'

'Yes,' Jigmai replied, with evident enjoyment. 'I am a fan of Amitabh Bucchan. You know Bucchan? Ah, he's very good at singing and fighting.'

'Would you like to read some dharma books?' asked Graham. 'I can lend you some of Chogyam Trungpa's books, *Cutting Through Spiritual Materialism* is a classic.'

'Ah no, that's okay, not right now.'

The chowkidar arrived with the batteries. We played the tapes, listening to Dylan again and again. Jigmai picked up phrases like 'it ain't me, babe' and sang loudly, accompanying the tune.

By 4:30, twilight was gathering and we could no longer prolong the meeting. Jigmai had to be in Mandi that night, and we had to get back to Sherabling. We watched as Jigmai packed his few belongings into a small briefcase with VIP etched onto the leather. He handed me his movie magazine with a voluptuous Bollywood babe on a glossy cover, as though it were a special gift. I took it, slightly embarrassed. It seemed evidence of the poverty of his provincial environment.

We drove in the eerie blackness of new moon on the jungle road towards Sherabling. The only lights were from the weak beams of the car headlights. Within half a mile of our destination the driver stopped and refused to go any further. The prospect of running out of fuel in such a remote place was terrifying. 'I would not be able to walk this road myself,' Jigmai said. 'We're not worried about it,' said Graham bravely. He opened the door onto the unknown and we walked boldly out into the night towards Sherabling, braced by our friendship with this strangely heroic, remarkable man. The jeep turned around noisily and chugged off in the opposite direction.

Sherabling was in the early stages of growth. After the initial love-struck encounter between Tai Situ and his Western 'yogins', we were slowly pushed further and further towards the boundaries of the monastery to make room for the growing number of monks. Graham and I had been fortunate to do our retreat in the one available house. When we finished we had to occupy one of the ten primitive cells along the furthest western edge of the monastery.

Each cement rectangle was no bigger than a person's length when lying on the ground with arms outstretched. Before building retreat houses, we lived in these cells, cooked using kerosene stoves, buckets of water carried from the main tap at the end of the corridor, and plastic basins for slops and the washing up. The dirty water would be thrown over the edge of the corridor into the jungle, onto the mounting pile of rubbish haunted by prowling dogs. We slept on hard wooden cots with flimsy, inch-deep mattresses. There was one small window at the front of the room near the door, which opened onto a cement runway leading to the kitchen. In summer, the tin roof heated to baking point and we simmered in our ovens. In winter, the cement walls dripped condensation and no amount of kerosene heating could change the humidity. In this precarious ecosystem we practiced elaborate meditations designed to purify negative karmas and accumulate merit.

As cultural realities weighed in on both sides, the master plan was to remove us from the monastic environment altogether. Tai Situ gave us permission to build retreat houses on the adjacent hillside. For us too, the push to get away was strong; away from the Tibetans, from prying eyes peering through private doors, staring minutes on end. Away from the acrid stench of shared toilets, from the monotony of rice lentils and curried veg in the kitchen, from gossip, from blaring horns at dawn, from the stampede of young monks to the canteen during breaks, from the shrill chorus of repetitions in the classroom, from communal dirt and alien customs. The honeymoon was officially over on both sides.

I began building a house on the furthest corner from the monastery. It was to be made of local stone on two floors with a kitchen downstairs and everything else upstairs: sleeping area, meditation cubicle, veranda, bathroom, and even an open fireplace. I was still carrying the template for a Welsh cottage; my architect, an American woman who had lived in Himachal for decades, was in love with mud. I had thrown into the design hotchpotch some wooden arches in the hope of giving the house a touch of elegance. But the local carpenter – actually a farmer – was unused to constructing anything more complicated than rectangular window frames. I looked on with dismay at the first wooden frames: they were cracked and warped. The stonemason suggested we contract the carpentry to someone in Mandi. Thus it was that I ended up in Mandi a few days later with my foreman, Paresh, a runaway from a tea plantation family in South India.

Mandi was at the far end of the Kullu Valley, three hours tortuous bus ride from Sherabling. Our bus reached the suspension bridge over the river Beas that marked the entrance to the town, at dusk. We checked into a hotel and slept off the dizziness that comes from lurching and swaying from side to side around bends, while grasping the rail as we hit the potholes.

The next morning at ten o'clock I went to Bijai Palace to say hello to Jigmai, while Paresh went to look for carpenters in the bazaar. His young servant answered my knock. Jigmai Sahib was still sleeping. Half an hour later Jigmai came into the sitting room drying his face. He smiled sleepily at me showing a puffy face and small bleary eyes. Two Tibetan children, bright and eager, were waiting for lessons.

We all went outside into the sunshine and sat on a stone wall as he talked to me, and taught them at the same time. At his insistence, I brought my bags from the hotel and placed them in the house. When I returned, he was sporting white tennis shoes, white pullover and white trousers. 'I challenge you to a game of badminton', he said balancing on his toes, his eyes glinting with anticipation.

We went into the garden at the rear of the palace. Weeds and stones choked out the remains of what had once been neatly arranged flower-beds. 'It would be nice to bring the flowers back here,' I remarked. 'When I came here from Tso Pema at seventeen,' said Jigmai, 'I created flower gardens so beautiful that the local women came every day to admire them. The gardens at Bijai Palace were known all over Mandi. Then I lost interest.'

He picked up his racket, balanced perfectly for several seconds on tiptoe, and served hard hitting the shuttlecock neatly into the corner. It was child's play for him. I ran from one end of the court to the other, each time the shuttlecock landed at an unexpected angle. He was light on his feet, supple as a feather. He seemed barely to move. Rather he controlled the game from one place.

'Come on, play,' he shouted enthusiastically 'Play, come on, play.'

I kept on running, laughing breathlessly. 'I'm afraid I'm not much fun for you' I shouted. After half an hour he came over to me and grinned. 'Tea?' he asked. I noticed he was cool; his breath was even. I was sweating with exertion.

We sat in his sitting room at a small table while he poured tea. Suddenly his mood intensified. 'What do you think of marriage?' he asked. I thought for a moment. 'It's great if you find the right person; otherwise it's hell, far better to be alone. I've never found the right man; it seems to be very difficult for me.' He pondered my answer without replying.

He excused himself and disappeared, leaving me to wander around the building unobstructed. The rooms were all sparsely furnished with the same solid, institutional furniture that characterised British boarding houses in the 50's. I looked at Jigmai's shrine, near his single wooden bed. It was a curious mixture of Hindu and Buddhist deities with a gaudy dayglo lantern, some Indian incense cones and a blazing pink poster of Saraswati, the Hindu deity of learning. Some Tibetan texts were wrapped in old brocade on the lower shelf. There seemed very little activity around the shrine, no evidence that anything happened there.

I wandered into the garden observing the state of neglect, when an old, gaunt monk, walking very slowly suddenly came into view. We stared at each other in amazement. A visible tension held his thin body together like a wire; anguish electrifying his spectral features. He was as curious about me as I was about him. I rose, clasping my hands together as in prayer. 'Tashi Delegs' I said, greeting him in Tibetan with a small bow. He continued to stare, detached, studying me like a scientist trying to classify a new species. I tried to tell him in the few syllables I possessed of Tibetan, that I was studying dharma with Situ Rinpoche at Sherabling. He seemed bemused at my collection of gestures, single syllables and sudden lapses. I turned away for a moment to watch a cat leaping on a mouse. In that instant he vanished like a ghost.

Jigmai returned around tea-time. 'I've met a strange monk who seems to be living somewhere in this house,' I said. 'That's Guruji,' he replied. I narrated every detail of our encounter. He listened with evident interest. 'So who is Guruji?' I asked.

'He's been with me since I was nine years old, since I was living in Tso Pema. He was captured by the Chinese in Tibet and tortured. His hair turned white overnight. He has never been able to forget that. He is half mad, but he is very respected and knows a great deal.'

'Does he teach you now?'

'He wants to, but I have stopped studying.'

'Why?'

'I left Tso Pema so I could enrol in Simla University for a BA in English Literature. But the Indian Government would not give me permission to leave Mandi, so I was obliged to continue my studies here. I started to drink a lot and gamble. I could not complete my studies and left the university.'

'Why do you not continue with the dharma now?' I asked with concern.

'My mind is disturbed,' he replied simply.

I felt his desolation like a stab at my heart. He spoke casually but his eyes were intense with the need to communicate. There was a brief silence. His loneliness was open and defiant, not tortured or covert. He was just what he was, and that gave him an aura of confidence and resolve.

'So… what do you think of marriage?' he asked without preamble. I considered the question, coming as it did a second time, carefully. After our morning's conversation the extraordinary thought had entered my mind that he would ask me to marry him. I dismissed it almost immediately. It seemed too improbable. But now I knew I was right.

'Does that mean you are asking me to marry you?' I asked very calmly. He considered it for a second. 'Yes.' He looked defiant.

I was astounded at the way these words had come out of both of us, as if we already had this conversation and it was stored waiting to be played back on a tape. This person who wished to marry me was no ordinary man. He was also young, inexperienced and somehow out of time. Provincial, I thought. His mannerisms, his style of dress, his expectations, his behaviour, his way of speaking – it was backward, somehow in a 50's timewarp. He badly needed a friend to support him through the chaos of Indian bureaucracy, Tibetan protocol and the political intrigues surrounding him. I was not in love with him but my heart was open and I felt a strong urge to help.

With all these thoughts chasing each other through my mind, I felt confused. 'I don't know yet', I replied. 'Let me think about it. I'll tell you soon.'

Evening shadows lingered in the room. In the far distance we could hear the hushed sounds of twilight pushing out the bustle of day. Vendors' plaintive voices wailed the last ice creams, hot spicey chai, channa dal. Birdcalls intensified, then faded into echo. The sweet musty smell of smoke from street debris mixed with the hot notes of cheap incense. Paresh returned exhausted from the bazaar. 'Sit down, sit down' Jigmai greeted him heartily, placing a glass of rum in his hand. We sat casually drinking and laughing as the dark curtain of night gathered around us. 'It's good to be here,' said Paresh. 'Everything feels right.' Jigmai's presence was like a powerful magnet that made a circle of protection around him keeping out all danger.

The second bottle of Old Monk rum clattered into the bin at Jigmai's feet, as he opened a third. 'C'mon, let's drink, cheers.' He lifted his glass and downed the brown, syrupy liquid in one go. We were, at his insistence, playing gin rummy and losing all our money. 'Gin Lummy,' he shouted, slurring the words as he pounced like a tiger and gathered all the cards together to shuffle the pack. Paresh took out a ten rupee note and laid it on the table. 'That's it. I'm out of the game.' Jigmai was the undisputed victor.

I sat next to him on the bed, feeling the warmth from his body. He moved closer until our bodies touched. Several years of celibacy had dulled the edge of passion, but I felt a strong need for the warmth of companionship. Paresh dozed off. I was yawning with fatigue. 'Mudjko ga ley lagao' Jigmai was singing in Hindi in a loud, drunken voice. 'Love me.' Or was it an imitation? The next second, he snapped out of it and began to make the sleeping arrangements. Beds, sheets, covers were brought in as he prepared the room for all three of us. Paresh pulled the blankets over his face and made the gentlemanly decision to retire.

Jigmai whispered loudly to me, 'We will sleep together tonight.' I nodded. It seemed completely natural, as though we had done this many times before. He turned off the light and entered the single bed beside me. His body was tense with anticipation. I lay quietly in his arms while his hands explored my body, each movement yielding a sharp gasp of surprise like a conqueror finding lost land to reclaim. His touch was heavy and indelicate. He climbed on top of me moving clumsily in performance of an unknown activity, while I guided his entry. We were talking in whispers, but his tone was becoming increasingly frustrated. It was as if our lovemaking was a game that he was losing. Suddenly he could bear his humiliation no longer. 'Aaaah,' he moaned. 'This is a tragedy.' 'No', I laughed, 'it's a comedy.' He relaxed and released himself. 'Is that it? Is that everything? Is it finished now?' he asked in an anguished voice. 'Is this what people do, what everyone wants and desires, what the poets write about?'

'We have just made love and for the moment it is over. But this is not really what it's all about, not at all,' I whispered. You have not really had the experience of making love. It will come later as we get used to each other. Don't worry about it. This is not **'it.'** I held his head and kissed him tenderly, like a child.' It doesn't matter, it will be all right, there will be much more to come.'

He lifted himself up on one elbow, his arm cradling my head and looked at me intently. 'You will be for me and I will be for you. We will be for each other, forever.'

My heart opened. It had always been my desire to form an unbreakable bond in love, to commit everything. I was silent for a moment. Then my eyes filled with tears. In that moment, I opened my heart to a man I barely knew.

The next morning we dressed hurriedly, embarrassed lest Paresh had heard our strange intimacies during the night. Jigmai summoned his servant. 'Bring tea. And get a coolie from the bazaar for Memsahib's luggage. Memsahib would like butter toast and also some marmalade. Hurry up, quickly. Go.' As we sat on the edge of the bed drinking tea together, I realised that in one brief night of confused intimacy, I had become the mistress of the house.

We walked through the streets of Mandi to the bus stand. A sullen greyness lingered in the chill morning air of late January, with a fine mist covering the view to the hills beyond. Jigmai was marching swiftly like a soldier on a parade ground. I fell in line with his bold fast steps. It was important for me to clarify what had happened last night. 'Jigmai,' I began, 'I really don't know exactly what you mean by marriage, but I would like to have a spiritual union. You know kundalini yoga?[3] I feel very strongly it is a practice I need to learn. Can you teach it to me?'

He looked away. It took him some moments to grasp the full meaning of my request. 'We' he said emphatically, 'do not do this.' 'We' are monks. Anyway there must be signs, sometimes dreams, which show the woman and the place and then you meet and everything is right. It is not like you just decide and do it. There are many things. You must be nearly enlightened to do this.'

His reaction made me feel foolish, as though I'd expected a cow to lay eggs. Still I persisted.' You are not a monk,' I replied.

'I am not a Lama either.'

'But you are a Rinpoche.[4] You are not an ordinary man.'

'I am not a Rinpoche. Who says I am Rinpoche?' he asked challengingly.

'Situ Rinpoche says you are very great, like the Dalai Lama.'

Jigmai looked pleased, momentarily excited, his eyes lit up with interest. 'Really, he said that?' He thought for a moment. 'Whoever says I am a great man must be a fool. We have to study, read texts, do many practices, meditate in caves for twelve years, or longer, then get all the signs. These are the real Lamas. Do you know anyone who is doing that these days?'

'You must become a real Lama,' I said with conviction. 'You must become a great Lama. I cannot marry you unless you become a Lama. I am only interested in dharma[5], not in worldly life.'

---

[3] sexual yoga using the sexual energy to transform passion into compassion.

[4] a reincarnate Lama

[5] the Buddhist path

'If I marry you, I cannot be a Lama. If I marry you, I can only be in worldly life.'

I was completely confused. 'But all these other Rinpoches get married and teach the dharma'.

'These days everyone is teaching dharma, but if you ask them to change fire into water or fly in the air they cannot do it. They can only run off to the West, get married and teach the Westerners, who don't know anything, or what a Lama is.' His voice was scornful.

Our conversation came to a dead end. He marched determinedly a few steps ahead, his accelerated pace cutting through the stares of the curious passers-by like a meat cleaver slicing sponge cake. Behind me trotted the coolie carrying my luggage. Walking slightly behind Jigmai but setting a pace of his own, came the bodyguard, sporting three days stubble, bleary eyes, and puffing on a beadie. Two young boys looked at Jigmai, then at me lasciviously, and back to him with a knowing grin. A group of young men stopped to greet him and shake his hand. 'Aha, Mohan Singh.' They eyed me furtively. Some young school-girls stared giggling behind their woolen Kullu shawls. They approached and hovered for a moment like a clutch of goslings, then backed away laughing.

Everyone seemed to know Jigmai. 'Namaste Prince,' 'Namaste Maharaj,' 'Namaste Mohan Singh.' Each greeting was followed by a long, hard stare at me. Some stares were curious, some incredulous, some lascivious. The stares from Tibetans were hostile. By the time we reached the bus stand I felt humiliated, as if I'd been paraded naked through town.

Jigmai bought the ticket, found a seat on the crowded bus and issued his last instructions. 'Write to me when you get back.' I sat down next to a thin, bird-like mother holding a miniature bird-like infant. 'I'll come and see you in two months time' I promised, 'after Losar.'[6] The driver jumped into his seat, the engine roared. I managed a thin smile and a little wave as the bus heaved and lurched out of Mandi.

The sun was shining from a brilliant blue sky as I stepped off the bus at the Sherabling stop four miles from the monastery. My feet were so sure of the path I could have walked it blindfolded. Over the stones to cross the river, across the railway track, down over the big boulders to the second river, a short climb to the village, around the newly cemented village tap, skirting the bamboo grove towards the cow barn, avoiding the toilet area, up a shelf of grey rocks, and then… there it was, the tree. It raised its gnarled black arms into the air, a portent of doom in the winter, yet in the spring, green buds appeared miraculously on its weather-beaten frame, and after the monsoon it looked as radiant as a young bride. Standing by itself on the boundary to the corridor of pine forest leading to the monastery, I thought of it as a gatekeeper, a black shape-shifting dakini.

After walking a quarter-hour through the pine forest listening to the conversation of gigantic crows overhead, I arrived at the retreat house. Graham was outside the house, reading a book quietly in the sun.

'Something unexpected happened in Mandi,' I told him. I paused, while he looked at me intently through his rimless spectacles. 'Jigmai asked me to marry him.'

He looked slightly concerned. 'Do you think he's serious?'

'Yes, he's in love with me.'

'What are you going to do?'

---

[6] Tibetan New Year

'I'm going to ask Situ Rinpoche's advice.'

'Good. I think you should finish the Nyung Nyes[7] first.'

For the next seven weeks without a break we continued the practice of fasting, praying and prostrating. We awoke every day at 3am and in the blackness of early morning took solemn vows not to eat meat, eggs or fish, not to sit in a high place, not to bedeck ourselves with ornaments and perfume, or to misbehave sexually.

The only interruptions were Jigmai's love letters. They were written on green lined paper with a margin running down the side. Most of them said almost nothing at all apart from the date and time of writing, and that he was fine and he wished I was fine and that he was waiting anxiously to hear from me. Since his writing was large like that of an elementary school boy, this would fill the page. In several letters he declared his concern for me, and his loneliness for my sweet company. But two letters were more compelling. On one he wrote the word LOVE in large letters in blood taken from his hand. There was a splash of blood extending from the word. I concealed it carefully, aware of its significance. In another letter he proclaimed, 'If I should lose you I will become some great criminal.' This too I concealed.

Just before the Tibetan New Year, a large envelope arrived at the monastery canteen addressed to me. There was no stamp on it. I opened it slowly and stared for minutes at a handmade peacock standing up proudly showing its feathers, which were carefully pasted onto the card. Inside was a neatly hand-written message with perfectly symmetrical letters.

---

7 fasting and purification practice of the Tibetan deity of compassion, Chenresig

Dearest Norma,
Thinking of you at New Year
And wanting to let you know
Sending this cheery message
Especially to tell you so
Thinking of you at New Year
And hoping that you'll know too
The special regard and feeling
That come with this card to you.

With love and good wishes
SN Jigmae

On the left hand side of the paper there were the Tibetan syllables, Om Mani Padme Hung, the mantra of compassion. I was very moved by the energy of the whole composition: the peacock, the carefully styled printed letters and the respectful thoughts that lay behind it.

The most important conversation of my life took place on the morning of the day I planned to leave for Mandi to see Jigmai. I walked up the cement stairs of the monastery, my nerves trembling, to see Tai Situ. The weeks of fasting and prostrating, together with the parasites clawing at my intestines, had left me nervous and weak.

Tai Situ was radiating golden calm, sitting on his throne in the window cubicle wearing a tight gold brocade vest and the maroon shawl of a monk. I prostrated three times and approached.

He looked at me intently, the lines of concentration appearing suddenly between his eyes. I braced myself to speak, but nothing came out. I didn't know how to begin. I didn't know what to call Jigmai.

I forced myself to speak. 'You know the Rinpoche from Bhutan?' Tai Situ tensed in total concentration.

'What is his real name, I don't know it,' I continued.

'Ngawang Namgyal.'

'Namgyal…? What did you say? What's his first name?'
'Ngawang Namgyal,' he repeated.
I tried to say it, but did not succeed.
'Anyway,' I leaned back on one arm, trying to look casual, 'he asked me to marry him and I'd like your advice.'

Tai Situ trembled with excitement. 'That is very great; he is like the Dalai Lama. Now he has nothing, but soon he will have everything.'
I felt awkward. 'I don't know if he's great, I've met him only a few times.'
'If he wishes to marry you, you should marry him. But make sure he's serious,' Tai Situ said.
I thought for a moment. I saw LOVE written in blood and remembered his words of eternal being for each other. 'He's serious.'
'You should have an Indian marriage.'
I was puzzled. 'I mean where the woman serves the man. But get married,' he spoke very seriously. 'Don't just have an affair'.
'I hardly know him.'
'Then go and find out.'
I hurried from the room, my head spinning.

I felt as if the blueprint for a lifetime of bliss had just been handed to me. I'd received the seal of approval. My Guru advised marriage to Jigmai. Therefore it became a spiritual instruction, which neatly met my quest for sacred love. Jigmai's refusal to link our marriage with a spiritual union got pushed aside by the significance I felt in Tai Situ's endorsement. Thus I embarked on an extraordinary adventure, one my own common sense would never have allowed me to enter. I plunged in, following blindly what I interpreted as the advice of my Guru.

CHAPTER 2

GURUJI

I took the next bus to Mandi to find out for myself who Jigmai was, looking around quickly for his familiar face in the crowd. Finally I spotted him. His glance rested for a long moment, incredulous, on my little girl pink shoes with crepe soles and buckle and my printed tiered skirt. He looked slightly annoyed. 'What took you so long?' he asked looking at his watch. 'I was watching every bus here since one o'clock. It's now four ten.' He could have been a sergeant major on a parade ground chastising a new recruit.

'I had to wait to see Situ Rinpoche before leaving,' I said. 'I got here as quickly as I could. There was no way to let you know.'

'Okay, come on,' he said herding me carefully through the busy street. His servant had already placed my luggage on his shoulders and was wending his way deftly through the crowd, towards Bijai Palace.

It was a relief to reach the Palace, away from the piercing stares of the men. While the servant prepared tea in a deliberately laconic fashion, Jigmai showed me around his quarters, which I had glimpsed two months before. Now I looked more carefully. On the bookshelves, amongst the compulsory reading for university literature courses, was the eclectic selection of books Graham had purchased in Delhi the year before- RD Laing, Carlos Castaneda. They looked unread.

I looked at the shrine. It still seemed vacant as if the human link were disconnected. But on the lower shelf there were more personal momentoes. I noticed a photograph of a small boy in monk's robes. His face was soft with the sweetness of childhood, his skin very white. His hands were placed palms down on his thighs. 'That's me when I was five,' he said quietly..

We had taken off our shoes to enter the shrine room. Now we padded through to the next room, a very small chamber with a single bed in it. 'We will sleep here,' Jigmai announced. A creaky door hanging off its hinges led to a large English style bathroom, with heavy porcelain bathtub on four legs, a wide sink with a non-functioning hot water tap, and a toilet, which never flushed. I felt a rush of anger that Jigmai's comforts should be so neglected. He read my disgusted look and bristled. 'I am the third most important VIP in India, next to the Prime Minister and the Dalai Lama.'

'They don't seem to be looking after you very well,' I replied.

His attention was on a large red plastic bucket to which he pointed proudly. 'When I heard you were coming I went to the bazaar and brought this for your visit.' I was baffled and amused. It seemed a quaint gesture. It took me several years to understand that this was the protocol of Hindu hygiene – welcoming an important guest with new clean washing facilities.

We left the bathroom by the main door and entered a small hallway with a very dirty kitchen leading off it. The servant was squatting on the floor watching milk boil on a dirt encrusted kerosene stove. We re-entered the sitting room and sat closely together on the sofa. Jigmai put his arm around me, pulling me towards him eagerly. His embrace was complete, without hesitation. I was his woman and I was there to do as he wished. In return I would have his protection. That was the tradition. Tai Situ had told me to have a traditional marriage and I knew that this is what he meant, but I had no experience of it. The roles in my previous relationships had always been undefined – and unsatisfactory. I had developed an idea of myself as a free spirit, evolving towards something beyond convention. My relationship with Jigmai would soon liberate me from that fantasy.

'Now, tell me about Situ Rinpoche', he said. I reported the conversation in full. 'Situ Rinpoche said it is great and that we should marry very soon,' I concluded. He showed more interest in other parts of my report. 'He said I would be king again?' he asked excitedly. 'Yes, he said, "now he has nothing but soon he will have everything."

'How can he know that?' he asked, almost belligerent.

'He sees the future,' I asserted confidently.

At this Jigmai stiffened. Thoughts I could not intuit were passing through his mind. He turned suddenly on me. 'Why did you discuss these things when I asked you to tell no one?'

'I had to seek his advice to decide what to do. He's my Guru, and he's not your enemy.' I couldn't conceive of embarking on this relationship without Tai Situ's advice. Perhaps I should have kept that secret.

'How do you know he is not telling you to marry me for some other reason? We are not allowed to marry. We are monks.' His suspicions aroused, he was heavy and unyielding, impenetrable as rock.

'But you do not wish to be a monk,' I said.

The tea arrived. Jigmai handed me the cup and saucer and we drank in silence. I felt dumb-founded, trying to bridge the gap between Situ Rinpoche's elated endorsement of the proposal, and the hard reality. I had not yet learned to yield into the shifting sands of Jigmai's mind. I pushed stubbornly deeper and deeper, trying to make it manageable, to change his instability.

'But how can I marry now?' he asked. 'I have no money, no home, no position.'

'Perhaps the Indian Government can give you something.'

'The Indian government will not allow me to marry a foreigner, perhaps to marry at all.'

'Why should they care about that? You're not a monk!'

'There are many things you do not understand. My people will not accept me if I am married with a foreigner. Then I am useless to the Indian Government.'

With no experience of the governing hierarchy of Bhutan, I could not grasp the politics. I had no idea that the spiritual kings of Bhutan had to be monks. So I said naively, 'The Indian Government can't decide whom you should marry, or if you should marry! It's your personal decision. You can't let them decide that for you!' I was sure that personal freedom had to be more important than politics. 'You must get your freedom;' I advised him fervently. 'Then you can do what you want.'

'Then I can be anything?' he asked softly, innocent as a child playing with an adult.

'You must become a Lama,' I insisted.

'I told you I will never be that', he said authoritatively. 'So please do not have the thought or you will be very disappointed.'

He paused a moment to shift gears before performing another act of stunning mental agility. 'I will be a businessman. I will go to Bombay. Vroom.' His hand glided through the air and hit the hard bed with a thud. 'Then I will make my business and live in a large house with lots of servants. At night we can go to disco. You know disco?' he asked, as if we had just met in a pub.

I was baffled and disappointed. Here was a spiritual giant talking about worldly distractions. I felt I knew what characterised a spiritual person and he was not conforming to it. 'I'm not interested in all that stuff,' I replied sullenly.

'I will be a taxi driver.' His hands gripped the steering wheel. 'They make a lot of money, no? I must have lots of money.' His hand zig-zagged through the air in several large arcs while he emitted the noise of engines roaring and brakes squealing, his gaze fixed ahead holding an imaginary steering wheel.

I was landing with a thud, but I couldn't work out exactly where I was. The reality I entered with Jigmai had a distinct flavour of its own, which I would taste again and again: flat, bitter and then, as it mixed with other, sharper ingredients, so pungent it transcended taste altogether to become quite surreal.

He was not an easy person to know. Our conversations frequently thinned out into silence. Instead, we developed a physical intimacy immediately. For four nights we slept entwined on the same small bed, in physical embrace. Jigmai was over-eager, impatient, and fiercely competitive – an overpowering intensity fuelled by the long procession, as he vividly imagined, of my previous lovers. His lovemaking was awkward, his touch heavy. He had not yet understood the subtleties of pleasure, the tantalising intimacy of communication that hooks a woman. I yielded, without looking back, without comparing. We were tucked away on a small hard bed in a back room of a ramshackle house in a market town of Northern India, tasting the compulsive sweetness of physical pleasure. I was honoured to be the consort of a man who had a place in history. At the same time, it was unreal, like walking into a film set and being handed the star part.

One afternoon a young man and his teenage wife came to visit. The girl looked shyly at the floor while her husband made conversation with his old school friend, Jigmai. Suddenly Jigmai announced he would take us somewhere very special. The four of us, accompanied by a bodyguard, left the Palace and after walking a short distance, arrived at a stone stairway leading off a broad alleyway. We climbed up steeply, passing several houses and a small temple on the right. After twenty minutes or more we arrived at a large stretch of open ground with a sweeping panoramic view of Mandi, the broad rushing river Beas and the snow capped Himalayas beyond.

Crowning this summit was a modest Hindu Temple. A toothless smiling old man pressed orange flowers on us and dotted the space between our eyes with a red chalky powder. We dropped some coins onto a dirty handkerchief spread out on the ground, took off our shoes and entered a cool inner chamber. A massive red deity with several arms stared fiercely in the darkened room. Jigmai circumambulated the statue quickly, left a small money offering and made an unceremonious exit. Once outside I asked the significance of the place. Jigmai delivered a summary of the legend:

'When Guru Rinpoche[8] came to Mandi, he flew up to this hilltop' he said. 'Below him the people of Mandi had gathered. He preached the dharma to them but they were stupid and did not listen. Then to show his great power and to save them from their own bad deeds, he killed the wicked ones and sent their souls to the pure land of Dewachen.'

[8] the 8th century founding father of Tibetan Buddhism

This was typical of Tantric Buddhist lore, stories of adepts who had gone beyond good and evil, and used wrathful methods to liberate beings. I was thrilled to be there in that place with Jigmai who was also said to be an emanation of Guru Rinpoche. It seemed numinous, imbued with significance deeper than the event itself.

The sun was shining brilliantly as we walked back down the steps towards the town. In buoyant spirit, Jigmai grabbed the arm of his old school friend and burst loudly into a Hindi love-song, stretching his arms out theatrically. He jumped down several steps singing all the while and gesturing while his friend laughed and played with him. Then he grabbed my hand and sang even more loudly, with bolder, more exaggerated gestures. A wave of embarrassment gripped me. I tried to free my hand from his, but his grasp only tightened. The shift from sacred history to Hindi movie was swift and seamless. I no longer saw him as Guru Rinpoche. I saw an overgrown school-boy playing pranks.

He held my hand firmly all the way down the steps until we reached the street. Saying goodbye peremptorily to his friends, we walked back to Bijai Palace.

And then I saw another image. In the darkened sitting room a spectral figure stood upright. Guruji: eyes wild, hair standing on end. Jigmai pushed me to one side to protect me from the onslaught.

Guruji began speaking agitatedly, his voice rising to a furious crescendo while his hands beat the air in wild gestures. He looked at me with contempt. Jigmai's voice was controlled at first, but soon he was shouting back emphatically and pacing the floor. I stood mesmerised by the vehemence of the argument. After about half an hour of furious exchange, Guruji delivered a lethal blow. He shrieked and spat on the floor at Jigmai's feet. Then he whirled around and disappeared.

Jigmai sat stunned, staring fiercely into space. After a few minutes he turned to me. 'He says you are a hippie, and you will be faithless and disloyal, the cause of my downfall, like the American woman who married the Choegyal of Sikkim. She left her husband when the Indian Government took over his kingdom. She betrayed him and he died afterwards. You will do the same to me, he said.'

I was shocked. I had heard the unfortunate story of the King of Sikkim and his American wife, Hope Cooke. The Indian Government took over Sikkim; the King and his family were put under house arrest. Hope Cooke panicked and decided to escape with their children. The King was a broken man and remained under house arrest until he died, alone – bereft of his kingdom, his family and his honour. In the East the story read differently. Hope Cooke had become the archetype of the wicked white woman whose disloyalty brings dishonour and ruin. 'But I am willing to marry you even though you are not a king and you have nothing at all. What did you say to him?'

'I said you were a dharma student, not a hippie, that you were very educated, and that you'd given up everything to come here and practice the dharma. But then he said you were a spy for the king of Bhutan and I could not answer that. Are you?' he asked looking at me sternly.

It was hard to breathe, like landing on the moon. 'I've never been to Bhutan, never met the king and I don't expect I will. I am not interested in politics, I'm interested in becoming enlightened,' I said flatly.

He looked skeptically at me. 'Only time will tell us all these things.'

'He's filling your head with suspicion and mistrust because he doesn't want us to get married.'

'I told him', he repeated, "She is the one I love and she is the one I will marry." Then he said, 'if you do that I will kill her.'

I was horrified. 'But he's a monk! How can a monk say that?'

'He said this is an obstacle year for me; that means my life is in danger. I should pray to my protectors. He said if I don't practice the dharma, if I do not become a monk and go instead into worldly life, I could become a great criminal.'

'That's when he spat at you?'

Yes. Fortunately it landed at my feet and not on me or I would have to throw him out of the house.

'He's your guru?' I asked incredulous.

'We call him Guruji out of respect. His name is Khenpo Choesang. My real guru is Dudjom Rinpoche. He wrote a recognition letter formally stating that I was the reincarnation of the Shabdrung. But now he lives in Nepal and I cannot go there, not yet.'

'Why don't you have a Lama who you can talk to, someone you can respect?'

'Most of these Lamas, they only know how to deceive the people.' He looked angry and disgusted.

There was a long silence while I looked at him puzzled and distressed. Were Lamas not heroic altruists, bodhisattvas? His eyes looked fierce as he retreated within unbearable memories. I placed my hand on his. He paused to bring himself back to the present, then said with conviction: 'There are only two great Lamas: Dudjom Rinpoche and the Dalai Lama.'

'Have you met the Dalai Lama?' I asked.

'Yes', he replied, 'many times. I went to see him last week in Dharamsala.'

I was intrigued by the protocol between two exiled kings. 'Do you prostrate to him?'
'No, he gets up to meet me. He says, "You are a king who has lost his country and I am a king who has lost my country. And therefore you will not prostrate to me and I will not prostrate to you." It was fascinating to hear such an exchange.
'What do you talk about with him?' I asked.
'He asks what I am doing and encourages me to study. Then I asked him about getting married.'
I listened intently. 'He said, you can get married if you wish, it's up to you, but it's simpler to be a monk. Family life is quite complicated.' Jigmai imitated the Dalai Lama's full-bellied laughter. 'I was getting ready to go when he whispered something to his attendant. The monk came back with a bundle of money. He handed it to me and said, "Here, this is for you. Now, go buy yourself some toys and play." And he laughed so hard some of the monks came in to see what was happening.'
I was astounded. 'How much did he give you?'
'Five thousand rupees.'
I pondered the meaning of this gesture. 'Maybe he thinks you need to have fun since you didn't have any in childhood.'

He locked the door, closed the curtains, came over to the sofa and placed my hand on his thigh. 'Yeah, darling, come here and play with me.'
'Please Jigmai,' I pleaded, 'do the protector prayers. I beg you, for your own sake, for me, please protect your life.'
He looked reluctant.
'You told me yourself the protectors are very strong in your lineage. They may turn against you. You must do the practice. After that...' I nudged closer and rested my hand lightly on his thigh.

'Don't try to control me', he warned pushing away my hand. 'Nothing can stop me except death.'
He got up abruptly and went to his shrine room. I could hear the haunting melody of the protector Mahakala chant, the clack of the skull drums and the sonorous ring of the bell. He returned half an hour later.

'Tomorrow morning you will leave, it is dangerous for you to stay here,' he said with concern. But tonight we will make love. Do you think five times is enough to get good practice?' he asked, enjoying the sport.

In the night he nudged me into semi-consciousness. 'Norma'. His voice was deep, loud and commanding. 'Turn off the tap; it's dripping.' I got out of bed like a robot and made my way dazedly to the bathroom. I was fully awake by the time I returned, and angry. 'Jigmai, don't ever ask me to do that again. Next time, you get up and do it yourself. I am happy to serve you, but I am not your servant.'

I was ready to leave the confusion of life at Bijai Palace and return to the order and tranquillity of Sherabling. I continued the fasting and prostrating practice in the attic room of my retreat house, now blackened with the thick oily smoke of burning butter lamps. I was alone now: Graham had returned to England to be with his elderly mother.

Jigmai's first letter after our meeting, written in capital letters on a blank sheet of paper, chilled me to the bone.

> Be careful. Do not walk alone in the forest or anywhere in the bazaar. You could get <u>raped and murdered</u>. Please take seriously. Also lock door. Do not go outside alone. You are in <u>grave</u> danger.

The words on the page were like a warning to beware the Ides of March. His deep compassion and concern for me was not the first emotion I felt. Free spirit that I was, I felt like I was getting dragged into an alien reality: a political murder. I was in the middle of a forest in my Guru's monastery doing a retreat. I lived alone, walked alone everywhere and enjoyed solitude. Fear was not in my mind and I didn't want anyone putting it there. I crumpled the letter and threw it on the charcoal brazier, watching it curl up, blacken and disappear.

A few days later I heard a distinctive knock on the door and looked outside to see Jigmai, mopping his brow with a large handkerchief, and breathing heavily. He looked distraught. He had slipped away from his bodyguards, taken a taxi from Mandi in his haste to see me, and walked four miles from the road to avoid detection. He came to the point immediately. 'One man has stopped me on the street in Mandi and said he knew you a few years ago.'

'Knows me? What does that mean? What's his name?'

'He's an Indian man.'

'Is he saying he had sex with me?'

'Yes.'

'Well it's a lie,' I replied vehemently. I felt sickened by the web of suspicion building around me. It made me feel imprisoned. 'I've never had sex with an Indian man. Never. I'm in solitary retreat, I've taken vows and I'm finding all this very disturbing.'

I prepared a pot of tea and poured the liquid into the cleanest cup I could find. Jigmai calmed down for a few minutes and then resumed the tirade that was turning into a set piece. 'That American woman who betrayed the king of Sikkim....' he started.

I knew what was coming and I felt despair.

'I can tell, you when the time comes,' I heard myself say,

'it will not be me who leaves you but you who will betray me.'

My words seemed to pacify him and restore his vigour. He came closer and put his arms around me 'Not now, I've taken vows, no sex, I cannot break my vows, don't ask me to do that. Please.' I felt his enormous power and it made me resist forcefully.

'I want you now', he said, pulling me closer until I could feel the heat from his body.

'No!' I shouted pushing him away.

'You don't love me, you love the dharma!' he bellowed in dismay.

My train of thoughts stopped. It was true; I didn't love him as he was. I loved him only when I could project a holy image onto him. When he didn't conform to my projections, I saw him as an intensely demanding, macho man. He was asking me to love him as a man. It was a defining moment in our relationship, like the moment the princess kisses the toad.

In one second I realised what I had to do. I had to serve him as he was, without any projections, unconditionally. I went upstairs to the shrine room and gave back my vows. I made a split second decision to cast aside my concepts of right and wrong, of spiritual and worldly, and take the leap of faith into blind love. Even the idea of serving an enlightened master, however ordinary he appeared, had receded into the background. I was just giving love to a man who asked me for it, needed it and deserved it.

'Where do you want to make love?' I asked when I returned downstairs. 'We can't do it here in my retreat space.' He thought for a moment. 'We can go outside.' I grabbed a blanket.

We climbed up the hill away from the monastery through the pine forest until we reached a sunny slope with a flat patch near a boulder. He looked at my body as I undressed. 'Your hair is so beautiful, I want to wrap it around my head,' he said caressing my wavy mane of dark hair and pulling it across his head. I looked at his face as he lay in the grass with the sun lighting his tanned skin, the glossy tuft of beard and long moustache curling upwards playfully, like Guru Rinpoche. 'Your face is so calm and sweet when you're lying down. It's how I would like to remember you.' He closed his eyes and smiled lazily, like a cat basking in the sun, as I captured the moment on camera.

We were undressing with mounting anticipation when we heard the tinkle of bells. A herd of goats was about to arrive, with their goat herder. 'Never alone in India', I said, jumping quickly into my skirt.

We walked back to the house and went upstairs. I had just enough time to throw my shawl over the compassionate thousand-armed Chenresig, whom I was calling on to purify the ignorance and habitual patterns of countless aeons, before Jigmai pulled off my silk underwear and entered me in the fullness of passion. Later, I pondered what kind of karma I'd made, but it wasn't something I was going to ask my Guru. In that deep part of myself which knows, I knew.

There are two types of Lamas, but most Westerners know only one type: the ones that present a picture of human perfectability – serene, compassionate, wise, with an extraordinary equanimity. That is the popular idea we have, embodied in the Dalai Lama – a smiling, kindly, saintly man.

But if one reads the stories of Tibetan masters, it's more complicated. The great masters have been paradoxical characters who often used shock tactics. They seemed quixotic, manipulative, dictatorial; sometimes even cruel. But all of these things were done to shock their students out of the rut of complacency and habitual patterns, examining their cozy assumptions about themselves and their relationships to the world.

This is the great dichotomy. In recent years the term applied to this kind of teaching is crazy wisdom. From the start it was apparent to me that Jigmai's behaviour did not conform to the first type. So I started thinking, is he the second? Is this irrational behaviour part of an ambiguous way of showing me something about myself? Is his irrationality part of his being a crazy wisdom teacher?

This was the question that would haunt me for the rest of our relationship. Was this crazy wisdom or just craziness, coming from the disturbances of his psyche? Was he a power maniac who was trying to possess me because he had lost everything else?

Running alongside this I could feel myself falling in love with him and he with me. So the question soon became, was I in love with him as a person or with some idea I had of him? When he said, 'you're not in love with me you're in love with the dharma', it forced me to make that instantaneous decision to accept him as he was. I decided simply to serve him, feeling the power of love would redeem both of us.

In that moment I started to walk a tightrope, making split-second decisions about where to place my next step; manoeuvring like a trapeze artist to weigh and balance every movement in the dance of love – with a great spiritual master who was also a dominating, macho man.

That was the moment I chose to walk a very dangerous path.

Two weeks later I was given permission by Tai Situ to finish the retreat. The amoebas were eating me up while I fasted. I was instructed to eat and take medicine. I had completed fifty-four sets of nyung nyes, one hundred and eight days under severe conditions: getting up before dawn in the freezing cold of a Himalayan winter, not speaking, prostrating all day while fasting, not drinking anything and the next day eating breakfast after sunrise, lunch by midday and going to bed hungry. Hunger, cold, sickness and exhaustion: it was very drastic medicine to arouse compassion for the suffering of the lower realms. I tasted its bitterness, but I did it because my Guru had prescribed it as a preliminary to the tantric meditation on the exalted Vajra Yogini, whose image continued to inspire me. It was a relief to stop.

Jigmai and I arranged a clandestine meeting to celebrate the end of the retreat at the Tourist Bungalow near the bus stand in Mandi – a place, unlike the renowned Raj Mahal, which Guruji would never think of watching. I arrived at the hotel in the early evening with my cassette player that could blast sound waves to rival Hindi pop music. I heard Jigmai's distinctive knock and opened the door. He walked in jauntily dressed in a t-shirt and white trousers that seemed unusually tight. The waiter promptly brought two bottles of Kingfisher, the local beer, and a plate of chips.

After downing them Jigmai relaxed, stretched out his legs and looked at his crotch.

'I saw a hippie sitting on a bench in Mandi last week. He was wearing a lunghi and his legs were spread open so I could see his cock. It was hanging out down his leg, it came to here', he said pointing in amazement to a place on his thigh. 'I was really surprised to see such a big cock.

'You know, sex isn't competition; it's communication.'

'What is the biggest cock you ever had?' he asked provocatively.
'I don't know. I wasn't measuring. I am definitely your first woman, no?'
'No.' He looked at my stunned expression and laughed. 'I was seven and I had full sex with a girl of five.'
'But how *can* you at that age?'
'I had an erection and I put my cock inside her and moved up and down, only nothing came out, like it does now'.

I listened, impressed by his candour. Everything was so open, so sharp, so entirely without shame or guilt. At the same time I couldn't help but wonder at his immaturity. It created confusion when I tried to align his rough edges with the perfect forms of his spiritual lineage. It just didn't fit, so I let go whenever I could and played – until the alarm bells started ringing, as they did, again and again.

He put on my favorite dance music, Robert Palmer, Sneaking Sally through the Alley. We began to dance without inhibition- leaping, swinging, kicking, spinning, singing boisterously like kids, screeching with laughter: Little Feat, Music from the Big Pink, Dylan, Van Morrison, Stevie Wonder, Marvin Gaye. We rolled on the bed wrapped in each other's arms while Joe Cocker sang, 'Just like a Woman'. And then....

Someone was pounding at the door. We turned off the music and sat still. I looked at my watch. It was an hour before midnight. The pounding continued. Jigmai went to the door and opened it cautiously. The waiter who had brought our beer and chips started speaking urgently in Hindi. Clearly there was an emergency. Jigmai shouted, 'Let's get out of here, quickly, Guruji is coming to the hotel, he knows our room number. Someone has informed him.'

We stuffed our bags hastily under the bed, shoved the cassette player into the wardrobe and locked the door. The escape was performed as deftly as if it had been rehearsed. Jigmai opened the window that led onto the balcony. He went out the window first, holding me by the hand as I followed and closed the window from the outside. From the balcony there was a straight drop of fifty metres to the ground, but right opposite our balcony was another balcony separated by about one metre. Jigmai took a bold stride and made it across to the next balcony, then held out his hand to pull me across. I leaped without looking down, grabbing his outstretched hand. The waiter was in the escape room opening the window for us to get inside. I lifted my skirt to climb in through the window, grabbing the waiter's outstretched hand. As I walked past him I felt his palm on my buttocks squeezing my flesh. I swung round to hit him, but he had already slipped past me and was whispering the next stage of the escape plan to Jigmai. We could hear Guruji pounding at the door of the room we'd vacated, his shouts of rage echoing down the corridor.

'Be very quiet', Jigmai whispered to me as the waiter slipped out the door. 'I have to go now', he said, 'I have to be in my bed before Guruji reaches there. I will have to leave you, darling. I will come and get you at six tomorrow morning and put you on a bus.' 'But the bus stand is right here', I protested, 'don't take the risk.' 'No,' he insisted. 'I must see you are safely on the bus'.

When the waiter returned, he escorted Jigmai through a back exit. The pounding and shouting continued for more than an hour. My head was spinning with confusion. I wanted to throttle the waiter who had dared to touch me. And as for Guruji, I hadn't expected a highly respected old monk to be so out of control. Jigmai was irrepressibly high-spirited, like a college boy, but underneath the male bravado, he was solicitous and protective. Was this confusion the benefit of offering my body to a great bodhisattva? My hopes and doubts started spinning again, chasing each other like the rooster, pig and snake at the hub of samsara's wheel. I finally dropped off to sleep.

****

After Guruji's dramatic midnight assault, I returned to Sherabling and moved prematurely into my new, rather grand retreat house, with a fireplace that belched smoke into the room, a damp waterlogged kitchen, cold as an icebox, and an Indian style toilet and shower – minus water. Apparently there was not enough water to supply the retreat houses, so I had to pay a didi, a servant, to come once a day and carry a container uphill from the monastery. The balcony, however, offered stunning views of the pine forest, with snowcapped mountains and the monastery in the distance.

As I was sweeping the cement floor with a disintegrating rush broom, I heard male voices speaking Hindi and a firm knock at the door. I turned around to see two official looking Indian men wearing identical khaki uniforms with badges. They were standing on the doorstep holding identification cards. 'Excuse us, Madam,' they said apologetically, 'we are from the CID.' I knew this was the secret intelligence service, like MI5. 'We have come to ask you a few questions. Do you mind if we come in?'

I ushered them into the dark dank kitchen. 'Please go ahead,' I said, feigning total unconcern.

'What is your relationship with SN Jigmai?'

'We are friends', I replied. 'I have known him for about one year.'

'Are you planning to marry with him?'
'I cannot say, I don't know.'
'Do you know the King of Bhutan?'
'No I have never met him, and I have never been to Bhutan.'

I took a deep breath and spoke. 'Look', I said, 'quite frankly, you think I am a spy because the old monk has told you. But he's only trying to make trouble for me. I have nothing to do with politics. As you can see, I am here in the middle of a forest and I have come to India to do my spiritual training. My Guruji has the monastery here and I came to take darshan[9] from him and practice meditation. I am not concerned with political matters. In fact I am supposed to begin my puja[10] in a few minutes.'
There was a pause; then they decided. 'We are very sorry to interrupt you, Madam', they said respectfully, and left.

I was struggling to steer my way through all these developments, recover my health and begin a new practice. Jigmai's letters did not inspire confidence in the stability of his life. But they had a charming vulgarity that made me smile.

> Norma-La,
> Here in this shit town of Mandi surrounded by unclean and vulgar people, the weather is unchanged for the last few weeks.
> I may go to Manali and some other towns of Himachal Pradesh on my routine tour, also I'm changing my residence so you won't find me here... Wait for my next letter to describe my whereabouts.

---

[9] blessing
[10] ritual prayers

The stability in my life came from another source: my Guru. One day I was looking out the window of my retreat house when I saw Tai Situ coming down the hillside towards my house, his sleeveless golden brocade shirt glinting in the sun. A young monk was holding a parasol over his head to shield him from the sun's rays. I ran out and invited him to bless my new retreat house. He came up the stairs, glanced at the shrine alcove to the right and went straight to the bed, built between a wall and a window facing south. Standing above the bed he made prayers that seemed to go on and on, while he scattered rice repeatedly over the bed. Then he turned to the shrine area and casually threw some rice on it as well. It was as if the sacred space was the bed and the shrine had only minor importance.

He didn't stop to talk but emanated an aura of golden harmony; a purity so fine it created a sense of balance. When he had finished, he made an elegant exit, moving so gracefully he seemed barely to touch the ground. It felt like the house was filled with particles of joy.

The tenth day after the Tibetan New Year was a special Guru Rinpoche day. There would be a massive festival with pilgrims from all over the Himalayas at Tso Pema Lake, which was a six-hour journey on a winding road through the Kangra Valley to Mandi, and another hour on a narrower road snaking upwards into the mountains. I made an instant decision to climb aboard a bus with a group of monks from Sherabling. As we passed through Mandi, I began to think very strongly of Jigmai.

In the late afternoon I joined the mass of pilgrims continuously circling the half-mile path around Tso Pema Lake. As evening approached, a crowd was building up behind someone important creating a rush of excitement as they tried to get closer. I followed the crowd expecting to see a great Lama with his retinue. I noticed a figure in a maroon cloak. It was Jigmai, flanked by bodyguards. I could hear the crowd murmuring his name, 'Shabdrung Ngawang Namgyal' as they pressed closer to present offering scarves. I caught up and walked beside him. He looked through me as if I were someone he had not seen before. I followed behind in turmoil watching him disappear into the Indian government guest- house.

It was the first time I had met Jigmai in his public role. Suddenly I had to recognise the great Lama who had no place for me in his life. Nothing in our relationship had prepared me for encountering my lover in his dynastic lineage as the mighty Shabdrung; and I didn't have the emotional maturity to deal with it.

At ten o'clock in the evening I knocked on the door. Jigmai opened it. 'I have to talk to you', I said.

'Not here,' he replied.

'Then come with me for a walk around the lake, there's no one there right now, it's empty. I really have to talk to you.'

We walked around the deserted lake with the waxing moon lighting Guru Rinpoche's power place.

'I don't care who you are' I started, my voice barely controlled, 'I don't care if this is a sacred place, or if it is the most sacred day in the year. I don't care if the Tibetans are watching, or if Guru Rinpoche himself is watching, I **want** him to watch. I **want** him to know. You can't sleep with me, make love to me, ask me to marry you, expect me to serve you, and then ignore me when we are in a public place!' I could not bear the humiliation of being denied as a woman.

A new emotional confusion was raging: not fear that he was not a Lama, but fear that he was. I could not look out of my self and absorb the overwhelming complexity of his life: revered figurehead, political prisoner, exiled king, and now secret lover to a free spirit.

Jigmai listened and said nothing. When my tirade abated he spoke calmly: 'Guruji is here, he will make a lot of trouble for you, you must understand, this is the way it is now. I'm not yet in control of my destiny. But by the grace of God', he said using a characteristic Indian phrase, 'I will be soon. I have to lead the korra[11] tomorrow morning, then we can go together wherever you like.'

I was captivated by his effortless ability to appease me and maintain his public role. He was totally in control of this game too. 'How can you get away?' I asked, incredulous.

'I will just go for one day as long as I am back in Mandi at night. We will go to the Palace Hotel if you like. Stop crying,' he ordered in a tone of voice that commanded obedience. 'You are not a baby.'

We completed the circuit without a single person seeing us. Then we separated for the night.

At dawn, I looked out my window feeling the buzz of excitement as the crowds gathered. I felt like a hungry ghost, those beings in Tibetan iconography with long thin necks too narrow to swallow food: they could see the feast but could not enjoy it. All I needed to do, really, was to let go of expectations, but of course I couldn't.

My life, my emotions were speeding up, racing out of control. One thing I knew with certainty: I was getting more and more involved with Shabdrung Ngawang Jigmai. He was boring deeper and deeper into my emotions, with his overpowering masculinity and his complicated double life. I was not meant to have a secret affair; my Guru had warned me. I reassured myself, I was not in love. I could

---

11 circumambulation of a holy place

still get out. The sexual alchemy had not yet happened, as if the electrical impulse hadn't been switched on.

I decided to stay away for the summer and monsoon, from all the complications with Jigmai, and the hostile environment created by Guruji. I needed to recover my health and even more importantly, my cultural sanity. I planned a few weeks in Darjeeling to take medicine from a special doctor there. I would relax at the renowned Windermere Hotel before flying back to London.

As it turned out, there was another scenario waiting for me, one that would show me I was not in control of my destiny, not at all.

CHAPTER 3

THE SHABDRUNGS OF BHUTAN

The Windermere Hotel was positioned strategically to the side of a prominent mound known as Observatory Hill where, it was said, a 'dorje', the Tibetan name for a sacred ritual sceptre, had fallen from the sky. 'Darjeeling' is actually a derivative of Dorje Ling, the place of the 'dorje'. Spectacular views of the five-peaked Kachenjungna mountain were only part of the attractions of the renowned Windermere.

The hotel was like a stage set from The Jewel in the Crown, with every detail of the British Raj in place – cast iron bathtubs on ornate legs, open fireplaces, tea trolleys, damask curtains with pelmets in the dining room, staff scurrying around in liveried uniforms. Its owner, an ageing rouged and lipsticked Tibetan aristocrat called Mrs Thondup-la, walked perfectly erect like a doll out of a box, complete with striped Tibetan apron, silk blouse and tunic, and – a slightly eccentric touch – a black patent leather handbag, which hung very straight from the crook of her elbow. Her father, she told me, over roast beef and Yorkshire pudding served in the dining room by liveried waiters, was General Laden-la. He had been instrumental in helping the British during the Younghusband Expedition, and therefore their family – quite wisely – had decided to move to Darjeeling, where they went into the hotel business. This was decades before the Tibetan exodus.

As I was sitting by the log fire in the library after dinner, she took out an album of photographs. The Windermere Hotel, she told me in proud, confidential tones, was the meeting place of Hope Cooke and the King of Sikkim before they got married. She opened the album and there in front of us was page after page of the young couple at the Windermere hotel sitting by the very same fire on the very sofa we were now on, followed by photos of their fairytale wedding in the Shangri-la kingdom of Sikkim. I looked in fascination at the unfolding of a story I'd heard so much about, and asked Mrs Thondup-la: 'Do you know anything about the spiritual kings of Bhutan?'

She began to tell me a story about the complicated marital links between the current Bhutanese kings and the Sikkimese royal family. 'No', I stopped her. 'I mean the spiritual kings, the Shabdrungs. 'No,' she replied perplexed at this sudden shift from gossip to history. 'I don't think so. Perhaps you can go to Habib Mullick', she suggested, her kohl lined eyes lighting up with excitement. 'His shop is in the town square and he sells antiques, books, everything. You might find something there.'

A prominent sign announced Habib Mullick's shop, dominating the centre of the town square. The double doors were open, so I entered, blinking in the dark. The electricity was down, the man wearing a boxy Turkish fez cap with a tassle told me apologetically. I walked past the wooden counters, trying to take in the detail. From floor to ceiling the room was overflowing with glorious objects. – Tibetan carved animals, wooden masks with ghoulish grins, heavy tribal jewellery, Tibetan felt boots, maps, fantastic sultans' hats, wide-brimmed Tibetan cowboy hats, gold brocade pantaloons, and shelves of books.

Immediately I saw a book that pulled me to it like a magnet: **BHUTAN** written in red letters, by the historian

Michael Aris. Here it was! Exactly what I had been looking for! I scanned the table of contents and turned to the final chapter on the first Shabdrung, Ngawang Namgyal, the founder of Bhutan,. 'How much?' I asked Habib Mullick. He opened the front cover. 'One hundred and eighty-eight rupees.' 'I have another one on Bhutan,' he said as I pulled out two hundred rupee notes. He went to take it from an upper shelf, dusted it quickly and brought it to me. **BHUTAN: The Dragon Kingdom in Crisis.**
'Nari Rustomji was the political adviser in Assam,' Habib Mullick explained, as I looked enquiringly at the author's name.

I opened Aris' book at random and found myself staring at a mural of the first Shabdrung in an impressively large brocade ceremonial hat. His face was wide, his nose broad, and a beard curled down the full length of his chest spiraling in a twist like a conch. One hand was touching the ground in the enlightenment posture of the Buddha. He was holding a long-life vase with two peacock fathers coming out of it. His eyes looked far seeing and compassionate. There was a physical – almost family – resemblance to Jigmai. 'I'll have both the books', I tried to say; 'I was breathless with anticipation.' Habib Mullick wrapped the books in tissue paper and placed them carefully in a clean cloth bag. I raced to the Windermere, clutching my treasure. Now at last I would find out who Jigmai really was.

That afternoon I sat in the library drinking tea. When the log fires died down at ten o'clock, I was still reading and re-reading Part Three of Michael Aris's **Bhutan**: 'The Zhabs-drung and the Creation of Bhutan'.

Ngawang Namgyal, the founder of the kingdom of Bhutan, known as the Shabdrung, was a larger than life character, unlike any spiritual master I had ever read about. I looked closely at another wall painting of the Shabdrung wearing a wide-brimmed black hat, right hand raised in a wrathful gesture. The same wide face was now showing a cropped black beard that covered the lower part like a mask. His eyes were fierce, but on close inspection, held compassion too. It was like looking at an outline of Jigmai, all the details fully developed and filled in.

The Shabdrung, Aris explained, was represented in sacred paintings with two different faces, one peaceful, one wrathful. In the more typical peaceful one, he wore the full robes of a monk, fingers touching the ground like the Buddha, his long beard twisted in a distinctive curl flowing down his chest. In the other, he wore the wrathful black hat of the 9th century Tibetan yogin, Palgyi Dorje, who had assassinated a Tibetan king, destroying the dharma.

I paused to reflect about this. It meant that Ngawang Namgyal was considered to be a Buddha. In Tibetan Buddhism, ordinary killing, out of conflict and hatred, is abhorred, even more than it is everywhere else; but there is another, rare kind which comes out of the purest most enlightened beings, who have overcome duality. To have that, one had to be enlightened. Many years later I would find these words of the Dalai Lama: "Violence and non-violence depend on the person's motivation. If a person uses appropriate measures to help another person, this is non-violence."

As I read, I could see that this story of Ngawang Namgyal's life was unlike the usual hagiographies of Buddhist masters, which cover up personal characteristics in order to dwell on visions, miracles and saintly activity. In it, an entirely different type was emerging – not the classical portrait of a Lama, but the wild, bold personality of a fearless Buddhist warrior – a shamanic man of power.

Namgyal was an extraordinarily charismatic character who used a combination of charms, like a sorcerer, to magnetise, dominate, and where necessary eliminate his many rivals and enemies, in order to establish a Buddhist kingdom in Bhutan. It was this complex legacy of supernatural powers and pure motivation that made him legendary, an epic hero, in the tradition of King Arthur: he was king, magician and Buddha all rolled into one. The life story of Ngawang Namgyal, first Shabdrung of Bhutan, as I discovered with amazement, was the history of Bhutan itself.

Ngawang Namgyal was born into an important aristocratic Tibetan family in 1594. From the moment of his birth all the ingredients of worldly and spiritual power were in place. His father was the prince-abbot of one of the major subdivisions of the Kagyu sect – the Drukpa. He recognised his son as the reincarnation of the omniscient Pema Karpo, literally the 'white lotus', a figure of immense stature in the Tibetan spiritual hierarchy. A monk, statesman, and scholar, Pema Karpo was also the spiritual leader of the Drukpa Kagyu. As frequently happened when there was so much wealth and power up for grabs, another noble family with a gifted child contested the reincarnation. The dispute went on for many years until both children were adults; and culminated in an incident involving death by ritual magic, the protector deities, and a precious bone relic.

Ngawang Namgyal had inherited a very precious sacred object – a bone relic belonging to Pema Karpo.This image of a deity with many arms had arisen spontaneously from the vertebrae of Pema Karpo's predecessor. The tiny image appearing in the bone was so fine it looked like it had been carved with the head of a pin; and so significant that it clearly established the possessor as the rightful reincarnation.

The rival claimant had the powerful ruler of the region, the Tsang Desi, on his side. They were desperate to get hold of this precious power object and devised a scheme. They claimed it as compensation for an accident in which some of their servants had drowned following a punch-up on a ferry with Ngawang Namgyal's servants. Ngawang Namgyal had, of course, refused.

When secret intelligence confirmed that the Tsang Desi was preparing to attack and kill him, Ngawang Namgyal pre-empted the attack in the first of several strikes he would make during his lifetime. He used his power of meditation and his legendary control of the protector deities of his lineage to perform what is known in Tibetan Buddhism as 'wrathful activity', destruction driven by compassion. As a result, three of the enemy princes died.

Ngawang Namgyal now became a man of destiny – the right person at the right time in the right place. The protector Mahakala appeared to him in the form of a raven, leading him to the Thimphu Valley in Western Bhutan, where he was told to establish his kingdom. Thus Ngawang Namgyal went into voluntary exile with his precious relic and began the heroic mission of taming hordes of bloodthirsty Bhutanese tribesmen into Buddhists of the Drukpa Kagyu order.

To achieve this he needed not only a charismatic personality, but also a little help from his supernatural friends. One of the first things he did was to propitiate the guardian deities of the Drukpa sect at a temple in the Thimphu Valley; and also the chief worldly protector of the temple.

When the Tsang Desi in Tibet mounted his first invasion against Bhutan in 1617, under the command of an officer called Ladgunas, Ngawang Namgyal retired to meditate in a cave. He was a mere twenty-four years old.

The invading forces witnessed a magical show as Ngawang Namgyal and his mighty troops appeared 'attired in tantric dress and accoutrements' – and they were terrified. Ladgunas was defeated; his head, heart and hands severed and offered to the guardian deities as 'secret supports.' A legend swiftly spread throughout Tibet, India and Bhutan, that "the great army of the Tsangpa had not been able to subdue this single yogin."[12]

Ngawang Namgyal then went into retreat in a cave, and performed a ritual invoking the supernatural powers of a wrathful deity to bring about the destruction of the Tsang Desi. The Desi and his wife died within a month. Upon hearing of the Tsang Desi's death, the Shabdrung performed prayers of thanksgiving to the protector deities to mark his victory. He made a declaration known as the "sixteen I's", which was incorporated into his personal seal. It is, in effect, a self-recognising testament of his spiritual and worldly status as one who has gone beyond duality, a Buddha. The testament included...

> I am he who turns the wheel of the dual system (of spiritual and secular law).
> I am everyone's good refuge.
> I am he who upholds the teachings of the Glorious Drukpa.
> I am the possessor of an unlimited view.
> I am he who refutes those with false views.
> I am the possessor of great power in debate.
> I am the hero who destroys the host of demons.
> I am mighty in speech that expounds religion.
> I am wise in all the sciences.

12 Aris, **Bhutan**, p. 212

I am the incarnation prophesied by the patriarchs.
I am the executioner of false incarnations.

The cave where he had meditated became known as 'the cave where demons have been subdued' and he became known as the Great Magician.

In 1627 two Jesuit priests, Cabral and Cacella, entered the court of Shabdrung Ngawang Namgyal, and lived eight months at his residence. The personality of this extraordinary man leaps out of the pages of their diaries. In a document called the 'Relacao', which Cacella sent to his superior in Goa – and which rests in the Vatican archives to this day – the Shabdrung is described as the King and chief Lama. His rule is known for its "great benevolence, the gentleness for which he is highly reputed."

In Cacella's words,
...the people have a very voluntary subjection to their king without any obligation on their part to defer to him or without any obligation to follow his doctrine, nor does he have power over the people to make anyone do anything; rather since his principal revenue is in what they give him voluntarily, he does not wish to have any of his subjects discontented and every one of them is very free to do what he wants, ... even his own lamas who are the people most subject to him.[13]

Many people from all over Tibet and the Himalayas were magnetised to the Shabdrung's court, they wrote, attracted by his varied talents as a man of letters and the arts.

They were also impresed with his discipline as a great meditator.

---

[13] Aris, **Bhutan**, p. 217

> He enjoys great regard for his gentleness, and not less for his abstinence from rice, flesh and fish, for he lives only on milk and fruits. At one time he passed three years in solitude living in a hut on a large projecting rock of a mountain without seeing or receiving anybody. With the aid of two ropes he drew up the food to his inaccessible dwelling place. He gave his time to prayer and in his leisure moments he made some images, one of which he showed us, an image of the face of God… carved in white sandal wood, small but excellently made. (*Early Jesuit Travellers in Central Asia,* Wessels quoted in Rustomji p. 50)

The Shabdrung had confided to one of the Jesuit priests that he would take full monastic ordination only when a son was born. In 1631 at the age of 37, he proclaimed a male heir with the birth of his only child, Jampal Dorje. (I looked in vain for any mention of his wife, or consort.) The next year he became a fully ordained monk.

Whenever the Tibetans attacked, they lost. The Shabdrung constructed great fortress monasteries, Punakha Dzong and Wangdi Phobrang to deter them. In the third Tibetan invasion a few years later these dzongs were attacked, but the Bhutanese again claimed victory.

In peace negotiations with the Tibetan ruler, the Shabdrung restated his claim to be the true reincarnation of Pema Karpo, and agreed to forego 'black magic rituals' if the dispute were resolved. The new Tibetan ruler capitulated, giving Bhutan to the Shabdrung as his domain. The dispute over who was the true reincarnation of Pema Karpo was resolved when the rival claimant died a few years later. His reincarnation became established as the Gyalwang Drukchen, the head of the northern branch of the Drukpa, while the Shabdrung continued to be the head of the southern branch of the school.

In 1642 the Mongols defeated the Tibetan ruler, the Tsang Desi, thus beginning the long period of the Mongol warlords' domination of Tibet. They had already created the title of Dalai Lama, which they had bestowed on a promising Tibetan monk of the Gelugpa sect, one hundred years earlier. By the time of the Fifth Dalai Lama, they had taken over Tibet. The Mongols under the Great Fifth, as he was known, attacked Bhutan a total of three times; and were defeated each time by the Bhutanese. Acording to Aris, it was not the Shabdrung's prowess as a military general leading an army in the battlefield that made victory possible, but his control of the guardian deities.

Feeling remorse for the number of deaths on both sides caused by years of battle, the Shabdrung dedicated himself to the construction of a large stupa[14] at Punakha. In his last years the Shabdrung occupied himself with the activity closest to his heart: disseminating Buddhist teachings and safeguarding the Buddhist community.

Ngawang Namgyal's activities in Bhutan became legendary. He had transformed it from a chaotic mass of warring fiefdoms governed by tribal chieftains into a unified Buddhist country, with himself as spiritual king. International recognition came in the later years when many important goodwill missions arrived at his court from neighbouring countries, and high-ranking lamas.

In 1651 he entered his final retreat and meditation, and the most enigmatic period in his life. Ostensibly, the Shabdrung entered retreat to counteract another Tibetan invasion foreseen in a vision. But it was six years before the Tibetans attacked – and lost, though at this point it was unclear whether the mighty Shabdrung was alive in deep meditation, or dead. The exact circumstances and date of

[14] Buddhist memorial structure containing holy relics

his death would be shrouded in mystery for the next fifty-four years, and can never be resolved.

The Shabdrung went into retreat at the age of 54, asking specifically not to be disturbed for twelve years. It was possible, Aris reasoned, knowing his leadership was so important for Bhutan's stability, he may have requested his chamberlain to keep his death secret, should it occur.

Whatever happened, it was clear the Shabdrung died in deep meditation. His chamberlain let it be known that the Shabdrung was in the after-death state, in the clear light, and could not be disturbed. This state of advanced meditation occurs in great masters after physical death and lasts from a few hours to, in rare cases, a few days.

In the case of Ngawang Namgyal, the after death meditation was adroitly stage-managed for years. Or was he actually in the state known as 'tukdam' where the physical body is dead but the meditation continues – for fifty-four years? During that time there was a realistic display of the Shabdrung's activity, albeit from his retreat cell. Decisions were seemingly made by him, letters written using his seal, food served through the trapdoor of his cloistered cell.

Fifty-four years went by before the country heard about the death of the Shabdrung. When the body was disturbed in 1705- by the reincarnation of Ngawang Namgyal's son! – it is said three lights went out from the mid forehead, heart and throat, and alighted in Sikkim, Bhutan and Tibet, where three reincarnations were found. The great Shabdrung had emanated three represenations of himself, embodying mind, speech and body. This superhuman spiritual accomplishment is possible for only the most enlightened masters. The mind reincarnation was enthroned in 1724.

Here Aris' history concluded. At the end of the book there was a photograph of the first hereditary king of Bhutan, Urgyen Wangchuk – looking every inch the victorious tribal chieftain – but no account of the takeover. No mention of the murder.

The body of Shabdrung Ngawang Namgyal was enshrined at Punakha Dzong in Bhutan where, to this day, a specially appointed cook and a chamberlain take care of the Machen (Great Mother, as the body is called) by preparing food and cleaning the environment. No one is allowed to enter and no one knows what state the body is in. It is considered the greatest sacred relic of Bhutan.

It would take many years to piece the whole story together, particularly the secret history of the murders of successive Shabdrungs. The first Shabdrung's exercise of wrathful powers, however pure the motivation, seemed to have unleashed the dark forces that lurk at the edge of the supernatural. There was a violent power struggle that continued for centuries after his death.

The successive Shabdrungs never succeeded in regaining the same degree of unified control over Bhutan as its founder had achieved. The epic quality of the first Shabdrung's magical victories gave way to a bloodthirsty struggle for power as the brigands who wrested control of Bhutan squashed and toppled each other like maggots crawling over a corpse. All six of the successive Shabdrungs from 1724 to 1907 were mere ciphers. They were frequently courted by one robber baron or another, or called upon to mediate in murderous disputes. They tried to discourage war and spent a good deal of their time in retreat.

"The Booteahs (Bhutanese) are full of fraud and intrigue and would not scruple to murder their own father or brother to serve their interest", wrote the Bengali agent to the British, who visited Bhutan in 1815[15] Political murders between warring factions, the burning of dzongs,[16] wars, smallpox epidemics, fires and earthquakes were common. Punakha Dzong – where Shabdrung Ngawang Namgyal's body lay in state – suffered no less than six fires, the body being escorted to safety each time by his appointed chamberlain. Six of the Deb Rajas, the regents, were killed, and at least twelve were deposed.

Although the institutions that the Shabdrung had created gave Bhutan a sense of cultural and national unity, politically and geographically the country soon reverted to the old tribal divisions that had prevailed before unification. The regional governors maintained in effect autonomous power. "Every baron was practically a king in his own province", commented Aris.[17]

Chief among these was the Ponlop of Tongsa, Urgyen Wangchuk, in east Bhutan, who in 1907 became the first 'hereditary' king founding a family dynasty, through a combination of brute force, political adroitness and magical good luck – much like a mafia version of the Shabdrung. The Wangchuks had something else that is said to have enabled their victory: the famous Raven Crown, now a symbol of Bhutanese royalty, but originally a magical battle helmet.

The Wangchuks were religious nobility: spiritual aristocras who could lay claim to the bloodlines of incarnation lineages. Religious nobility had wealth, power, and respect, the command that comes in Buddhist lands, from being the brother, father or sister of a revered

---

15 Aris, **The Raven Crown**, p. 46

16 fortress monasteries

17 Aris, **Bhutan**, p. 264

reincarnation. Frequently they became titans blown up with spiritual pride.

Urgyen Wangchuk soon established himself as Ponlop of Tongsa by eliminating the current Ponlop. By the time Wangchuk was twenty-four he had vanquished all enemies of the east and west and consolidated power by appointing his relatives to key positions.

It was then that matters took a decisive turn in a set of auspicious circumstances that politicians crave. In the wake of Younghusband's invasion of Tibet, Wangchuk gained favour with the leader, Sir Francis Younghusband himself, and became a mediator between the Tibetans and the British. The chieftain, whom the British saw as a "jolly, astute individual who was the de facto ruler of his country",[18] had the opportunity to become a statesman. His mediation was instrumental in effecting a settlement, and as a reward the British made him a Knight Commander of the Indian Empire. To further consolidate himself in his push for monarchy, Wangchuk then asked Lord Curzon to make him Ponlop of Tongsa for life. Curzon declined. Nonetheless the British played a key role in destroying the Shabdrung's legacy because they were interested only in secular power.

British support lent itself more to ceremonial show, as important to the Empire as it was to the Bhutanese. In 1906 Urgyen Wangchuk was invited to Calcutta by the Raj to meet the Prince of Wales and the Viceroy. He was greeted like an Indian prince, saluted with fifteen guns and given a gift of gold coins. In his thank you letter Wangchuk pledged allegiance "to the Supreme Government, hoping that as the sun and moon are like parents of the whole world, we

[18] Aris, The Raven Crown, p. 88

also will enjoy the blessings of their beneficent rays for ever and ever till the cessation of worldly existence."[19]

Unsurprisingly, this regal declaration was a prelude to a bid for the monarchy. On December 17, 1907 in the presence of a British Political Officer, Urgyen Wangchuk was made king of Bhutan by unanimous consent. The great seal of the founding Shabdrung (the current Shabdrung was only four years old at the time) was imprinted on the document, giving him and his heirs the kingship.

Charles Bell, British Political Officer, was impressed. The King "had lessened, as far as one man could do, the lawlessness inherent in this hardy but primitive people."[20] As a conciliatory gesture, Wangchuk installed the young spiritual king at his monastic seat at Talo. When Wangchuk died at the age of sixty-four, it is said he repented his acts of violence

When his son, Jigme Wangchuk, inherited the throne, the gates of hell that had been left ajar opened wide. In 1923 he was installed at Punakha in the presence of the 7th Shabdrung, the twenty-two year old Jigme Dorje. (Curiously, they were both the same age and both called Jigme.) Colonel Bailey, representing the Government of India, attended the ceremony to present the insignia of the Companion of the Indian Empire.

Conflict between the hereditary and spiritual kings started when the Shabdrung, who had no temporal power, exercised a very small favour, which threatened the King's authority. The King's suspicions increased when the Shabdrung sent his brother under escort to meet Mahatma Gandhi in India, to enlist Gandhi's help in restoring his waning powers.

---

[19] Aris, The Raven Crown, p. 94

[20] Aris, ibid, p. 100

Relations worsened to the point of open confrontation. When the Shabdrung's attendants heard that a troop of soldiers was about to storm Talo they begged him to leave. He refused: "I am a monk, not a soldier. They will not harm me for I have done nothing wrong,"[21] he said.

Three hundred armed men – among them Lamas – dressed in full battle regalia reached Talo on October 29, 1931. Shouting war cries, they split into different groups, each group entering from different gates and descended on the terrified residents. Although they besieged Talo for nearly two weeks, they were reluctant to commit the cardinal sin of assassination.

Orders to kill the Shabdrung came from the king's winter court. On the night of November 11, 1931 the Shabdrung asked for a new set of clothes, but they were uncomfortable and he decided to sleep naked. When warned of the danger, he replied, "If my death is of any benefit, it is all right for me. I am not afraid to die. For me it is like changing my clothes." He fell asleep. Just after ten o'clock, eleven men entered the room with torches. They encircled the sleeping Shabdrung, pinned him down, grabbed his throat and kicked him in the scrotum. A silken offering scarf was stuffed down his throat until he stopped struggling. The next day it was announced that the Shabdrung had died in his sleep, aged twenty-six.

---

[21] Wangchuk, **Of Rainbows and Clouds**, p. 31 ff.
The secret assassination of 1931 would not be revealed until 1999 with the unusual publication of a book **Of Rainbows and Clouds** written by one of the four queens of the current ruling king, whose father was the uncle of the murdered Shabdrung. King Jigme Senge Wangchuk had married all four daughters of the family of the murdered Shabdrung in a bid to meld the spiritual monarchy and the hereditary kingship, thus consolidating his power.

The body was disposed of hurriedly, bypassing the usual elaborate arrangements for the forty-nine days lying in state of a high Lama. Twelve days after his death the Shabdrung was cremated on the lawn at Talo. Everything was reduced to ashes except his heart, eyes and tongue, which miraculously did not burn, and should have been preserved as holy relics. One of the murderers, a reincarnate Lama, pointed a stake at the heart and jabbed it to bits. Witnesses, who are still alive, reported that people cried aloud, dogs howled, and the Shabdrung's horse was seen rolling in agony when his master's ashes were immersed in the river. The whole valley, it was said, reverberated with wailing.

The only Bhutanese account of the event at the time suggested suicide. "Saddened by the deeds he had committed from listening to the plots of these evil persons, the Shabdrung died on the first day of the tenth month."[22] The 8th reincarnation of the Shabdrung was also murdered during the reign of the same King.

In Nari Rustomji's book, written in the late seventies, I came upon a chilling passage about the 9th Shabdrung, my Jigmai, whom I had met in 1980. The book exposed the assassination of the Prime Minister, Jigmie Dorje, a close friend of the author, Rustomji. Dorje had told Rustomji many times that "as far as he was concerned, the institution of Dharma Raja" (that is, the spiritual king) "was as dead as the dodo, and that he would not under any circumstances permit its resuscitation. His loyalty, first and last was to his King" – the hereditary monarch – "and if any young lad was luckless enough to be identified as a potential Dharma Raja, the Bhutanese were adept in fixing an 'accident' to hurry him to his Nirvana".

[22] Aris, **The Raven Crown**, p. 122

By 1962 Jigmai's extinction had become crucial to the King of Bhutan, because war had broken out with China. The Prime Minister was concerned that the child of six might be abducted by the Chinese and set up as their puppet, thus threatening "the authority of the rightful ruler" of Bhutan. He sent frantic SOS messages to his friend Rustomji, who was Adviser to the Governor of Assam (bordering Bhutan), trying to locate the child in order to kill him. But Rustomji was working to a different, and kinder, political agenda. He brought Jigmai and his guardian to stay with him "in the safer environs of Shillong". From there he brought the child to the Dalai Lama in Dharamsala. "The maneuverings in certain orthodox quarters to restore him to his traditional dignity in Bhutan, are, needless to say, not given official encouragement," commented Rustomji.[23]

Rustomji was an important figure in Jigmai's childhood – the Indian officer who had protected him from certain murder at the hands of the Bhutanese Prime Minister. But he was still a pawn in the game between India and China. No wonder Jigmai was cynical and suspicious! He had been hunted from earliest childhood, his mind disturbed by deceit and betrayal. The mighty Shabdrung of Bhutan was forced to live in exile in Mandi, unrecognised and powerless. Jigmai's fondness for Shakespeare suddenly made perfect sense.

In 1987 he told me he had met the King of Bhutan at a meeting arranged by the Indian Government at the Ashoka hotel in Delhi. 'He said to me,' recounted Jigmai, 'I am inviting you to return to Bhutan, but prove to me that you are the reincarnation of Ngawang Namgyal.'

'What did you say?' I asked.

---

[23] Rustomji, p. 92

'I said, "I don't have to prove anything to you. You should check for yourself and find out everything. When you are satisfied so that you know who I am, come and find me." Then I turned around and left the room.

'What do you think?' Jigmai asked me. 'Did I say the right thing?'

'Yes, if you want to put him in his place. What do you think would happen if you went back to Bhutan? Would they kill you again?

'I am not sure. I can't think about it. The thought itself makes my body shake.'

Eventually the king worked out a more manageable option. He made a public apology to the Bhutanese people for the evil committed by his forefathers, married the four daughters of the assassinated Shabdrung's family, and with due pomp and ceremony, brought a precious image of the murdered Shabdrung back to his seat at Talo Monastery where silk ceremonial offering scarves were draped over the bejewelled bronze gilded body. But the living Shabdrung exiled in India, was never formally acknowledged. King Jigme Wangchuk and Shabdrung Ngawang Jigmai never met again.

References:

Bhutan, M. Aris, Aris and Phillips Ltd, Warminster, England, 1979

The Raven Crown, M Aris, Serindia Publications, London, 2005

Bhutan The Dragon Kingdon in Crisis, Nari Rustomji, Oxford University Press, Delhi, 1978

Of Rainbows and Clouds, Her Majesty the Queen of Bhutan, Ashi Dorji Wangmo Wangchuk, Bookwise (India) Pvt Ltd, New Delhi, 1999.

CHAPTER 4

THE VISION

London 1981

After my research into the life of the Shabdrungs I felt awe for the original Shabdrung but despair for Jigmai. He was not free to marry, I realised, or to live a normal happy life, The Shabdrungs, it seemed, were all monks. The question remained: was he actually going to take his place as the Shabdrung? For the first time I understood the political dimensions of what I had fallen into. Should I continue the friendship in spite of the obstacles, or take them as warning signs to get out?

Safely back with friends in London I dared to express my concerns. I wrote a letter to Jigmai bewailing the backwardness of Indian attitudes towards women, explaining how difficult it was for me to be seen as a sex object, to be secreted in a hotel room, to have the Indian police watching me, and to be on guard against a crazy old monk who wanted to kill me for being a spy.

He interpreted the letter as a personal criticism, a prelude to my departure. The dream shattered instantly for both of us.

Hello! Norma,
Received your very interesting letter and came to know its all contents. I would like to suggest you that if you feel so terrible to stay here in India and face many rights of life then better to stay in west and get marry with some young chap and enjoy yourself. Why knowingly you are putting yourself in agony and misery? It was of course very nice to read your mind about the Indian culture, somehow I would like to tell you wether a man or woman is from east or west one day it has to merge with the earth so dear, I can't see any solid reason of having such a bad view about these poor creatures. You are in Dharma so I think at least your development of mind or concept of worldly things should be above than that of an ordinary people. But learning so much of Dharma and wasting huge sums of money again if you feel like captivated by the glittering of western society and its show then I am sure no one can stop you going back from where you originally came. But the time will come when you will regret on your own deeds but that will be too late. Anyway I am sorry for writing such an othentic letter or remarks.
As I hear from Paresh, your house is almost finished I think...
Apart everything I'm happy to know that you are enjoying and passing your time nicely. Forget about getting marry with me and don't be so scared of having an eastern husband anymore. My mind does not change but the time is changing swiftly.
Rest everything is all right. Hoping to see you in India soon. With all good wishes and sweet memories.

N. Jigmai
Mandi, India

Good Bye – and good luck to you Dear Norma. Kept on waiting you to write me first but you preferred some one else from your beautiful England.

With the effect the
deep
Love, deeper than the depths of sea
Shattered into small rivers, and the drout brought agony to
ALL.
(In the margins was written) Soon I may go somewhere else
"DO NOT BURN IT. KEEP IT AS A MEMORY."

I could feel his sadness, but for the first time I felt free. I wrote an appeasing letter expressing remorse for hurting him; he asked for my arrival time at Delhi Airport. But again it seemed that some force beyond my own will was guiding this relationship.

The day before my departure for Delhi, I met Joyce, a wealthy Californian who lived in splendour in Holland Park. Joyce was young at forty- eight, her expensive chunky turquoise jewellery and long exotic peasant shirt showing a taste for the bohemian international lifestyle. But it was her engaging personality which was far more striking; her lively sparkling brown eyes seemed to miss nothing.

We drove to a forested area outside London. During the walk she talked with her associate, while I walked with my friend, Judith. Joyce and I exchanged the barest of pleasantries. We went back to her enchanting home in Holland Park for dinner. The walls were lined in silk brocade and luxuriously textured patterned velvet. Pictures of fantastic creatures, esoteric books, exotic displays of feathers and crystals gave the feeling of a cabal, a secret society.

Joyce turned off the lights, lit the candles and served quiche and salad on exquisitely patterned china. Then during dinner, she suddenly turned to me and asked, 'Who is that extraordinary man who is always around you? He is very powerful.'

My fork stopped in mid air. I looked at Judith sitting next to me for explanation. 'Joyce is clairvoyant', she said quietly.

Spontaneous clairvoyance at this level was new to me, but I couldn't help knowing that Joyce was really seeing Tears came into my eyes as I knew in my heart I wouldn't be able to get away from Jigmai. 'He is the spiritual king of Bhutan' I replied, 'and he asked me to marry him. But there are so many obstacles. I want to help him, but I'm not in love. I don't know what to do.'

'He seems very old.'

'That's because he is a very high Lama with many reincarnations.'

'He is a very important man, a very great being. But you are not seeing that. Right now he has nothing, it's not showing. Look' – she came out of her vision momentarily to address me directly. 'You're not treating him properly. It won't happen the way it's going now. If you want this to happen I can tell you how to do it, but first I'm going to tell you about your own lifetimes. You are something special as well. You've had past lives as a monk in Tibet, but for now I'm going to tell you about your lifetimes as a beautiful woman. You have your own lineage as a very beautiful woman.'

She looked into space, and seemed to be reading images that were coming to her. I listened, fascinated.

'First you were the consort of a king; it looks like Egypt, ancient Egypt, about 2000 years ago. He had many consorts but you were his favourite. You're in silk pantaloons; your hair is long and red, tied in a knot at the top of your head held with a jeweled pin.

Now I can see you as a grand lady married to a man whom you're not happy with. You're living in a large luxurious house in Venice and you spend most of your time with a secret society, something similar to the Knights Templar.

In some ways the happiest time you've had was when you were living in a cave in the desert. People are coming to you for advice; you're known far and wide as a seer. You have a horse which you ride everywhere. In this lifetime you are free of the world.'

'Now I can see another image', she continued. 'This time it's in the future. I see you in a beautiful saree. You're in a mansion entertaining with your husband by your side. He has a very high position, something like a Governor of one of the Indian states. You're looking at him laughing at his great wit and charm, and he's drawing you into a special space you've created together. You're a powerful couple.
Now I can see two beautiful children, a boy and a girl. They're your children. But I should tell you this. He's going to have a lot of women and although you're the woman he loves, it's going to hurt you a great deal. Think about it.
This is only one slice of the pie,' she warned. 'It's there, you can have it, but you have to completely alter the course of events now.'

I was in turmoil. Could any of this be true? But what she said about Jigmai, **was** verifiable.
'Now I'm going to tell you what you have to do if you want all this to happen,' Joyce continued. 'You have to play more, lighten up, laugh, play with it all, enjoy it. Let go, let him take the lead, loosen up, and submit to him. Let go; let him have what he wants. Give yourself to him. You can have some very happy years with him,' she said.

There was barely time to catch the last bus to Kentish Town. The streets were deserted. as Judith and I eased into our seats. 'What an extraordinary world we have been in!' Judith gasped in awe 'I knew Joyce was clairvoyant but

I've never known her to do anything like that. She must have felt you really needed to know the whole story. It was as if something was guiding her.'

I was more impressed by synchronicity, the last minute timing of the meeting. Perhaps Joyce was spinning her own Californian fantasy. But that it had happened now, made it feel like a sign, a portent indicating an inevitable and dramatic event.

That night, as I slept on a mattress on the floor of the squat in Kentish Town, my mind began to change, to accept this new vision of a mature, professionally empowered Jigmai, still a renegade inside, but a man of power, with his unusual Western wife by his side, respected and accepted. It was as if I had drunk a magic potion and was under its spell. In one night I fell in love with Joyce's vision of a loving couple in a divine union with two beautiful children flanking us, the fruit of our bliss.

I didn't ask myself who my ambition was for, myself or him. And I didn't listen to the warning.

Act Two

Everybody has his own path, his mission, and even if you take your Master as a model, you must always develop in a way that suits your own nature. You have to sing the part which has been given to you, aware of the notes, the beat and the rhythm; you have to sing it with your voice which is certainly not that of your Master, but that is not important. The one really important thing is to sing your part perfectly...

(M. Aivanhov, What is a Spiritual Master? p.70)

CHAPTER 5

TANTRIC SEX

October 2, 1981.

> Today is a day when my life moulded to a new direction. I am freed by the Indian government to an empty sky. Now I will get a chance to image myself and do actual work in my own way.
> This news was broke to me by the DC Mandi at 9:30 am. May Kunchog grant me strength and power to bright my life.
>
> *from the diary of SN Jigmai*

There was something different about Jigmai when he met me at the airport in Delhi the next evening. The immature boisterous, awkward man in a tight ill-fitting suit and blue cotton turban, who called himself Man Singh, was no longer there. A subtle hint of sophistication seemed to be lying just under the surface, waiting to extinguish the old crudeness. 'Let's go to the Maharani Hotel,' I said impulsively. The Maharani was usually off budget for both of us. 'I have so much to tell you. But how did you manage to get out of Mandi?'

'I also have some news. I just received my freedom from the Indian government. There are no more bodyguards unless I will request it. The SP will call on me and make reports and they are still keeping my VIP salary and status.

So I got everything I asked for.'
I was overjoyed. 'That means you are free to marry?' I asked.
'That is why I asked for it, but now I am wondering how I will image myself, what I will do. I have been freed to an empty sky.'

The taxi reached the hotel. When we got into our modest suite Jigmai sat on the king size bed and ordered me to close the curtains. He seemed very much in control.
'Now tell me about your fortune teller lady.'
I gaped at him. 'How did you know?'
He ignored my question. 'Go on darling, tell me everything.'
His voice was so seductive; I sat on the bed beside him.
'She said you were very great, and we could be happy together, that you would be holding a high position within the Indian government and I would be accepted as your wife. We would have two beautiful children. But I had to change my way of behaving. I had to submit to you, to lighten up, be playful, give in to your commands.'

I laughed, teasing him. Our bodies moved together, perfectly synchronized for the first time in the act of erotic love. 'This is how a man fucks when he loves a woman', he said. As we moved together I forgot about time. And then we separated.

He looked at his watch. 'An hour and fifteen minutes', he said proudly. I laughed. 'You have incredible control. I've never met anyone who could make love like that. How did you learn that amazing position?'
'I looked at the pictures of the couples at the temple of Khajuraho. You know they built those temples to distract the monks because Buddhism was taking over Hinduism. So what is your opinion of Indian customs now, darling?'
'I'd like to know more about them. Perhaps you can teach me. It obviously needs a very qualified teacher, and an

interested student willing to open herself,' I said, keeping as straight a face as I could.

He lay down on top of me, gently at first, then more strongly until his full weight pressed on my body. It was like being crushed by a bulldozer. 'Don't', I gasped, 'you're suffocating me.' He continued the pressure until I stopped struggling to get free. Then I found I could breathe and the pressure became quite bearable. He bit my nose, gently at first, then harder and harder until I yelped in pain as his teeth bit bone. 'That's more than a schnozzle bite,' I said, rubbing my nose.

'I love you so much I feel I want to eat you,' he said.

'You know,' I said feeling his intense restlessness, 'you should be the general of an army, or the king of a country, or ...the governor of a state. You're a warrior, a man of action. You shouldn't be focusing all your energy on one woman.'

He sucked my nose eagerly like a baby sucking a nipple, and then gently, sensually, slowly entered me again.

****

Two days later Jigmai came to my retreat house at Sherabling and initiated the bed, which still had bits of rice on it from the blessing. He had become an adept at the art of lovemaking and conquered me confidently, with a devastating combination of eroticism, love, and power. His life force energy flowed constantly into me.

'Our bodies fit together', Jigmai said suddenly one night as we lay together. 'Let's measure it and see'.

We stood naked against the wall with the tape measure and compared our height, then lay in bed and measured ankle to knee, knee to hip, hip to armpit, neck to elbow and elbow to the tips of our fingers. Our measurements were all identical. But in breadth, he was twice my size.

He noticed a drop of blood on the sheets. 'I want a bottle of your menstrual blood,' he said abruptly. It was a command. I could feel a cold dread creeping over me.

'No', I said appalled,' what do you want that for?'

'I want to put a drop on my forehead. It's supposed to attract women.'

'That's crazy', I shouted. 'I can't do things like that. Where do you get these ideas?'

We dressed and sat on the balcony.

'I have a text on magic, many texts', he said casually. 'In my lineage we are very perfect in magic.' I remembered Ngawang Namgyal, the Great Magician and knew he was not lying. 'Do you see those four people walking on the hillside over there?' he asked pointing to the ridge opposite my house. I looked and saw four people walking in a line on the footpath.

'I can make them fall down the hill. But I will do it only if you tell me, and if one of them gets hurt or killed, it's your karma.' I looked at him. It did not seem to be a joke; more like a challenge.

I began to feel afraid. 'I'm not interested in making that kind of karma. I'm only interested in practicing the Buddhist teachings. Why are you asking me, anyway?'

Indignation was rising in me like a claw clutching at my throat. This volatile man was tossing all my ideas about right and wrong into the air with reckless abandon! Just when I thought we were at peace, he became provocative. When I thought we were perfect lovers, he became jealous. When I followed the dharma, he boasted of his dark powers. When I gave up and settled into submission, he turned into a baby.

Once again I was walking the tightrope wondering whether Jigmai was a crazy wisdom master or merely crazy. The history of Tibetan Buddhism is full of crazy wisdom Lamas. Drukpa Kunley, 'the divine madman of Bhutan', wrote songs recording his sexual pleasure with young innocent girls, extoling the tightness of their vaginas and the fullness of their breasts. It was considered a great blessing to have sexual contact with an enlightened master: the semen was the essence of his compassion. When Drukpa Kunley's women meditated afterwards they reached a state of clarity and bliss. The songs of the sixth Dalai Lama were love poems to the various women he adored, some of them prostitutes.

And then there was the controversial Chogyam Trungpa, a contemporary Lama, who downed saki like water, had sex with his devotees, staged shocking scenes involving nudity and humiliation and gave extraordinarily precise teachings that targeted the culture of Western spiritual materialism. Some of his students were convinced he was a master in the tradition of crazy wisdom yogis. But to some he was a sexually depraved guru who became a cult icon and died of alcoholism. In the shadow-lands beyond boundaries, reality is what you perceive it to be.

Though I had asked Jigmai to teach me tantric sex, when he denied he was a Lama, I surrendered, accepted him as he was: an extraordinary lover and challenging companion. None of his 'craziness' seemed motivated by what I could recognise as traditional expressions of loving kindness and compassion. But he was said to be a tenth level bodhisattva, virtually an enlightened being, who reincarnates out of compassion to guide others. It was taught that conventional reality, for a tenth level bodhisattva, was like a dream or illusion it wasn't the fixed solid entity it was for ordinary people. Compassion and wisdom, I thought, had to be deeply embedded in his spiritual genes, no matter what.

I knew a bodhisattva didn't have to be a Lama, that he could take any form whatsoever, but nothing in my training prepared me to encounter somebody as quixotic and unpredictable as Jigmai: one minute an erotic lover emanating from the pages of the Kamasutra, the next a sorcerer with magical powers from a remote past life, the next a fierce, indomitable, heroic warrior, ready to slay the dragons of religious hypocrisy. He seemed to slide in and out of a web of personalities in multiple dimensions. The truth was always staring me right in the face but it was too close and too simple to see. Jigmai was a master of the greatest sport of all: illusion's game, the play of appearances.

Three weeks later on November 5, 1981, the 16th Karmapa died in Chicago. He had been ill, but nonetheless the news of the passing of our lineage Guru left a deep hole in our hearts. The 16th in the lineage of the Karmapas was, like his predecessors, renowned throughout Tibet for his miraculous powers. He came to the West in the early seventies, when I first met him in Hay-on-Wye, and he continued to sow the seeds of enlightenment through his extraordinarily powerful spiritual presence. He seemed to embody the still point, the source of creation. No one who met him failed to revere him. His passing seemed to make the world suddenly darker.

I decided to join the group from Sherabling who were journeying to Rumtek monastery in Sikkim where the forty-nine days ceremonial rites would be held. I wrote to Jigmai and said I would be away for two months. Within days he arrived at Sherabling.

'Why are you going to Sikkim? He paced up and down the mud packed floor. He seemed overpowered with possessiveness.
'I'm going to the Karmapa's funeral. He's my Guru', I maintained resolutely. 'I **have** to go to Sikkim.'
He was ranting now, charging himself up for the battle with religious hypocrisy. I began to weep with despair. I could feel the whole structure of my existence slipping away, and a dark fear overcame me, as if I was about to be marooned without hope of rescue. I began to fight for my life.
'You can't control my life like this. I'VE GIVEN YOU MY HEART, NOT MY SOUL', I found myself shouting.

'Goodbye and enjoy yourself!' he shouted as he walked down the stairs out of the house. I thought I could hear fragments of phrases, 'dangerous man' and 'Buddhists not revengeful but I am.' And then, more clearly, 'You will never be able to forget me.' I watched him disappear from the hillside into the forest.

Conflicting emotions were tearing me apart. At a human level I understood Jigmai's reactions to my independence. This male possessiveness was against every expectation I had from studying the Buddhist teachings. Why, oh why, was this man in my life? Did he need my support or was he going to drag me into his dark underworld?

I felt as though I had turned a key and opened the door into an alien world, a place where logic and reason were giving way to a world of magic and intrigue, with scheming Lamas conniving for power. Little did I realise I was seeing through Jigmai, the dramatic landscape of Bhutan, with its very dark shadow.

My foundations were beginning to crack. I was losing my moorings, struggling to retain a grip on anything recognisable. I tried to remind myself that Jigmai was not my guru. I had made this clear to him and he had seemed to accept that we were not guru and disciple but lovers, a man and a woman. I told myself that in the Karmapa's sacred environment the cracks would heal, and everything would make sense again.

The next day I packed my bags and left for Sikkim.

Sikkim November 1981

Dr Wangyal's house was perched on stilts on a hillside, like all the other houses lining the road to Rumtek Monastery. He was standing on the balcony as we trudged down the steep hill from the monastery where the bus had dropped us, with our sleeping bags stacked on top of rucksacks. We had been traveling for three days from Sherabling.

Dr Wangyal was beaming broadly, showing teeth stained with beetle nut, a Bhutanese addiction. 'Welcome, Sherabling!' he grinned. The beetle juice dribbled out of his mouth onto his flat red cheeks. His short wide legs, with small flat feet pointing outwards, gave him the comic appearance of a penguin. 'Ladies' dormitory', he laughed waddling into the shrine room to show us sleeping space for six on the wooden floor. The four men were more fortunate and occupied a variety of beds in a spare guest room.

It was so cold we gravitated towards the wood stove in the kitchen which Dr Wangyal's wife, Dolma, was stoking with wood. 'I've prepared a welcome drink for all of you', he said, handing us each a wooden glass filled with millet and hot water with a straw protruding from the brew. 'It's called tumba', he said, gurgling as he sucked his straw. Every time the water level decreased, Dr Wangyal jumped up promptly to fill it up. After an hour we were as merry and red cheeked as our host. The millet was fermented and turned into pure alcohol as the hot water was poured on top.

'No need to rush', said Dr Wangyal, popping a fresh beetle nut covered in a green leaf into one side of his mouth. Now he looked like a panda with a delicious grub in its cheeks. 'The ceremonies won't be starting for one week. They are packing His Holiness' body in salt. No one can go inside except the rinpoches.'

I was eager to explore the renowned pilgrimage places of Sikkim, one of the major sacred lands of Guru Rinpoche. 'Let's go on pilgrimage and come back in three weeks,' I suggested to Isa, a robust, Spanish woman with olive skin. It was late November with bright, sun-filled days and cold, bone-biting nights when we started walking from Pemayangtse, an important monastery, to the mountaintop hermitage of Tashiding, the foremost sacred site in Sikkim.

There was no direct route linking the sites enroute in a clockwise circle – the korra or movement of the pilgrim. We ventured along the rim of mountains on foot -sized goat trails into the untouched garden paradise of Sikkim – through fragrant cardamon forests into sunlit orange groves, crossing a river over a swaying, frayed bridge, to a lake set deep in the midst of an ancient forest, so tranquil it looked enchanted. It was Khechuperi, a lake blessed by Guru Rinpoche. At another place, near a river where hot sulphur springs formed huge healing tubs, there was an opening into the rocks. A small entranceway like a porch led to a great cavern where a natural skylight threw a shaft of light onto an unmistakable outline – the enormous body print of Guru Rinpoche. At Tashiding a huge boulder concealed terma or sacred treasure, which Guru Rinpoche had placed there in the 8th century.

Everything seemed imbued with Guru Rinpoche's presence, even the cascading chutes of water forming icy pools into which we plunged, the exotic orchids and spices, the very air we breathed. Every time I saw an image of the Guru with his curling moustache, his fearless stare and warrior-like trident resting upright in the crook of his arm, I understood Jigmai was truly his emanation: an unpolished diamond with the same fearless quality underneath.

By the time we returned to Rumtek, it was as if I had walked the inner circle of a magic spell, seeing Jigmai beyond his worldly veils, on his spiritual level. The different appearances were meshed, the mythic linking in with the personal. I was beginning to fall in love with a man who, much of the time, I didn't even like. Here, away from him, I could find him in my heart again.

Rumtek Monastery December 1981

The courtyard in front of the monastery was so packed with devotees we were barely able to negotiate a passage through it to get closer to the temple. Tibetans, Bhutanese, Westerners, Sikkimese, Indians- all mingled together in an exotic display of customs and costumes. Some Tibetans had crossed the Himalayas to be at the ceremonies.

Boisterous Bhutanese men were clothed in knee length checked cloth tunics with long wool socks covering sturdy calves, their black hair and red stained teeth reminiscent of medieval peasants drinking blood. The women had identical straight black hair in a short pudding basin cut and ankle length checked tunics with heavily embroidered belts at the waist. Beetle juice lay in thin red stains on the ground, evidence of the preferred vice of both sexes.

The Indian army had set up large khaki tents all over the hillside from which they offered mountains of free food and even shelter to all the participants. Every day significant contingents of devotees were arriving. Trungpa Rinpoche, by now a famously iconoclastic guru, had arrived from his adopted home of Boulder Colorado, accompanied by a group of American students dressed like professionals in impeccable business suits and shiny black shoes. They made short formal bows everywhere like the Japanese, and chanted prayers in a thumping drum-beat, to give more authenticity to their awkward English translations.

On the day of the cremation, thousands of people jammed into the stairway of the monastery to get to the top floor where Karmapa's body was lying. I joined the caterpillar queue weaving inch by inch towards the summit until I was finally deposited right beside the huge white stupa containing the sacred body. The four heart sons of the Karmapa were seated with their monks at the four cardinal points, each wearing the resplendent ceremonial crown of the Buddha of that direction.

I looked around at the inner circle. Dilgo Khyentse Rinpoche, the official Guru to the Bhutanese royal family, occupied a prominent position. He possessed not only the girth of a giant but a presence vast as the sky. Seated with his monks around him he looked like an oak sheltering small birds at the trunk. It was impossible to imagine him playing politics, no matter what his close relationship was with the family of hereditary kings.

I glimpsed a shimmer of black hair, as though a flock of ravens had just flown past. The Bhutanese royal family were entering the reserved space in the most prominent position just outside the sacred mandala. I began to see through the eyes of Jigmai and felt something sinister: the sudden hush, the swing of their long glossy raven hair, the swish of their brocades and silks, the respectful escort of monks as they were seated on high brocade cushions in regal isolation. I quelled my feelings: it was too important a day to give in to distracting emotions.

It was mid-day; the sky was bright blue without a wisp of cloud. We were startled by a sharp blast of gunfire as the Indian army fired a twenty-one gun salute. At precisely the same moment the cremation fire was lit. As the flames licked the funeral pyre, everyone looked into the sky and saw a perfect rainbow circling the sun. It was a miraculous phenomenon, like the earth quaking when the Buddha became enlightened.

Later, another kind of omen slipped into to my mind as I recalled the extraordinary events of that day. I couldn't forget the strange hush, the swish of silks and the raven hair of the Bhutanese royal family. It was an image as dark as the rainbow around the sun was light. I was filled with Jigmai's sense of betrayal, as if he were planted inside my body. I made an appointment to see Dilgo Khyentse Rinpoche to ask him a simple question: are you supporting the hereditary kings of Bhutan?

The translator was sitting next to Khyentse Rinpoche who, like a mountain, barely moved. He was naked to the waist; his long grey hair tied loosely in a topknot falling casually over his shoulders. Every cell in his body was in a state of deep relaxation and he radiated an unshakeable profound tranquility. His wife – a tall, thin, aristocratic woman in her fifties – walked in and out casually.

After a brief introduction explaining that I was living at Sherabling and was the companion of Shabdrung Ngawang Jigmai, I came to the point.

'I understand', I said to the translator, 'Dilgo Khyentse Rinpoche is the Guru to the royal family of Bhutan. I know the history of the assassination of the Shabdrungs by the grandfather of the present king, which seems to mean that the inheritors of the throne also inherit the karma of murdering a bodhisattva. As Rinpoche is their Guru, does it mean he supports them?'

The mountain wasn't shaken but I thought he was very slightly perturbed because of the way he answered. He was quiet for a moment then talked softly, almost in a whisper to the translator. I didn't realise that this was his usual manner of speaking.

'Rinpoche says that karma is not inherited, although being born into a family is the result of causes and conditions, but everyone makes their own karma. Secondly, the dharma is not just for good people, but to alleviate the suffering of everyone, no matter what their karma is. And that he cannot refuse to teach someone if they request sincerely because of their bad karma. In fact, where the suffering is greater there is more need for dharma.'

I refused to be pacified. 'But he is confirming their position as the rightful royal family and accepting their offerings.'

Contemplating my response, Khyentse Rinpoche *did* look slightly perturbed. 'His motivation is to give the gift of dharma to all who need it and request it,' said the translator.

The interview was over. I clasped my hands together and bowed, thanked him and left the room.

I wasn't sure about anything any more. My foundations were not just cracking but shifting. Jigmai's story of betrayal had opened up a new abyss in my mind.

Mandi, February, 1982

After returning to Sherabling from Sikkim, I sent several letters to Jigmai in Mandi. When a month had passed and there was no reply, I began to feel a strange absence as if he were not there anymore. I experienced a longing to conceive a child, to put new life into my body, and began taking some strong Tibetan medicine to boost fertility. One day I knew this was precisely the moment to act. I hatched a plan to disguise myself and go to Mandi.

I walked hurriedly into Mandi Milk Sweets Shoppe and Restaurant, sat down at an empty table, took out a piece of paper and wrote, 'Urgent! Meet me at the Raj Mahal. I am in disguise! Norma (alias Amrit Singh)' The waiter, whom I recognised as a friend of Jigmai's, came over to my table after a few minutes. I was wearing a salwar kameez, the local Punjabi dress, large gold-hooped earrings, glass bangles, plastic mules with high heels, and a pink shawl around my head covering one long plait tied with a stripy coloured elastic band ending in brass baubles. My hair was parted in the middle with red powder in the parting. I had darkened my skin, put black kohl under my eyes and painted my lips with red glossy lipstick. At last, I thought, I look Indian, and no one will notice me.

But the waiter did. With his gaze resting on the red bindi between my eyes, he said, 'Madam, every good wish on your new marriage.'

Not quite sure who I was supposed to be, I replied hastily, 'I am very well, thank you, and I have just returned from a holiday abroad. I understand you are a friend of Man Singh and I have an urgent message for him. I don't know exactly the location of his residence so I need to send a messenger. Can you help me, please?'

The waiter looked at me, folded the note I'd passed him into his jacket and left immediately on his scooter. I went to the Raj Mahal and took a room, booking myself in as Mrs Amrit Singh from Chandigarh. The receptionist eyed me at length. 'I think you have been here before, Madam. Which room would you like?'

'No, you must be mistaking me for someone else. This is my first time in Mandi. I'll have your best room; but let's see, perhaps the ones at the back would be more quiet and cozy.'

When he closed the door, I looked in the mirror and laughed, remembering Joyce's advice: 'Play, do something unexpected, be inventive; enjoy the game.'

There was a loud knock at the door and Jigmai's voice. 'Hello, Norma!' He came inside quickly locking the door behind him. He looked at me with a mixture of alarm and dismay. 'What is all this stuff?' He touched my clothes, fingered my hair and red bindi. 'I am in disguise,' I laughed. 'I didn't want anyone to recognise me.'

'When I got your message', he said frowning, 'I thought there was something wrong. I thought you were in distress, I didn't understand what is disguise. I thought it was an emergency and you needed me to come at once. And then my friend told me you were recently married. So I came running.'

'This?' I asked pointing to the bindi between my eyes. I had no idea that the bindi signified a married woman. 'I thought every woman had it, so I put it on.'

'You look like a common Indian woman. Go into the bathroom,' he ordered, 'and wash this stuff off. Take it all off!'

'I had to come like this. Where have you been, anyway? I sent you letters; there was no reply. I was worried you had disappeared.'

'I went somewhere very far away', he replied enjoying his mysterious answer.

'In India?'

'Yes', he replied, 'on the border with Pakistan, to the line of control. I was in the Indian army for two months.'

I sat down abruptly. There were so many sides of this man that I barely knew. I tried to study him more carefully. 'Tell me.'

'Take all that red powder off', he insisted. 'I can't look at you that way.'

I took a shower, wrapped a towel around me and started to dress. 'I don't think you need to dress, darling', he said, taking off his clothes. 'Tell me about the army.' I said. 'What happened?' I poured myself a glass of hot water and took a large dark brown pill, the last of the Tibetan medicine. I climbed into bed and nestled into his arms as he pulled me close.

'I wanted to have some training in fighting. You know how I like fighting, darling? I think you have some experience of my character, no?' he said, playfully.

'I feel I've had some training myself in the last year,' I replied dryly.

'But it was not in my karma to do it,' he continued. 'My horse went lame and I couldn't ride it anymore. Then the unit commander gave me a gun and ordered me to kill it. (He lifted an imaginary rifle to his eye, squinted and took aim.) POW! POWPOWPOW! I started to take aim, but tears came into my eyes. I went over to the horse and stroked its head. I thought I must take care of the horse, not kill it. I gave him the gun back and walked away.'

My heart filled with love at his tale of spontaneous compassion and I kissed him tenderly. I was delighted to lie on top as he lay on his back. His face looked composed and peaceful in repose. We remained in union without moving for what seemed a long time. As the minutes went by I became absorbed in the lightness of his being. The man I knew wasn't there anymore. There was simply a presence, more like a buddha, in deep meditation. After a long time I saw his lips moving in what seemed like prayer.

He looked radiant.

His prayers became a rapid mumble that increased in volume and then stopped. He went into the bathroom still saying the prayers, and washed his hands. I knew before I even touched myself that there would be no sticky residue inside me. He had used our sexual energy to pull his semen upwards, filling his whole body with bliss. It was the alchemy of transformation, the teaching I longed for more than anything else.

'I didn't realise you could do that.' I said in amazement.

'Do what?' he replied innocently.

'Don't try to pretend. I know exactly what you were doing. Kundalini of course, tantric yoga.'

'How do you know?' he asked with interest.

'Because you didn't lose your semen,' I replied. 'And there was no passion.'

'Do you remember the story you told me about the sixth Dalai Lama?' I continued. 'Everyone thought he was having sex with prostitutes, but then he demonstrated his mastery of passion by urinating off the balcony of the Potala and sucking the urine back up his penis. You must be a tantric master,' I said with respect, 'like the Sixth Dalai Lama'.

He didn't reply, but remained very calm as if the meditation were continuing.

'But why did you choose to do it that way just now?' I asked.

He maintained meditative equanimity. I started to get dressed slowly, feeling I might be intruding. As I approached the door to depart, he broke his silence. 'I'll give you a baby,' he said as if reading my thoughts. 'I will definitely marry you, but it will take time.'

'How long?' I asked helplessly.

'Four or five years,' he said calmly.

There was nothing to hang onto. Slippery as a fish – he was a double Pisces – and changeable as a chameleon. I remembered his warning: "don't try to control me. Nothing can stop me except death." I did not possess perfect patience.

'Look', I said, trying to find common ground. 'You came after me when I was not interested in worldly life, you proposed marriage to me, and with the advice of my Guru I accepted. But since then you've become more and more evasive. Yet you've taken over my life so that I'm totally involved in yours now. I've fallen in love with you,' I said; 'and I feel desperate, like a trapped animal.' I was crying in anguish.

'Let's be friends, let everything go its own way, not arrange meetings, not plan anything,' I said tentatively.

'But we must write to each other,' he said. 'I also need you, darling.' He held me tightly entwining our bodies together.

'Do you think we can do it?' he asked.

'I can if you can.'

'You write to me first,' he said.

I returned to Sherabling in urgent need of help.

****

CHAPTER 6

THE MAGICIAN

Sherabling March 1982

Tai Situ rolled the dice three times. 'It's possible to get married, but not very soon.' he said interpreting his divination. 'About five years.'.He looked thoughtful.

'What can I do?' I asked, distressed. 'I can't wait that long, it's impossible.' I felt like someone crawling through a narrow tunnel, too far in to get out. I had been captured on every level: spiritually, psychologically, emotionally, sexually, and I was too weak to fight. The only possibility was to keep going, to get through to the other side. Then, I reasoned, we would be happy, living Joyce's vision.

'It would be very good *for him* if he would take you as his consort', Tai Situ said meaningfully. I was surprised to hear these words so soon after Jigmai had used me as his tantric partner.

'I would like that also', I replied, 'but it's not up to me. I can't do anything about it. I can't control him in any way.

'What happens', I asked suddenly, 'if the man does this practice and the women does not?'

'Then the woman can become weak, because the man is drawing on her sexual energy. It's much better if both partners do it.'

'It seems like I've had nothing but obstacles in this relationship,' I said. 'First it was with Guruji, then with the

CID, now Jigmai himself. He's impossible to relate to. He changes personalities continually. He's in a different world to ordinary people. And now I don't have the strength to get out.'

'There *are* obstacles', he said. You should sponsor pujas[24]. I will write it down for you, then you go to the nuns at Tilokpur, make your offering and show them this piece of paper from me. They should do it right away. It will take at least one month.'

He wrote seven names in Tibetan on a piece of paper and handed it to me explaining each one. The one that stuck in my mind was Mahakala, the black wrathful protector. I did as Tai Situ instructed. Then I waited, confident I'd enlisted all the help I could get.

Between March and May there were three letters from Jigmai.

Dated 1/3/82

Hello Dear Norma,
Thank you very much for sending your wishes on the eve of Losar and my birthday.
Tell me what sort of suffering has brought you to the place which you mentioned in your letter.
Rest is fine.

With best wishes,
SN Jigmai

How is your health?

---

24 Ritual meditations

8/3/82

Hello dearest Norma,
I'm fine here and writing to you to remind my memory once again. Don't think I'll let you go out of my hand so easily. You must teach me English and make me perfect in this subject whenever I'll ask you to start this work. As you know, I'm not perfect so let me become perfect then it is very much possible I may go abroad to make money only in case if I won't become the King of a country.
Don't be in a hurry at all and make yourself ready to face and show your depth of love, for which you claim to be.
Write to me soon. Rest is ok.
With all my love,
SN Jigmai

22 May

Dear Norma darling,
I am in good health here and hope you may also be the same at your lonely retreat house....
It is raining a lot here and almost impossible to walk around the famous bazaar of Mandi. I hope you must have not forgot the charming market and the naughty people of Mandi, ha! ha! Tonight when I am writing this letter to you I really had a hard time to find piece of paper which is under my hand at the moment and will be soon in your snow like hands, which each finger has a full of blazing flame of love and care for darling. Answer me dear whether my intuition was correct or wrong.
Dear baby, I am feeling a bit hungry, so very soon I will be going to Raj Mahal to have my dinner. And do you know after that what I am going to do? Well, I must tell you I had decided to watch an English movie on the video, so called 'Confession of a Pop' for adults only. I think I come among the adults, what is your idea about it darling.
I shall write to you about the story of this movie because it is not possible to mail the letter till tomorrow. I did a bit of washing today so I think I should have a shot of whisky at

Raj. It is raining all the day and even now when I am getting ready to walk.
My sweet baby, see you later and will continue writing after returning from movie. I love you so much. Bye Bye.

It is 7:25 pm IST. Date 22 May Sunday.

Dear Norma darling,
Good morning baby, I am sorry that I failed to continue last night. I was very exhausted and the movie has board me too. I start today with some good lines,
I love you more than I can say
I miss you more than I can say
Don't you know how much I need you.
I'll love you twice much more tomorrow.
You win – I loose.
Love is all mystery.
That's why I want you Baby.

The movie was full of fucking scene and was so boaring that I left it before it finished. There was nothing special in it to write or describe to you. Today I am feeling bit funny… It is a clear morning and my clothes are also drying. Last night's Raj trip was pretty expensive, may be you can check by yourself as it was Rs 37/00.
May be I got lot to do today, since I may leave for Manali tomorrow. And ink inside the pen seems to be finishing so I may as well finish my letter soon. Because as you know it is very annoying if the ink ran off while writing. So I don't want to take a chance. Please baby; don't forget my love and purity in my heart for you, since it's very difficult to say whether I may be able to see you again or not. If I remained successful to come back from Manali to Mandi, and again Mandi to Manali, then I will definitely come to Sherabling one day, and would like to make love to you darling.
At the moment very much love from me, and several kisses to you….

with love, Jigmai

Within a few days, Jigmai arrived and stayed. We were in a state of grace, the dazzling long days of late summer expanding with a new sense of freedom. The land around Sherabling was wild and full of power places, which I'd explored on my own. In the mountains were pine forests with hidden streams covered by gnarled intertwining rhododendron trees, their flowers forming brilliant red arcs like lights in a tunnel. But my favourite wild haunt was a natural swimming pool in the river, which seemed inhabited by nature spirits.

We walked through an Indian village with mud houses painted in shades of ochre, the summer heat drying the long bundles of winter wheat. Buffaloes with elegantly curved horns shambled across the path, moving slowly to drink from water troughs outside the mud brick houses. We walked along the railway line and then climbed straight down a steep cliff to the pool of water formed by a circle of boulders where the river widened. It was as large as a small lake, with many boulders scooped out into human shapes, smooth and flowing like Henry Moore sculptures. It was a natural paradise, a secret water garden where I had spent many blissful afternoons swimming naked.

Jigmai stripped down to his underwear; I took off everything except my silk shorts.

'This is a very powerful place', he said. 'There are nagas[25] here. You must not come alone.' He shuddered.

I entered the pool first, beckoning him into the water like a child. He slid down the water-smoothened rocks over a small waterfall into the deep pool, shouting like a warrior entering the battlefield. He grasped my arms tightly in fear. I tried to teach him to float face down in the water but we ended up holding hands, arms outstretched, head

[25] water spirits

to head like two fish eyeing each other. We returned slowly through an ancient eucalyptus forest. The white mottled trunks of the giant trees stretched overhead like a protective canopy, as we walked hand in hand, alone, innocent as children in a fairy story. The next day I accompanied Jigmai to Mandi where I caught the overnight bus to Delhi to pick up some money.

It was in Delhi that the most bizarre, unimaginable episode in my life was waiting to happen, as if some unseen hand were orchestrating events. The help I had prayed for materialized in a completely unexpected form. I don't know whether to call it black magic, the hand of the dark underworld, or white magic, the benevolent help of guides and protectors. As I discovered, there was a thin line between the two.

It could have happened only in India where the superficial chaos of the physical world masks a more profound reality; and a deep vein of spiritual attainment has permeated every facet of life for thousands of years. The heart of India, as I discovered, was profoundly magical and synchronistic. Here anything was possible.

Delhi June 1982

I paid the auto rickshaw ten rupees for taking me from the bus station to the grand entrance of Dalmia's Guest House on Sikhandra Road. Dalmia's, in the most exclusive part of New Delhi, was a shabby colonial style house built during the Raj with high ceilings and spacious rooms. The chowkidar[26] showed me to a large empty dormitory with four beds and four ceiling fans for thirty rupees a night. It

---

[26] caretaker

was June and the pavements of Delhi were buckling in the heat. The air outside was like a blast furnace, so hot it singed the hairs inside my nostrils with each breath.

Dalmia's was owned by one of the wealthiest families in India, but there was a court case for its possession as part of a divorce settlement. In the meantime the family rented out rooms. There was only a certain kind of person who would stay at Dalmia's. Cognoscenti. It wasn't in any of the travelers' guidebooks. Only people who lived in India knew it. And because the rooms were grand but the amenities antiquated, it attracted those who appreciated the bygone elegance of the Raj, but were prepared to tolerate dilapidation in exchange for charm – and a lower price.

Every day for two weeks I went to Grindlay's Bank on Barakhamba Road to check if my money had arrived from England. Every day the answer was no, not yet Madam, please come again tomorrow.

There were few guests brave enough to endure the heat of Delhi in June. A couple in their mid-thirties who were studying sitar in Benares, a Frenchman who was on his way from Goa to Manali to sit out the summer heat in the mountains, an English couple working for an NGO in Nepal, and a black man from Nigeria studying at Nehru University in Delhi. We all made friends quickly and gathered in the evenings on the veranda to complain about the unbearable heat, drink cold lassi and play cards.

'That's it, now I got it,' the black man playing opposite me said suddenly, looking at his cards. He looked up at me. 'Your man is a king, and I would say,' he continued thoughtfully, 'he's also a Pisces.'

'A double Pisces,' I corrected him, 'and he's a king without a country.'

That is how I met Patrick Boone Ikehi, a Nigerian studying law at Nehru University, the son of an eminent politician whose father had been murdered. 'You are having a very difficult time with your man', he continued, as we retired to a bamboo sofa in a corner of the veranda. 'He is very possessive. He has lost everything so he's putting everything on you. He wants to possess you, to dominate you completely, almost to crush you. He's taking away your own power and you're letting him because you are completely open to him.' I listened with intense concentration. I had told him nothing of Jigmai. 'You have no protection. After he has dominated you he won't be interested in you anymore. You have to block him; you have to become powerful again.'

As we walked towards his room, I was galvanized by his insights into Jigmai's character and my predicament. Here at last was someone who could see the truth. Not calling Jigmai 'great, like the Dalai Lama'; or giving me a rosy picture of the future if I submitted to him; but someone who could read his character as it was, who seemed to be in touch with the depths of my experience. An ally. 'I can help you', Patrick Boone continued when we reached the privacy of his room. 'Do you want me to tell you what I can do?'

I looked at his face, trying to measure him through the barrier of black skin, maleness, and alien culture. A man trying to have sex with me was something I could smell a long way off. I couldn't catch the faintest whiff of it now. 'Okay, tell me.'

'Let me tell you who I am. I am an Ikehi; that's a tribe of people who are shamans. We are Christian, but we still have the rites, we still have the old ways. We are black Christians; we have powerful black medicine to overcome possession. Come to my room at the university. I'll show you a picture of our founder. I have everything there. You can come with me tomorrow. '

'What exactly are you going to do?

'There is only one way to remove his power, and that is through the same method as he put it there. I have to pray to our father using the special prayers and rituals he has taught us, and then when his power comes into my body I will extract the possession from you. Do you understand? It's a ritual; it's the surgical removal of energy. You're a beautiful woman I can see that but for me you're a sister. I can help you.'

'I can't do that,' I said appalled. It may destroy our connection.'

'I'm telling you: he's a powerful magician. Do you remember anything that sounded like a spell?'

I recalled immediately Jigmai's mutterings before I left for Sikkim that had now grown into full-blown threats. ***'Remember, I am a very dangerous man. Buddhists are not supposed to take revenge, but I am a revengeful man. You will never be able to forget me.'***

'That's it', Patrick Boone replied. 'That was when he bound you. He's a very powerful man. You're no match for him. He's used his power to get you; you have to get free of it before you can keep him.'

Slowly my doubts were ebbing away. He must be genuine, I thought, otherwise how could he see Jigmai's character so accurately? No one else had been able to see how he had abused his power. It was something I'd known but never wanted to admit, even to myself. There were many stories of deities using a human form to help a devotee in need. Could Patrick Boone be an emanation of the black protector Mahakala, activated by the pujas?

I had entered into the irrational magical substratum of India, with its astrologers, palmists, and priests; where saddhus in loin-cloths wander the roads holding Shiva tridents, bus drivers stop to pray at roadside shrines to the gods, and snake charmers sit on city streets playing the flute to undulating cobras. It was still exotic but not alien to me. After years of absorption in Tibetan meditation, I also believed in the power of mind to call forth invisible dimensions.

'Okay', I said. I could feel dread in the pit of my stomach. 'I'll come to your room tomorrow and see how I feel, but if we go ahead, it has to be surgical, like an operation. Then I can keep my bond with him intact.'

'I promise you', said Patrick sincerely, 'I am here to help you.'

The grounds at Nehru University were practically deserted. It was summer, the evening light thinning into the blackness of a dark moon, when Patrick ushered me into his room. I looked at the photograph of the founder, Father Ikehi, in his flowing white gown and long black beard, eyes blazing with spiritual passion like a black Jesus in the desert. I noticed the bone horn and small silver cup like a chalice on the table. Patrick lit a candle, while I sat on the bed and watched him pray. 'Father, hear my prayer, let me cast out the spell from our sister, who has fallen in love with a great sorcerer. Let me be pure and clean and let the result come perfectly as we wish.'

'Pray with me,' he said, 'pray with your whole heart; use your meditation to concentrate on this. We have to do this act together. You're an important part of it. Wish with everything you have. Pray to your Buddha; pray to your God; pray to your Guru. Your happiness depends on it.' His voice was rising almost in a liturgical chant.

I sat up and went into meditation, calming my thoughts, cutting through fear and doubt. He went into a trance, his body shaking. I saw a light in his eyes and assumed he had made contact with the Father. He donned a clean white long Indian cotton garment. The ritualistic procedure began and I surrendered to it emotionlessly, as I would an operation.

Afterwards he prepared me for the next stage. 'We have to do this every night for three nights,' he said as we sat in a taxi taking us back to Dalmia's. 'Now that it is new moon the power is increasing. We can do it here tomorrow night,' he said as we paid the driver and walked into the guest-house. 'No need to meet at the university anymore.'

By the next night I had made up my mind to see this arcane ritual through to completion. I had been diagnosed with a disease and it had to be removed. We went into Patrick's room at Dalmia's and locked the door.

The third night there was a sliver of moon in the sky. 'Now you are really free' he said triumphantly after performing the ritual. 'But it is not the end. You have to go tomorrow and find him, leave early in the morning. You must find him within three days.'

'I don't know where he is, he's moving his house from Mandi to Manali but for one week he could be anywhere between Dharamsala and Manali. I don't know how to find him.' I felt panic rising in my throat.

'You will find him. It is meant. I can see it. When you find him this is what you have to do to complete the ritual. You must make an offering to him. Buy some fruit, fresh dates, fresh grapes, bananas, melons, a box of milk sweets and some nuts- almonds, walnuts. Take a large plate and prepare it carefully with flowers and sweets in the centre and the fruit and nuts around it. Leave it on the table. Offer it to him as soon as he enters the room. If he takes it and eats heartily, especially if he eats some of everything, then he's yours, his possession is over.'

'But remember this.' He raised himself to his full height and towered above me, all six foot two inches of him. He turned to face me: 'Don't ever tell him about me. No matter what happens don't tell him about this or it will be ruined. Don't even mention my name. You will lose him and you will never have him again.'

The next morning we walked together to the bank. At last my money had arrived. As I counted the notes, Patrick said, 'One more thing, and this is also very important. Give him some of your money; tell him it is an offering to do business so you can be together in the future.' I nodded. 'I need $100', he added looking at the stack of notes disappearing into my handbag. 'My money hasn't arrived and I need to pay some bills before I leave India. I think I'm worth that much to you.'

I handed him a $100 bill. 'I would like it re-paid,' I said emphatically, 'otherwise I will feel you did the whole thing for money, that you conned me.'

'As you like, Ma'am,' he replied grinning. 'It will come back to you, I promise.'

Our parting was uneasy. Something powerful had been set in motion and it was far from over.

My plan was to look for Jigmai first in Dharamsala, then work my way towards Manali. The thought of three days put a pressure on my heart that felt like an electric hammer. A fear gripped my chest, tightening every muscle in the solar plexus. There was no mental space to think rationally, no distance from the obsession to find him. Every nerve in my body quivered; my breath came in short gasps.

It was evening when I reached the Bhagsu Hotel in Dharamsala where Jigmai and I had stayed on previous trips together. It was on a spur of forested ground above the main bazaar with the snow clad Himalayas in front.

The receptionist knew nothing about an SN Jigmai. I scanned the guest book anxiously, a dim panic spreading over my nerves like a person drowning in quicksand.

I rushed out into the pot-holed streets with the chaos of buses, taxis, rickshaws and beggars assaulting my senses. I ran to catch the night bus for Mandi where I would stay overnight, reaching Manali the next day. By that time it would be day three.

The bus to Manali followed the course of the river Beas winding slowly through the mountains, as the driver stopped at all the roadside shrines to make his prayers to Ganesh, or Shiva for good luck. The heat of Mandi had been exhausting, as I had walked the streets the previous evening, desperately seeking Jigmai. Bijai Palace was boarded up, as if no one had ever lived there, and no one in town knew Jigmai's address. He had flown leaving no footprints in the trackless sky.

As we climbed past Kullu, the air freshened and the smell of pine forests calmed the stress of the past few days. We reached our destination at four o'clock, just as the afternoon sun was throwing off the heat of midday. I got down and started walking towards the bazaar.

From the moment I set foot in Manali I understood why it was renowned throughout the Himalayas as the land of the gods. The air was pure, with an intoxicating fragrance. The quality of the hashish, which grew freely in the mountains, had spawned a thriving hippie culture. Walking quickly, I passed a German bakery, a restaurant called the Mona Lisa, and a small Tibetan emporium proudly proclaiming to be HH the Dalai Lama's Charitable Trust.

After deliberating a few moments, I braved myself for the Tibet Emporium and asked if anyone knew SN Jigmai, a Lama from Bhutan: a short stocky man wearing layperson's clothes. They stared at me as I feared they would, and I left hurriedly. Of course, he would never visit the Tibet Emporium.

I sat outside on a stone near the Tourist Information Centre in the middle of town and watched the road, remembering Patrick Boone's prediction that I would certainly meet Jigmai. I don't know how long I waited. Finally I got up with a sigh of despair.

Just then an ambassador taxi came up the road and stopped beside me. The door opened as a hand reached out pulling me inside. Jigmai! As we embraced, I started to cry. He talked excitedly. 'I was looking for you! I went to Sherabling, then to Mandi this morning and then took a taxi to come here. I knew you were looking for me, that we had to meet very soon.' I was trembling with emotion, relief and joy cascading through my body.

'I went into the Tibet Emporium looking for you,' I cried. 'I felt so desperate, no one knew of you.'

'You asked for a short fat man in ordinary clothes who was a Bhutanese Lama,' he said, scornfully, lifting his hand as if to strike a naughty child. Once again I could only marvel at his clairvoyance.

He instructed the driver to go to the Tourist Lodge by the thundering river at the bottom of town, in front of a bridge leading to sulfur hot springs. 'Stay here tonight, darling', he said booking the room for me.' I will come to you at around 9 o'clock. I have to see my friend Sey Rinpoche at 7 o'clock tonight. We planned a little party'.

'Please, darling', I requested, when we got to my room, 'come to me here before you go to the party, just briefly, for half an hour. I have something to give you and I need to hold you, to be with you. It feels like a long time, I need you so much,' I said cuddling into his lap and kissing his neck.

'I'll be here at six thirty', he said looking at his watch. He closed the door. I could hear his steps on the wooden veranda leading to the street.

I waited ten minutes, and then walked into the bazaar. Within a few minutes the ingredients for the feast were in place: a mixture of fresh fruit, nuts, honey, a box of milk sweets and a small bottle of rum. The Tibet Emporium provided a large Chinese plate with dragons. There were wild roses in a hedge near the guest-house and I plucked a few. I showered with cold water, put on a printed silk sarong and sandals with wedge heels. There was even time to paint my toenails and plant some of the wild roses in my hair. The plate was perfect for the flowers and milk sweets placed in the centre, with the fresh fruit in thin slices in two circles around it, the nuts adorning the edge. I sprinkled the offering with a mixture of honey, rose petals and rum.

Jigmai walked in at 6:30 promptly. I was glowing as he embraced me. 'Ah, Norma, so beautiful,' he said kissing me on the lips. 'Look what I have prepared', I said proudly, pointing to the table. 'It's my feast offering to you.' He looked at the plate perfectly adorned with delicacies on the wooden table. A small white tablecloth covered its coarse surface, and candles lit it in a soft glow. I offered it to him with both palms outstretched. 'Ah, this is delicious,' he said tasting the apple covered in melted honey and rum, relishing the taste of one fruit after another. Very soon it was all gone, even the nuts at the edge.

'You know the business you wanted to start?' I said to him. 'I've thought about it and I would like to offer you some of my money to get it started. I can give you $1500. I'll send it when I get back to the West. But please remember, it has one condition. It is to be used so that we can be together soon. Please promise me that, darling.' He wrapped his arms around me tightly. 'Thank you, yes I can promise you that. I love you so much, my darling.' We stayed in embrace for several minutes, the warmth of our bodies mingling, lost in the sweetness of love. 'I won't be long,' he said getting up, 'I'll be back in a few hours. Wait for me. And make sure there is no other man in your arms.' He roared with laughter as we kissed at the door.

I looked out at the foaming river and smiled. Patrick Boone Ikehi's magic had worked. Jigmai's 'spell' was over; I was empowered again. Whatever happened, this was my moment of triumph and it tasted like divine nectar.

The transformation was remarkable, as swift as turning a page and starting a new chapter. But this time we were co-authors. Jigmai came with me to Sherabling and watched while I packed my bags. As we were leaving he noticed an old trench-coat hanging in the closet. The raincoat was a traditional British macintosh, of the vintage worn by Sir Winston Churchill.

'Where did this come from, darling?' he asked. 'I've never seen it before.'

'Judith was doing retreat in my house while I was in Delhi and she must have left it here.'

He took it off the hanger and tried it on. It fitted perfectly with the belt buckled on the last notch around his hips. 'It makes you look completely different,' I said pondering the new look.

He went into his luggage and pulled out a plaid cotton sun hat with a small brim like a trilby. 'What do you think, darling?' he asked, looking in the mirror.

'You could be a detective from the 1930's,' I said casually.

'That's it', he replied excitedly, standing to face me. 'I'm Harret Rixon.'

'Who is Harret Rixon?' I asked in bewilderment.

'He's a detective in a novel I was reading. I really liked the name: Har ret Rix on', he said pronouncing each syllable carefully. 'Now you must call me Harret, nothing else.'

A curious connection suddenly popped into my mind. 'When did you read this novel?' I asked.

'About a month ago, in May,' he replied. 'Why?'

'Because when I read your letter to me in May calling me 'my darling baby,' I immediately thought you were being influenced by something. It sounded like a detective story.'

'You are a good detective yourself, darling', he said, kissing me.

'So what is my name?' I asked teasingly.

'Mrs Rixon, of course'.

'Wonderful, Harret, let's go.'

He gave me a penetrating look. 'You know the reason I am with you?'

'No, tell me.'

'Because you're the only woman who is strong enough to take me.'

Harret picked up my bag and carried it all the way to the bazaar, where we boarded a bus to Delhi. Harret and Mrs Rixon signed the registration form at the Conaught Palace Heights Hotel and stayed for two days drinking tea and taking cold showers. Harret escorted me to the airport to take a midnight flight for London. Before leaving he made me promise to write him immediately, swearing eternal love for his darling Mrs Rixon.

CHAPTER 7

THE HONEYMOON

Harret Rixon, Manali and Goa 1982

The first letter from Harret when I reached England was delightfully casual and loving.

Dear Darling,
I don't feel like writing 'dearest' to you because you are the only one who is dear to me. Well, I'm fine here and passing my days nicely and remembering you a lot. I got your letter from London and am so joyed to read few sweet lines of your reaching England safe and sound....
Darling, thank you very much for your writing to Canada for money. Moreover I would love to see you regain your health, but anyhow it is O.K. I love you very very much.
Here the weather is quite tricky. I think the monsoon is on its full swing. I'm little drunk by the time I started writing you. You know what I'm like when drunk.
So dear you are still trying to find out the relationship of our birth signs. I think the book (Liz Greene's *Relating*) relates very near to our position, what you say? I'm here surrounded with many westerners and am trying to figure out the depth of love among them, maybe I'll write to you my comments in next letter.
If you find anything for me to do here in India please write to me. Have a nice time in Scotland darling. I send you my love and kisses.

Harret

Manali 4.8.82

Hai Darling,
Received your money so thanks a lot. It was so easy to get money that even I don't have to go to Delhi...
Now maybe from this very month of August I may start my business. I hope to make good profit and able to build good capital. But for this I require your good wishes and desire to see me milllioner soon...please tell me how you are doing in Scotland? How bright is future, and if you had started working? Here at Manali perhaps the same old game has started, so on my letters just put my false name, so I may get every letter without the notice of wolf's. ...
Quite often I dream about you and my heart longs for you but as you know I have good patient so it is O.K. Please send me your photo of sweet sixteen and family members if it is possible. Somehow I would like to see them. My love for you remains the same. I wish you to have a nice time in west.

With love,
Harret

Dear darling Norma,
Received all your letters except the photo which you mentioned in your latest letter. I'm very well and passing my days smoothly. In fact I wanted to write to you so much but did not do it, simply I'm lazy. Few days back I was in Delhi making reservations for Bombay and I remembered you a lot. Every road of New Delhi was reminding me of you and passed old days in your precious and sweet memories of company. Of course, some bitter ones also (just a joke).
...Please darling, take care of your health and you don't have to cry for a little mismanagement of life. I shall be leaving Manali on 29th September. I shall write to you soon, dear love.

I send you kisses,
Harret
Manali 20/9

My darling Norma,
I'm writing this letter to you from Goa that you know how much I love you and of course how deep. Oh darling, you are everything to me O.K. Ah!
Last night when I wrote above lines I was under intoxication so if something wrong please don't mind.
I am here in Goa badly strucked because I lost money and everything but you don't worry darling. I started from Manali on 29th of September and arrived in Goa on 7th of October. Here the climate is quite hot, and the beaches also don't look so beautiful, Somehow I am little sure you won't like it very much.
How the wheel of our fate keeps changing it is really hard to say. It was in my mind that from Goa I'll write to you in piece and really a heart welming letter to you, but I think it was not in our karma to do so. Anyway I will write to you whole the incident after more time but not now.
...Don't worry about me, darling and I'll not forget acknowledging my gratitude to you for your financial help to me, which made me see day dreams. I don't know how much time it takes but I'll definitely return your money. Please take care of your health. I wish you all success in your life, dear.

With all my love,
Harret Rixon
Goa

The letter from Goa took over a month to reach me. In the gap of silence I intuited that something was awry, and wrote a small note in a very different tone. It had an unexpected impact.

I can't understand what your silence means (I wrote). But if it means your relationship with me is unclear, please remember that the money I gave you had one condition – that it be used in such a way that we be together as soon as possible. It never occurred to me that you would not honour my wish, but now that you've chosen not to communicate with me, I'm understandably concerned about your motivation. If it's not used with the right motivation, the money will do no good. My plans are also uncertain. My love for you remains the same, but I feel sad at your silence.

Dear Norma,
Well I'm here at Manali again with sheer desperation and your letter welcomed me in a very distinct way. Any how, tell me how is your health and state of mind, darling?
I really feel sorry for writing letters late casually. But what so, even letters I kept on receiving after some times has always the complaint saying you haven't got any letter from me. I really don't understand what is it? Yes Norma, my darling, I had to admit that you have some supernatural power and that as you said in your letter, your money will do no good. Really, it did not do good since I lost all of them including some which can be estimated around 25,000/ Rs. Few days before leaving Manali I got a letter from you saying you do prayers for my good business; probably this must be the result of your bad feelings for me. Some how I don't mean to hurt you in any way, why? Because I loved you and been loving you up till I received your this heart welming letter on the date of 17/10/82 at 5pm.
But listen, one thing which I would love to tell you, you had underestimated my character. I can do anything but, I'll never do and perhaps can't do one thing and that is to steal someone's money. Sometimes you claim yourself to be knowing me very well but if you have this kind of impression that I will take your money and will disappear, then perhaps you failed to know me. I will NEVER DISAPPEAR before returning your money, so you need not worry. This is not Jigmai's loose words but the sound of his blood which is honoured by the reincarnation and its depth of humanity; cherishes by declaring – HE WILL NOT DISAPPEAR WITHOUT RETURNING NORMA'S MONEY WHICH IS WORTH RS 25000/. If even then you don't have faith on me then you can go to your GURU Situ Rinpoche and ask to throw a mo[27]. I wrote a letter to you from Goa

27 divination

1. Losar handmade peacock card, 1981

2. Jigmai, 1981

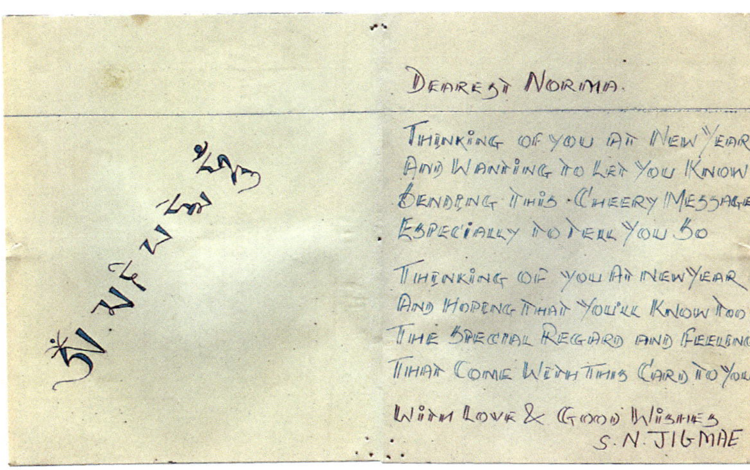

Dearest Norma.

Thinking of you at New Year
And wanting to let you know
Sending this cheery message
Especially to tell you so

Thinking of you at New Year
And hoping that you'll know too
The special regard and feeling
That come with this card to you

With love & good wishes
S. N. JIGMAE

3. Jigmai's handwritten Losar card, 1981

4. Cremation of HH 16th Karmapa on the roof of Rumtek Monastery, Sikkim, 1981.

5. Indian army firing gun salute at the cremation of the 16th Karmapa, Rumetk, Sikkim, 1981.

6. The cremation stupa of HH. 16th Karmapa on the roof of Rumtek Monastery, Sikkim, 1981.

Rumtek photos by the late Shri Madhusudan Singh, courtesy Meera Madhusudan

7. *Jigmai at Sherabling, 1982*

8. *Pilgrimage at Rajgir, 1982*

9, 10, 11. Sherabling

12. *Sherabling, 1983*

13. *Sherabling, 1983*

14. swimming near Sherabling, 1983

15. my house at Sherabling, 1983

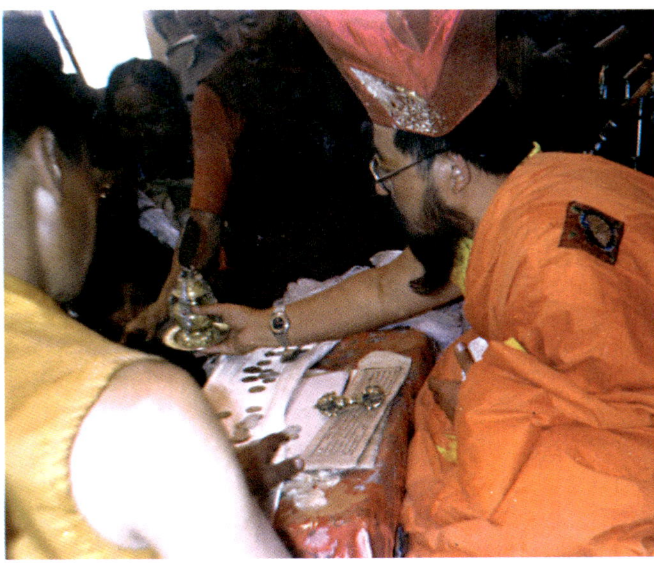

16. Shabdrung Rinpoche (Jigmai) giving blessing in Zanskar, 1984

17. Shabdrung Rinpoche, Zanskar, 1984

18. Nirula's Hotel 1985

19. Shabdrung Rinpoche, 1990's

20. mural at Pedong Monastery of Shabdrung Ngwang Namgyal

21. Shabdrung Ngawang Jigmai circa 2002 shortly before his death

22. image of Shabdrung Ngawang Namgyal, Punakha Dzong

23. Punakha Dzong

24. Punakha Dzong built by Shabdrung Ngawang Namgyal

25. kutshab or representative of Shabdrung Ngawang Namgyal, made by himself, Punakha Dzong

26. Green Tara made by Shabdrung Ngawang Namgyal, Punakha Dzong

27. Retreat hut at Tango Monastery where Shabdrung Ngawang Namgyal meditated for four months to manifest the apparitions that drove away the Tibetan invaders.

28. Tango Monastery

29. The shrine of the Kudung of Shabdrung Ngawang Jigmai, Pedong Monastery, 2006

30. A monk conducting the ritual ceremony before the Kudung of Shabdrung Ngawang Jigmai, Pedong Monastery, 2006

31. A monk serving food to the Kudung of Shabdrung Ngawang Jigmai, Pedong Monaastery 2006

32. Yangsi Shabdrung, the reincarnation of Shabdrung Ngawang Jigmai, at one year two months on arrival in Bodh Gaya, December 2004.

33. His Holiness the Dalai Lama and Yangsi Shabdrung Rinpoche, Dharamsala, 2004

34. Yangsi Shabdrung Rinpoche

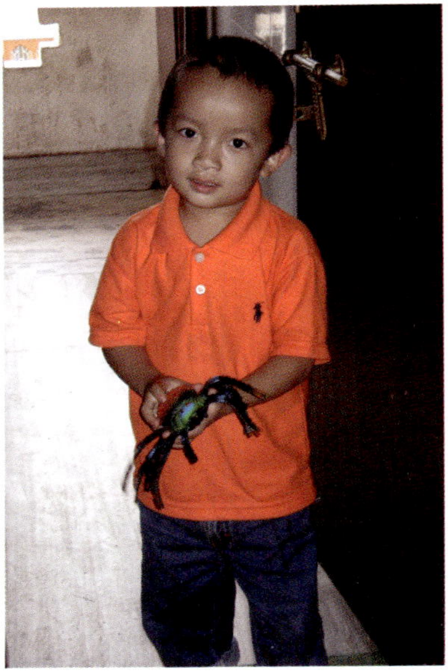

35. Yangsi Shabdrung Rinpoche, Bhutan 2008

narrating "It may take some time to return your money". But now it won't take more than a year. Please tell me in which currency you would like to take your money? American dollars or some other.

... Again before finishing my letter I will not forget to say, thanks for your help. What so ever happened is one's own luck, so Thank you very much Norma for your help. And you can't be blamed for writing such a hard letter. But what to do darling I'm also not used to hear such kind of things which hurts my inner conscious. You can remain silent for forever if you feel. But take care of your health. Before receiving your letter I been always remembering you and badly wanted you. But now I should try to forget you and think no more about you.

If this letter of mine is little heavy on you then please forgive me.

SO GOOD BYE MY LOVING HEART NORMA AND GOOD LUCK.

(This last line, part of an unreadable paragraph, was crossed out with a dark blue pen.)

PLEASE DON'T READ LAST STANZA.

Yours Jigmai
Manali

Dated 19/10/82

Dear Norma,

I guess you might have received my letter written to you on 19/10/82 and must be in full of angry. This letter follows to request don't be annoyed. Loosing temper is no good for health. Now onwards you shall get frequent letters from my side, so the danger of my disappearance may not threat you. I don't care whether I get reply from you or not, because it is immaterial.

... Rest is bad for me, thus good for you.

with regards,
Jigmai
20/10/82

Dear Norma
Few days ago I wrote a stupid letter to you and so I feel that might have disturbed you. I doesn't mean to trouble you so please don't take that seriously and try to forget about all that, because that is nonsense. It is also true that I'm not getting all of your sweet letters too…

with all my love,
Ngawang Jigmai
21/10/82

Delhi December 1982.

I arrived back in Delhi in December after six months absence. There was a certain anxiety to get back, as I wasn't quite sure who I was going to meet: Jigmai, Harret Rixon, or possibly someone else. A mixture of Jigmai and Harret, as in the letters, seemed the most likely.

I scanned the faces on the other side of the barrier for a minute or two until I saw him. He was wearing a checked shirt open at the neck and a pair of grey trousers underneath a smart brand new trench coat. Harret, then. There was no denying the expression of sheer joy on his face as he opened his arms wide to hug me.

'How is your health, darling? You are looking strong. When I first saw you I thought you might be some new foreigner lady who has never been to India. You were walking so fast.' He looked admiringly at my new blue velour track-suit.

'I am well, as you can see. How are you, darling? I asked looking at his trench coat. 'Or should I say Harret?

He laughed. 'I am enjoying, only some few upsets which taught me good lesson'.

'The money?'

'Yes, I'll tell you when we get to the hotel.'

'It was upsetting for me as well. It doesn't seem a good

sign, but I don't understand how it happened. Where are we going?' I asked as we got into the taxi. I sniffed the air to take in the peculiar sweet stench of exhaust fumes, human sweat, smoke from cow dung fires, held in colloidal suspension with cloying incense. 'Ah, Shiva's fart – still there' I thought, and relaxed.

'Dalmia's Guest House, where you told me you enjoyed before you left India. Sikhandra Road', he said to the driver.

My body tensed. Would he find out? I went over every possibility in my mind, recapturing every movement there before I had become Mrs Rixen. No, there was no reason to worry. Everything had been done very discretely and in any case, no one had been watching. There had been only the faintest presence of the chowkidar when I'd been there in June.

'Good, I really like that place. I hope it won't be too cold though. The rooms are very large and they probably have only a one bar electric fire.'

'All the Westerners in Manali already left for Goa. They say they have wonderful time there at Christmas; lots of parties, smoking hashish, drinking coconut fenni and free love'. We laughed and moved closer until our legs touched.

The taxi driver drew up outside the large house on Sikandra Road, and let out a long blast on his horn to wake the sleeping chowkidar. The gate opened and we entered the driveway. I started to feel a cold dread and shivered. Jigmai took my icy hand and led me upstairs. He turned on the light as we entered a large draughty room furnished with a double bed, wardrobe, mirror and glass overhead light. Through the door I could see the cracked tiles of the en-suite bathroom. Exhausted, I sat down with relief. It was not the same room where the 'ritual' had been

performed in June. Jigmai turned on the electric fire and looked at me with concern.
'You look tired, darling. I think something has upset you.'
'No, it's just the long journey and the relief of finding a nice quiet place to stay. But you promised to tell me the story of how you lost the money. I've been wondering about it for months now.'
'I'll tell you in the morning, not now. You must take rest.'

I took off my clothes and jumped quickly into the bed pulling the covers tightly around my neck, mesmerized by the soft pale skin of his smooth buttocks, the roundness of his belly. The heat rushed into my body. 'Any other man in your arms?' he asked. 'No', I gasped, 'there's been no one since you. And you?'
'Yes, I did,' he replied, 'but only once. I thought I would try another woman to see what it was like.'
'Where?' I was surprised.
'In Goa.'
'A hippie?'
'Yes. I met her at a party and she wanted me.'
'She asked you?'
'Yes, so I gave her one good long fuck, but it was only fucking, not making love. You're the only one I love, darling.' I surrendered in some deep part of my being; I just let go of jealousy and enjoyed the moment.
'I enjoyed that story', I said when we had made love several times. I felt freer sexually than ever before. 'Now tell me about the money'.

He sucked my nose then bit it playfully. 'First I bought a motorbike to have some fun for the summer. Ah!' he said remembering, 'it was wonderful. We went everywhere; up and down all the roads, through Manali'. His hands moved in an arc conveying the maze of twisting roads.

I could hear the Dalai Lama's laughter when he gave Jigmai five thousand rupees. 'Here take some money and play', he had said. That's what money was for, as far as Jigmai was concerned. He had completely ignored the condition I had imposed, to use the money so that we could be together. Who is 'we'?' I asked controlling my anger.

'Sey Rinpoche and me' he replied. 'Then I sold the bike and bought some kilos of hashish to sell in Goa. I put them in my briefcase and took the train to Bombay, then the bus to Goa. I got off the bus, went to the toilet. I left the briefcase outside with my luggage for very short time, maybe three minutes. When I come back the briefcase was gone. I was badly struck. Really shocked. There I was in Goa with very little money and nothing to sell. But don't worry, darling, I will repay you every paise.'

I couldn't imagine anyone doing anything more stupid. Was he that naïve? And why was he involving himself with illicit business anyway? 'Don't you think it's a sign that you should not be doing this kind of business?' I asked sternly. 'After all, look who you are: Shabdrung Rinpoche, a very high incarnate Lama. I am sure it's the protectors warning you.'

'You're right, my darling' he said dismissing my question brusquely. 'You are my darling, aren't you? Now let's go to sleep. I want to go back to Goa with you. We can spend the winter there and enjoy. What do you think darling?' I could hear him speaking, but it was enough for one day. I slid gratefully into sleep.

****

We waited like refugees in the cold, winter-darkened station, huddling in blankets, trying to board any train that would take us to Bombay.

'Life is strange, isn't it', I said. 'Here we are in the middle of the night in Pathankot waiting for a train to go to Goa. I would never have thought this possible a year ago. What are you thinking?' I asked, turning to fathom his thoughtful expression.

'I am twenty-six and I have done nothing with my life except to fall in love with a Western woman,' he replied frankly.

'Well, you didn't want to be a Lama, you didn't want to study the dharma, you said you wanted to be just Jigmai. Now it's Harret.'

His reply went so deeply into my mind, I would never forget it. 'I wanted to step outside the mandala to see what it was like. I wanted to be a self-made man.'

'How can you be a self-made man with your kind of karma? You're already the reincarnation of the Shabdrung. Do you mean self-made in this lifetime?'

'Yes, not taking anything that was already there for me. Otherwise I could be a Rinpoche with a monastery, sponsors, devotees, and teaching the dharma. But like that it will be missing something, never know how it is to be on the street, like this. It's also important. But this way I also will miss something.'

'That's very brave, very fearless.' But not wise, I thought, saying no more.

For a moment a window opened into his universe. Falling in love, getting married, having children – it was just common life, not what he had reincarnated for. His mission was so much greater than his need for personal happiness and love. Would he have to sacrifice love for the greater good? The tension made him lonely, vague, melancholy, and alienated. He turned it into playful or ironic humour, and in the evenings, a restless moodiness fuelled by alcohol. As Dylan said, 'Ya gotta serve somebody'. If he didn't he would be wasting countless lifetimes of spiritual evolution.

We boarded a train at two in the morning without a reservation, and lurched like sleep-walkers from compartment to compartment, looking for one that was empty. At three in the morning we settled finally for a berth in a second-class compartment with only a hard wooden bunk bed. With the blankets forming a tent over us, we found the intimacy of our own space, making love urgently as the train squealed and heaved through the dark night, submerging the cries of pleasure that are eerily so close to pain.

Goa, December 1982

Colva beach in South Goa was a long stretch of sand with fishermen's huts dotting the miles of sea front and a few cafes and restaurants at one end. It had the reputation of being the most unspoiled of beaches, with only a few Westerners, who wanted tranquility and isolation rather than the sex, drugs and rock parties for which Goa was famous.

Harret Rixen, appearing now as a Japanese traveler in baggy pyjamas and t-shirt with a Western wife in a hip variation of salwar kameez – followed the young village boy laden with luggage to a modest sea front house about one quarter of a mile along the beach. The sun heated up the golden sands at mid-day baking our feet even through sandals. The house had a 'room to let' sign painted neatly on a board. We walked onto a large veranda with several rooms leading off it, and spoke to the owner, a native Goan with a weather beaten face. Jack Fernandez was a fisherman, and a crucifix wearing Christian. His smiling young wife seemed, like all Goans, to be stuck in a 50's fashion time-warp – knee-length pleated skirt, white nylon blouse, bobbed hair with a fringe. Jack showed us a medium sized room with a cement floor, double bed, shelves and mirror, and windows looking out onto some coconut palms. It felt concealed enough to give us the privacy we craved. He pointed out the bathing facilities – a cold shower outside in a cubicle, which all the family used. 'And the toilet?' I asked. Jack waved his hand towards the great outdoors. 'There are plenty of pigs here,' he said laughing.

'We want to stay for maybe two months, what is your best price?' Jigmai asked. Jack looked thoughtful. 'Seventy rupees one week' he said. 'For both of us,' Harret stated leaving no room for doubt. 'Yes, okay sir, you are the boss.' Jack joined in Jigmai's laughter as they shook hands closing the deal. 'Harret Rixon', said Jigmai, 'and this is my wife Norma Rixon.'

'Honeymoon?' asked Jack.

'Uh, yes', said Jigmai, 'honeymoon. Second honeymoon,' he corrected himself, realising we were too old to pass in India as newlyweds.

'Where are you from sir?' asked Fernandez trying to make sense of Jigmai's Mongolian features and his loose white cotton Punjabi style pyjamas.

'Japan', said Harret laughing heartily. 'I am a Japanese businessman.'

'What kind of business?' Fernandez asked innocently?

'Fish', said Harret. 'When I get back to my country I will send you a big pfish.'

They both laughed. Harret's outrageous humour gave us the privacy we needed. Fernandez and his wife kept their distance.

In the village market we bought a kerosene stove, two plastic buckets, cooking and eating utensils, and set up a small kitchen near a wooden table. In the evening we walked barefoot on the beach scrunching the cool wet sand between our toes. As the fishermen unloaded their nets we marveled at the different shapes of sea life – octopus, squid, lobster, crab. We chose the red jumbo prawns, the most prized of the catch. After the fishermen had left, there were remains of fish on the shore-line, mostly eels gasping and struggling to get back into the sea. One by one I picked them up and threw them into the water, watching them swim away quickly.

For the next two weeks we barely left the room except to wash, go to the toilet, buy food – and swim. I swam everyday, alone, with Jigmai watching. He could not swim and though he wanted to learn, he was wary about entering the water. For those first two weeks our passion seemed endless, constantly recharging itself. Love became our world, wrapping us tightly in its intimate spell.

We walked on the wet sand watching the waves gather force as the evening tide rolled in. The breakers came nearer and nearer, wetting our feet, then our ankles and finally splashing our knees. Jigmai grabbed my arm and huddled under my shoulder to protect himself, like a child in danger, reaching for its mother. 'You have so much fear of the water', I remarked. 'I think you must have drowned in another lifetime.'

'Yes, that's how it happened,' he acknowledged. 'I can remember it still. They threw me over a cliff but I hung onto a tree. I ran back to the monastery. Then again they came to my room, but before they could knock the door I jumped out the window. I fell down ten floors but even then I did not die. Again they caught me and threw me

into the river but the river took me upstream instead of down. I was half dead.'
'It was a miracle?' I asked
'Yes. That is what people say.'

'But again they caught me and tied a boulder to my body and threw me into the river. I can remember the water going into my nose and filling my lungs. So that time I drowned.
'How old were you?' I asked stricken with grief and anger at the same time.
'Thirteen', he replied. 'But nobody knows the exact date because people were afraid to keep a record.'
A sudden thought came into my mind. 'The victory was yours', I replied with certainty. 'They tried to drown you but you came back as a fish, a double Pisces. It means you are indestructible.'
He smiled lovingly. 'You must teach me to swim, my darling.'
'In the morning, when the water is calm', I replied. 'But the main thing is fear; you have to overcome your fear of the water.'

The sea was rolling gently as I coaxed Jigmai into the water, opening my arms towards him like a protective mother. He came jumping over the undulating waves. I had taught swimming many years before, and tried to convince him to submerge his head. He screwed up his face tightly and held his breath so that nothing could penetrate. The idea of breathing out underwater was impossible to convey.

I changed tactic and tried to teach him to float but his body was tense and heavy. When a wave washed over him, he jumped to his feet and started flailing his fists into the water, fighting with it. 'Bastard!' he said, as if the water had betrayed him by turning into a wave. 'You can't fight water', I said gently, holding his arms. 'You have to go along with it, let it roll over you, submit to it. It's like meditation. You can't fight with your thoughts. You have to go along with it and realise its nature. It's the same with waves and the ocean. It's all water, just go along with it; make friends with the waves. Relax into it', I urged.

We tried every day for one week until he could float somewhat cautiously but in only the calmest sea. After that we came to an understanding that water wasn't something he could conquer in this lifetime.

'Tomorrow night is New Year's Eve', Jigmai said. 'Tell me, my darling, what is your wish.'

'I wish we could get married and live happily ever after', I replied.

'I mean, what is your wish for New Year's Eve. What do you want to do? There are lots of beach parties'.

'No, nothing like that', I said forcefully. I want to spend it alone with you.' I thought for a moment. 'Shall I tell you how I would like to bring in the New Year?' He nodded. 'I want to have some delicious food, like jumbo prawns and scallops; and drink coconut fenni. And then I want to make love to you. At the last stroke of midnight I want us to be in union with the sound of the waves pounding on the beach. I want to experience the perfection of love with you at the very first moment of the New Year. Do you think you can arrange it, darling?'

'Yeah, let's try. I am quite sure about it, particularly freedom of love at midnight.' He laughed. I feel we have practiced enough for that.'

At sunset the next day, we walked on the beach and bought the jumbo prawns and scallops. I would cook them with butter and garlic and prepare a home-made mayonnaise with a salad of grated white radish and coriander leaves.

This was to be an exquisite appetizer accompanied by coconut fenny and salted cashews, for which Goa was famous.

At one hour to midnight we lit candles and incense and began the feast. We sat on the bed savouring each morsel and eyeing each other, aware of our nakedness underneath the flimsiest of tropical clothing – a sarong for me and a lunghi for Jigmai. As we drank the fenni and ate the prawns I could feel my body temperature mounting. He invited me to sit beside him and touch him, but I was already there as his lunghi slipped to the floor. At eleven thirty we started to hear fireworks but were already deeply entwined. We began to prolong the crescendo as the church clock started tolling the countdown to midnight. At the last chime of midnight, as we joined together in the perfection of love, he whispered in my ear, words which I shall remember for the rest of my life, repeating them like a liturgy.

These extraordinary words, however bizarre they would have seemed to me once, thrilled me now. Sex and death were the most important moments for transformation. I felt honoured by my lover, elevated to the highest level of the feminine, like a dakini.

Time passed in the way it does for lovers caught in the spell of their love. One morning I awoke feeling unusually hot. My body ached when I tried to walk; the lower part of the belly was painful and swollen. The doctor diagnosed pelvic inflammatory disease and gave me a two-week course of antibiotics to take immediately. 'And absolutely no sex', he warned. 'That will make it worse.'

'Don't,' I gasped in pain as Jigmai overpowered me. 'The doctor said it would make it worse. DON'T DO IT'. Each thrust was like a stab. I gasped in pain. I wanted to scream or cry for help but instead the opposite happened. I muffled my cries and submitted to the pain, accepting it as I'd accepted the pleasure. The same act that had produced exquisite ecstasy was now producing piercing pain. After a week the pain started to decrease, the swelling went down, and the infection disappeared.

I didn't ask myself whether Jigmai's motivation was utterly selfish, or somehow benevolent. Was he a selfish male animal or a divine madman purifying the karmas of passion? We were now so inextricably intertwined there was no way to stand back and judge. I couldn't even try any more.

I no longer denied his contradictions; I lived with them. At one and the same time he was infantile, stupid beyond belief, lazy and undisciplined, but ironic and playful as a jester. He could be ruthless, sentimental, demanding and carefree, all within a few minutes of each other.

These paradoxes were maddening, exhilarating, confusing and sometimes deeply painful, but they were all part of the fast moving drama that kept me bound to him. How could I fix on one thing and act, when there was nothing solid to grasp?

Underpinning all these contradictions was the utterly irrational, magical power of love. It was intoxicating; and we were hooked. I kept thinking that eventually we would get to the end of these contradictions and turn into a stable couple with two children. In the meantime I would have to be patient, loving, and non-judgmental. Of course, it was impossible.

The honeymoon was over. It was time to settle down.

CHAPTER 8

THE PILGRIMAGE

Delhi 1983

Dr Mangala Telang looked at my case history carefully. I had just filled in a questionnaire describing every illness I'd ever had. She questioned me about the two instances of pelvic inflammatory disease. 'We will have to analyze your husband's sperm count first to eliminate that source of infertility', she said. 'My husband is a Lama, I replied 'and will never consent to having his sperm examined. 'Do you have sex frequently?' she asked. 'Yes, at least twice a day'. 'Then make sure you have sex tomorrow morning and come to my office at ten o'clock. Of course', she added conspiratorially, with the faintest smile, 'make sure you don't wash.'

The next day I returned for an examination. 'Well, we can eliminate that possibility', she said looking at her microscope. 'Your husband is 100% fertile. I suggest an x-ray of the uterus to see what the damage is.' Within a few minutes I had the result. 'Your fallopian tubes are blocked due to pelvic inflammatory disease which first occurred over ten years ago. You can get an operation for this now to open the tubes', said Dr Telang. 'It's called microsurgery and the most advanced doctors are at Hammersmith Hospital in London'.

I suppressed the urge to cry in despair. The more I pursued it, the more Joyce's vision seemed to recede. 'Shall I go through with this operation?' I asked Jigmai later that day. He looked unconcerned. 'Of course you can if you like. It's up to you. It's you taking the risk so you must make the decision.' I felt oddly relieved. There was no pressure to make a decision now.

The snow was still on the mountain peaks when Jigmai and I returned to Sherabling. Somehow the drama of my passing illness had grounded us as a couple. We began to form a friendship with two other devotees of Tai Situpa living at Sherabling; Sven was a tall bearded Dane, and his Polish wife Danuta, gaunt with pale skin and high Slavic cheekbones.

One of Danuta's many qualities as a passionate devotee was her belief in the spiritual merits gained by offering her body to the Lamas. Jigmai, the highest of incarnations, and a lay- person with no retinue to maintain boundaries, was a perfect object for her devotion. She earned her place by giving everything she had, generous to a fault. Her body, to my great relief, was an offering that Jigmai showed no interest in accepting.

'Jigmai!' Danuta cried, opening her arms wide to greet him. She passed me a plate of fresh fruit and a bag of small ripe mangoes, which Jigmai loved. He stretched his arm out to clasp her by the hand but she clutched it and put it around her shoulder, wrapping his arm around her neck. He removed his arm and led her by the hand into the house. 'Come, let's enjoy.' They sat on the upstairs balcony watching the display of birds at twilight. Droves of parakeets flew in a green cloud; the most exotic, a bird with a feather duster tail, seemed to sweep the twilight air.

I walked upstairs bearing a tray with a plate of freshly made french fries, a bottle of rum and five glasses. The usual card game was reaching its usual conclusion. 'Jigmai!' said Danuta with playful exasperation. 'You have won all our money again. It's not fair. You know everything so it's not possible for us to win.'

'It's just a game, Danuta, just a game' he laughed, counting his money. 'Just to kill the time'.

It was his favourite expression and one that I hated.

'Listen, Jigmai', she said earnestly holding his hand. 'Everything's just a game for you because you're enlightened. But for us, we have to work hard.' She tilted her head to one side and fixed him with an adoring gaze. 'Please come on pilgrimage with us to Bodh Gaya. Instead of wasting time here playing cards, let's go to the holy places.'

To my great surprise and pleasure, he answered immediately: 'Okay, let's go.' He stretched back putting his feet up on a cushion and closed his eyes, smiling with mock contentment.

On the appointed day we walked in a group carrying our rucksacks, five miles through mud brick villages and pine forests, crossing the turbulent river to Baijnath by leaping from stone to stone. We met Jigmai as planned and boarded the coach.

Bodh Gaya, 1983

Bihar was notorious as the poorest state in India, where generations of caste warfare had created violence and chaos. Goondas or bandits ruled the roads but the trains were considered safe.

We had only one compartment with four berths. The fifth, booked in another compartment, had been double booked. Jigmai solved this delicate problem by gallantly declaring he and I would share one berth, barely wide enough for one person. The only sleeping position possible was to lie with our heads at either end of the berth so that his feet were towards my face and mine were towards his.

Although I knew how disrespectful it was to point one's feet towards a Buddha statue or holy person, I somehow didn't connect that to our situation. The setting was so different to that of a sacred environment – a monastery, a throne, or shrine- that I simply didn't think of it. All night an unconscious warfare ensued as he punched my feet down to the floor and I curled them onto the berth again. In the morning I was about to ask him for an explanation of his behaviour when I was startled out of my rational mind.

I awoke to find him putting on my skirt- fortunately elasticized – and my blouse, which barely fit over his wrists. The skirt reached to his knees, leaving his muscular calves exposed. With his bare feet in cheap Indian rubber thongs, he walked casually down the corridor to the toilet. As he moved along the narrow passage past the passengers in this outlandish getup, their eyes followed him, and then they returned to their conversations. There was no comment, no staring, no whispers, or laughter. Walking slowly and naturally as if nothing unusual was happening, he sat down opposite me drying his face and stared nonchalantly out the window. In that moment I saw clearly that he was truly a crazy wisdom yogi practicing an advanced meditation to surpass conventional boundaries, reminding me in particular of his transcendence.

Gaya station was like a Tibetan painting of the hell realms. A sticky, sullen heaviness hung in the air even at six in the morning, with an acrid smell like tar, as if we had walked underground into a subterranean level. Beggars such as I'd never seen before crowded around us, dangling emaciated limbs, or miniature infants, to get our attention. 'We are ghosts from the invisible realm. Let us be visible and rejoin the world of the living,' they seemed to say. One wretch grabbed my hand and pinched the skin to show the fatness beneath the surface, then dangled a skeletal claw in my face. Jigmai said something authoritatively in Hindi and the mob parted as quickly as it had formed, leaving us with an unruly gang of rickshaw wallahs competing for the fare to Bodh Gaya. We decided to forego the cycle rickshaws – the cheapest form of transport in India – and took instead two auto rickshaws – motorized three wheelers that belched black sooty exhaust.

It took almost forty-five minutes to travel the fifteen kilometers to Bodh Gaya. A fresh breeze greeted us from the island of stupas as we approached. Dominating the site was a central stone memorial rising majestically fifty meters into the air, whose origins could be traced to King Ashoka in the third century BC, and excavated by the British archaeologist, Alexander Cunningham at the end of the 19th century. This marked the place of the Buddha's enlightenment. The road went towards the stupa and then veered sharply to the right into a village of shacks – teashops, makeshift restaurants, and stalls selling Buddhist paraphernalia. A five minute tour was enough to see that the only solid structures were the temples for pilgrims and monks, the 'embassies', as it were, of every Buddhist country in the world.

We gathered at the stupa for a twilight korra. It was March and the summer heat had driven out the pilgrims who had attended annual winter events, such as the Dalai Lama's teachings. Graham consulted his Tibetan calendar. 'Tomorrow is full moon', he said, 'great for doing prostrations around the stupa'. Everyone was excited at the prospect. 'If we get up early enough', I said, 'we can do it before the heat sets in'. 'Even if it gets hot, it's good. The harder it is, the more merit', Graham said, stern as a schoolmaster proclaiming benefits of cold showers and healthy discipline.

Jigmai looked bored. 'Time for my roti,'[28] he said, patting his round belly. He sniffed out a Punjabi dhaba, a restaurant on the street where cauldrons of rice, vegetables, dal and meat were simmering in aluminium pots over charcoal fires. With the hiss and squeal of the pressure cooker marking time behind us, Jigmai pulled out a pack of cards. He leaned back on his bench with a serious expression, shuffled carefully and dealt the pack. In his white undershirt and baggy beige trousers, he could have been a professional gambler. By the time the food arrived we were penniless and drunk. After eating, Graham rose from the table. 'I'm going to bed. Goodnight, Jigmai, goodnight all,' he said wearily. None of us had expected to be on a pilgrimage sitting next to the most sacred Buddhist monument in the world and gambling with a great bodhisattva.

In the morning I awoke early, donned an old tracksuit, put on my straw hat, took my sunglasses, and tried to tiptoe quietly out the room. Jigmai woke with a jolt and sat up straight, as though startled by a vision. He looked shocked and vulnerable. 'Norma, where are you going? Come here.' I sat down on the bed and took his hand. 'I had a dream just now', he said 'very powerful. I saw Chenresig, as clearly as I am seeing you. He lifted me up and turned me upside down, shaking me, banging my head

---

[28] literally bread, sometimes used to mean dinner

on the ground. "Wake up", he said, "wake up, wake up." He said it three times, just like that.'

'I don't think that needs any interpretation, does it?' I continued holding his hand gently. The dream seemed a good omen, truly a wake up call, I thought. I left him rubbing his eyes while reciting the familiar chants with which he started every day. The only one I knew was the mantra for auspicious interdependence, which he usually did in the bathroom while washing.

There were three concentric circles around the stupa: the inner korra, which was a small circle, the middle korra and the outer korra, which was a good quarter mile in circumference. I opted for the middle korra while Graham, Sven and Danuta decided to go for the outer one. As soon as I started my prostrations, I realised how difficult this would be. I had no padding for my knees or gloves to protect my hands from the grit of the pavement. Very soon I could feel the sweat pouring down my face. Some time later I noticed Jigmai watching me from a nearby stone column. As I was approaching the end he pulled out his watch and looked at it meaningfully. '7:30', he said, 'time for breakfast'. I continued my prostrations till the full circle had been completed.

As I approached, Jigmai looked in disgust at my dusty clothes as though I'd been playing in the dirt like a naughty child. I touched his shoulder. 'Wash your hands,' he shouted in alarm. 'Don't touch me with your dirty hands'. He moved his shoulder to one side, as though touched by a leper. The inconceivable merit of prostrating around the stupa on the full moon seemed to leave no impression on him whatsoever.

And yet his compassion on the street was as natural as his love of food. The beggars were out in formidable battalions as on every full moon day. While we placed a coin in each tin plate, Jigmai bantered with them in Hindi, like a benevolent king caring for his children. Instantly, their faces brightened and they became human again.

He was a man of the people: talking to beggars, sleeping in the cheapest hotels – when he traveled without me- eating the most common food, wearing casual clothes. Whereas many Lamas sported a gold Rolex, his wristwatch with its ordinary chrome-plated band was straight from the local bazaar. His only luxury was a wide gold ring set with a stunning ruby, which he had been given by a Sikh friend; the ring, as he told me proudly, of a king.

It was mid-day when we reached the second holy site – Rajgir, or Vulture's Peak – where the Buddha had taught the second turning of the wheel of dharma. The summit, crowned by a magnificent Japanese stupa, was on a plateau amidst jagged overhanging rock cliffs with views of the dusty plains below. Jigmai was in playful Harret mode, striking a variety of poses like a school- boy out on a picnic. He ran over to an arching acacia tree with full blown bright orange-red blossoms, put his arms behind his head like a Bombay film star, waggled his hips and posed for the camera while we relaxed at his feet, laughing. In the background was an imposing stupa marking the historic spot where the Buddha brought into the world his sublime teachings on transcendent wisdom.

The streets of Rajgir were baking with ferocious heat as we descended into the poverty and pollution of an Indian town. There seemed no way to alleviate the misery of the beggars except to drop a token coin into their tin pots. Jigmai looked directly at each one, said something in Hindi; and again they looked satisfied, their humanity restored, as if they had been fed.

Then we all saw something that made us stop in our tracks. A horse was lying in the gutter beside the road, ribs exposed, rasping a last breath. I untied a red blessing cord from my neck and went to tie it gently over an ear. The flies were buzzing around his head; his eyes were closed. I whispered mantras into an ear and saw Danuta and Graham also saying mantras and tying blessing cords. 'Please do something, this poor creature is dying', I requested Jigmai, touching his hand.

'Don't touch me with your dirty hand', he shouted. I jumped back, stunned by his wrathfulness. He walked around the horse for a few minutes gazing at it attentively, and then rejoined our group with what seemed total indifference. The next minute we watched, transfixed, as the horse got to its feet and walked away as if nothing had happened; as if it were all a dream, an illusion, and death and dying had no reality.

'What did you do?' we all asked Jigmai, eager for an explanation. 'Nothing', he replied blankly. He seemed pleased, but as surprised by the transformation as we were. 'Jigmai!' Danuta rushed over to him, 'It's a miracle, what you've done is a miracle.' Her eyes were brimming with emotion.

I was also convinced it **was** a miracle, which Jigmai's presence had somehow triggered. It was truly impossible to imagine that the horse would have got to its feet and walked away. These silent impressions of Jigmai's powers as a mahasiddha were beyond interpretation. I stored them in sealed packages, dropped them into my memory and left them there.

****

In the coolness of early morning we walked the streets of Varanasi jammed with the kind of traffic only India can produce – bullock carts transporting goods of all kinds, palanquins of corpses covered in white shrouds, auto rickshaws overloaded with passengers, and the occasional curtained white ambassador taxi, the car of officialdom.

We rounded a corner and dived into a small clean restaurant. 'Paunch lassi,' said Jigmai to the waiter, ordering for the five of us. 'Ah', said Graham, licking the first drop of the delicious liquid from the rim of the glass, 'at last. Lassi in Varanasi!' We clinked glasses shouting 'Lassi in Varanasi!', emptied the contents and sat back contented.

'Okay', said Graham after we had downed the second glass, 'now we are ready for the burning ghats.' Jigmai frowned. 'Why do you want to see that? It's a cremation ground, a very dirty place. 'We can't go to Varanasi and **not** see the burning ghats' Graham argued. In the West death is completely covered over. We really should go there to deepen our practice.'

Jigmai boarded the rickshaw reluctantly, complaining all the way. 'I don't want to see dead bodies. I don't want to think about death. It will come when it comes.' His reaction was puzzling, as though he were ignoring a fundamental Buddhist principle.

The rickshaw wound through narrow alleyways passing temples splashed in ochre, with statues of Ganesh or Shiva set within small courtyards, alongside stalls selling miniature statues, prayer beads, lingams. The rickshaw driver stopped. He could go no further, he declared. Now we had to walk to the ghats.

We followed a line of sadhus wearing the barest of loincloths, carrying staffs with tridents on top, small tin pots and bundles over their backs. The path went down a hill, wound around a few corners through cobbled alleyways, and then we emerged onto the legendary Ganga.

The ghats were compartments in the river divided by long flights of stone stairs from the streets. As far as the eye could see they stretched along the shoreline. Directly below the stairs in front of us was a line of fires marking the burning ghats. We followed a funeral procession of mourners dressed in white behind a corpse covered in a white shroud. A stack of neatly cut logs lay at the side as a crew of men like galley slaves in dirty lunghis were stoking fires that apparently never went out. We watched the fire licking a freshly prepared corpse, saw the flesh blacken and shrivel, smelled the fat dripping onto the fire, heard the skull pop as the pressure of the heat opened it. Street dogs prowled for remnants from the funeral pyres. The mourners had withdrawn and were sitting on the bank chanting prayers. We sat on a nearby rock and watched, like spectators of live theatre. Graham had taken out his prayer beads. Sven and Danuta were on either side of Jigmai, who hovered in the background looking impatient.

'Let's go now,' said Jigmai mopping his brow with a handkerchief. 'It's too hot. This place is for the family mourners, not tourists' he muttered. His disdainful look instantly cut through our fascination with the spectacle of death.

We arrived at the Tourist Bungalow in Sarnath at dusk, the hour before sunset when Buddhist pilgrims circumambulate the holy shrines. In the gathering twilight Jigmai and I separated from the group, to walk arm and arm into the Deer Park, like lovers recently reunited; Harret and Mrs Rixon again. Just as it started to drizzle with a light evening rain, we came to a clearing in the forest and saw a gathering of peacocks and peahens. The peacocks were strutting with their fans displayed like divas, singing loudly with a heart-rending wail, calling their mates. The peahens responded and each in turn joined with a peacock to walk side by side in the darkness as the rain created a misty curtain. It was like an initiation into the primordial dance of love.

'I have never seen anything like this', said Jigmai holding my hand more tightly. 'Nor have I', I replied. 'Whatever happens we will always have this to remember,' I said, filled with an exquisite bittersweet longing. 'Let's make a promise to remember this always.' We kissed tenderly, deeply, until the rain soaked our heads and ran in streams down our faces.

'What is the purpose of doing this all kind of thing?' Jigmai asked suddenly on the last day of our pilgrimage. We were removing our shoes to enter the precinct of the memorial temple and prostrate to the sacred relics. 'It's better to take it easy and enjoy. We have been running here and there every day for so many days I can't remember. Just going round and round doing korra. Let's sit under a tree and enjoy.' 'What do you have in mind, Jigmai,' asked Graham, pointedly. 'Just follow me and I will show you', he replied.

We put our shoes back on and followed him to a large bodhi tree offering shade from the burning heat. Settling on the thin brown grass under the tree we watched in mock horror as once again he pulled a pack of cards from his pocket, cutting and shuffling with intense concentration. 'Please, not here, darling', I pleaded. 'It's a holy place'. But Danuta joined in Jigmai's excitement. 'Okay, let's go', she exclaimed. 'Gin rummy', she threw her head back and laughed. 'Wherever you are is a holy place,' she said with utter conviction. 'You are a buddha'.

'I don't really want to play cards now', I said. 'Today is our last day, isn't it? I want to make some offerings, do some practice.' Jigmai looked at his watch. 'Ok. I'll meet you in an hour outside the gate. Don't talk to any strange men', he said good- humouredly.

At a quarter to four I went into a small restaurant near the gate to quench my thirst before meeting Jigmai. There were only a few cushioned benches and tables. I passed one table full of Tibetan students and sat down at another facing the door. It was then I noticed Jigmai sitting with some Tibetans right in front of me. He must have seen me walk in. Puzzled, I got up, went over to his table and said pointedly, 'Hello, may I sit down?' The Tibetans looked at me curiously and moved over. 'Oh, yes, hello,' Jigmai said with elaborate vagueness. 'How are you?' he asked politely, as if I were an acquaintance he could only vaguely remember.

My body became numb. I sat awkwardly for a few minutes waiting for an introduction but the conversation in Tibetan continued. They called him Rinpoche with great deference. It was clear they knew who he was. I looked directly at him but he blanked me as if I barely existed. Like a woman in a black veil, I had no face and no name. I was invisible.

I panicked, rose from the table and ran wordlessly from the restaurant, down the street, into the Tourist Bungalow. I packed my bags as if chased by a demon. The train ticket was on the desk, with our five names on it; we were supposed to leave later that night on the Shiv Ganga express to Delhi. I grabbed the ticket, heedless of how it would upset the group, and arrived at the train station five hours ahead of our departure. I went into the ladies waiting room, sat on a ripped leather chair and clutching my straw hat, stared into space, in shock.

A few hours later, Jigmai, Sven, Graham and Danuta came rushing towards me. 'Norma, why did you run away with the tickets, how could you do that without telling any of us, we had no idea where you were!' Danuta cried. Jigmai held me by the arm. 'I thought you had disappeared, that something terrible had happened to you.'

I turned away mutely. The relationship was over. I wanted to erect a gigantic wall around myself and make it impenetrable. I sat in misery, with the scene of Jigmai's denial in front of me, trying to extricate myself from that haunting vision. We boarded the train in a state of wild commotion, like victims of a disaster who had lost their bearings.

Jigmai sat beside me on the berth. His protective arm around my shoulder felt heavy, like a chain. He whispered into my ear, 'Norma, please come back to me, it was a mistake, I wasn't expecting you to walk in and I didn't know what to do. They were old friends, and I am a very secret man. I don't want the Tibetans to know anything about my private life. They always gossip. Please come back to me.'

I removed his arm from my shoulder and maintained silence. His pleading continued for hours until it was nearly midnight. I got up to make my berth and lay down, covering myself with the woolen blanket. In the chaos my straw hat had fallen to the floor and lay crushed beneath some luggage. Danuta picked it up, tried to restore its glamour, but failed. She handed it back to me. 'Norma, your beautiful hat…' she said sadly. I grabbed it from her hand and hurled it in disgust out the ventilation window of the compartment. Danuta stared after it, an expression of shock on her bewildered face.

Jigmai's laughter exploded into the mute compartment. 'Oh, that was wonderful!' He roared until the tears came down his cheeks and he had to gasp for breath. Even when he lay down he kept on laughing. Wave after wave rocked into that miserable lonely recess of rejection and abandonment stored in my emotional body until it broke my obsessive silence. The absurdity of the whole drama dawned on me and I joined in, releasing the tension. I let go of the excruciating pain I had experienced and let the present take over. By the time we arrived in Delhi, the story of the straw hat had become a legend.

Bonded again in love, we took a hotel room, and returned to our comforting roles as Harret and Mrs Rixen. 'I love you so much', he repeated, looking passionately at my body as I undressed. ''Please', I said, 'don't make love to me unless you are committed to marrying'. After the traumatic rejection in Sarnath, I saw marriage more than ever as the only way to become visible. 'That is already decided, I will definitely marry you', he vowed. 'When?' I asked yet again. 'In two years', he said. 'Is that a firm promise, a 100% commitment?' 'Yes', he said with conviction.

Invigorated by our commitment, our bodies united again. Afterwards we talked about our future together and an operation to restore fertility when I returned to the West. Having a child now became part of the plan.

CHAPTER 9

THE SPELL

Sherabling 1983

'What meditation do you want to practice now?' asked Tai Situ when we returned to Sherabling from our pilgrimage. 'Vajra Yogini,' I said without hesitation. The red, naked dakini, dancing with wild-eyed abandon, had become part of my visionary landscape.

'I think you should do the Guru Yoga of Milarepa,' he said. 'Vajra Yogini is in that as well.'

Milarepa is an icon in Tibetan Buddhism. His life story was even more dramatic than anything I'd experienced with Jigmai. And it had some of the same elements: black magic, murder, trickery, disappointment, humiliation, and rejection. Finally he purified his bad karma and transformed through Tantric meditation methods into a buddha, going from sinner to saint in one lifetime; truly a Tantric Buddhist archetype.

Jigmai looked over my shoulder as I studied my meditation text. 'Dulgya', he said selecting one Tibetan word, unexpectedly serious. 'Do you know what that means?'

'It's translated as 'place of taming', I replied.

'Yes, it is place of taming, but I will tell you why it is important. Every Lama has his place of taming, the place

where he has to accomplish his work. Unless he finds his 'dulgya,' his activity will not succeed.'
'And what is your place of taming?' I asked.
'Ngawang Namgyal's place of taming was Bhutan,' he said. 'No doubt, it is Bhutan'. He looked concerned.

The sky was brooding with clouds unusual for that time of year. They became dramatic, outlined with lightening and bursting out in light strokes of warm summer rain. We ran into the garden and threw seeds into the ground – lettuce, salad, herbs and sunflowers. When the rain stopped we planted seedlings in the soft wet ground– gardenias, hydrangia, bougainvillea, zinnias, calendula. Jigmai turned into a playful nature spirit balancing amongst the rows, holding his hands out and dancing. He came and nuzzled my ear like a child. We sat on the balcony looking at the snow mountains, smelling the wild roses, while the storm clouds parted overhead and the birds called plaintively in the still air.

'What do you think of our relationship?' he asked unexpectedly.
I thought back over the last four years. 'It hasn't been easy', I replied truthfully. 'But it has grown a lot. What do you think?' I asked.
'It's like you say, something that grows and changes. It's like watching a child grow and develop. It gives the same kind of satisfaction.'
'It's a feeling that we created something together, isn't it?' I asked.
'Yes, my darling, you've said it exactly.'

In between his visits I was nurtured with love letters.

Friday, June 28

My dear darling NORMA,
I love you so much, even quite hard for you to understand. No one on this earth can perhaps have that love, apart from you, from me. Do you know what is love? What love means to me?
I am fine here and about to do something very soon. Please don't have any doubt about my love for you. I wish you to have a successful retreat, as well as cheerful one of course. I always desired nothing else than your happiness. I will let you know everything what I will do. Please keep everything within yourself.
Please write to me soon. Wishing you to be happy.

With love,
SN Jigmai

As well as the outpouring of eternal love, there was a premonition of imminent change, and a sense of secrecy. It kept me on my guard. This point counterpoint was the music of our relationship, a dissonant background theme to remind us that there was a bigger agenda over which we had no control.

There were frequent visits, for a month at a time, when we became a domestic couple wrapped up in our own world. He would come in the early evening with a small rucksack, filled with old monk rum, a round of English cheddar covered in wax, sent by post from the Swiss Dairy in Kalimpong, a few t-shirts, underwear and a plastic bag of toiletries.

He began to grow a beard that spiraled into a conch-like twist, like his predecessor, Ngawang Namgyal, whose beard touched his navel. We lay in bed watching the rain, playing cards, drinking rum, nibbling home fried chips and making love. In the evening Jigmai would go downstairs and cook a meal, frying tomatoes, cheese, chillies and oil in a delicious relish.

Life seemed to be a slow preparation for a major event, which was just around the corner. He was biding his time like an actor waiting for his cue to come onto the world stage, possibly as a king. His future was still undefined. Nor was I sure what my part would be in it, but I knew with certainty, I was the woman he loved.

I entered the solitude of retreat. Ten hours every day of visualization,[29] mantra, and devotional prayers to the king of yogis, Milarepa: to come right now and transmit the blessing of his enlightened mind. Tears of devotion rolled down my cheeks as I sang the hauntingly beautiful devotional melody: 'je mila shepa dorje, la sol wa deb'. 'Jetsun Mila, I beseech you'.

Days turned into weeks broken only by Jigmai's letters.

October 19, 1983.

Dearest Norma darling,
... I think you might have started retreat, and must be doing lot of meditation. I wish you to have very successful result of what you are doing. I really miss you so much and sometimes think how bad I was with you. Even then you were very sweet and nice to me. Oh! You are wonderful Norma. But I never meant to be bad with you, ...May be when we meet again we will love each other even deeper and with better understanding...

I hope dear that everything is going fine with you, and so you are enjoying everything at Sherabling. I really want to see you soon. It is 12, so you say it is midnight. Therefore

29 imagining an image in the mind and focusing on it

I will go to sleep now. Goodnight darling. Many kisses
XXXXXX with all my love
Jigmai

Love Norma
Love Norma
Love you so much Norma
Jigmai

Sunday, October 23

Dearest darling and part of my life Norma,
Few days ago I drop few lines to you through a registered letter. I hope you might have got it. …
I will definitely be coming on your birthday, if no accident happens on the way. I am going to order for a birthday cake and a bottle of beer. I'll be bringing some pictures sent by Sven and Danuta. It is very cold and raining since yesterday evening. I'm staying in two houses now. It is bit difficult to decide where to stay, because gap between two houses are so long.

See you soon darling,
With all my love
Jigmai

On November 10th he arrived through the woods at twilight, shouldering a heavy rucksack, and sweating with exertion. He took out beer, rum, tonic water, cakes, candles, chocolates, and a separate bag of red rice from Manali. 'It's for your birthday dinner tomorrow night', he explained. My heart was on fire with love.

By the end of the evening we were both high on spirits. The festivities continued the next evening with a dinner he cooked on the wood stove. The finale came with a blaze of lights on a chocolate cake, which had miraculously appeared aglow with candles. 'Happy Birthday darling', he said lifting his glass. We drank to everything possible –

the completion of my retreat, which had only just started, long life, good health, our relationship, his success as the Shabdrung, and of course, our love.

I re-entered the solitude of ritual and prayer. After an interlude of extraordinary intimacy and joy, another letter:

> Dearest darling,
> Few days ago I got your letter. I'm very fine and enjoying nice time so far. I wish you to have much more enjoyable time. I really do love you. You really gave me wonderful time. I can't remember better time than this without any fighting. I'm little drunk and stoned too while I'm writing this. That's why I'm so immotional as you know I always is like so.
> Here it is not very cold and pretty dull as it used to be most of the time. I'm thinking of moving out of this place as you know the reason. But so far I'm struck here. As promised I'll drop a card or few lines in a letter. Wait till my next letter comes to you.
>
> With all my love and hug.
> Jigmai

On January 14, 1984, Jigmai again intimated a change in the near future.

> My dear Norma,
> ...once again the life seems to be sailing at ease and curving towards a great change in the near future. Although I haven't got any indication but I can feel and see something.
> ... Maybe very soon I'll come to see you....
>
> With love,
> H. Rixon.

February 1984

Jigmai sat on the bed watching me sweep the mud floor, putting his shoes to one side. He had arrived late the night before. I had only one more month of retreat and since I wished to complete it without interruption, we agreed this would be the last time we would meet until the end.

He continued sitting in silence for many minutes, his gaze unwavering, fixed on the window. I checked the view. The spring landscape was fresh with buds, but it was the same as usual – shrubs, pine trees, birds, a path to a small stream, and a pine forest beyond, stretching to the hills. I walked downstairs to bring in the milk and noticed a letter under the milk pot. The Tibetan cook who prepared my food for the retreat would leave whatever post arrived for me on the veranda, usually under a stone. The bold handwriting was unfamiliar so I turned over the letter quickly. There was no return address. I walked upstairs to open it.

Jigmai rubbed his eyes and turned to face me. 'Now my life is going to change. Guru Rinpoche has just appeared to me.'

'In a vision?' I asked startled.

'Yes. He just appeared to me.'

'Does this happen very often?'

'No, not often but it happens time to time. When he does, some change is there. I was waiting for this.'

'I am very happy it happened here. It will bless this place.'

I opened the letter. There were a few words on a blank sheet of paper:

'Dear Norma,

I am sorry it took so long to return your money but I have kept my promise to you. I hope everything is working and you are happy.

Patrick Boone Ikehi

Instantly, I felt pulled into a vortex like a spell. I tried to keep my mind focused on the present but a hundred dollar note escaped and fluttered onto the floor. Hands trembling, I picked up the note hastily and put it back into the letter.

'One hundred dollars! Why is someone sending you one hundred dollars?' Detective Rixen inquired suspiciously.

'I lent it to someone I met in Delhi last year and he has just returned it,' I explained casually.

He looked at me, his eyes becoming hard. 'You would never lend someone that much money, definitely not someone you happened to meet by chance. Who is this man? How did you meet him?'

'No one significant,' I said struggling to remain calm. 'Just someone who was waiting for his money, and I had just received mine:' My mind was racing. 'We were staying at the same guest house, at Dalmia's.'

'Must be some reason you lent it to him. You wouldn't take a chance like that with someone you just met. What was his name? Where was he from?'

'I didn't know him very well. It wasn't important. Anyway', I added defensively, 'it's my business and I don't want to talk about it.'

Harret Rixen was a first- class detective. He knew how to work a suspect. I was good at keeping secrets but very bad at concocting cover-ups. My defensive tone was just the trigger he was waiting for, the clue to the crime. He pulled me to him and sat me on his knee. 'Darling, why don't you want to talk about it, if it's not important, just tell me what it is, I will understand. We should not have any secrets from each other. You want to get married, don't you?' I nodded, falling into the trap. 'Then tell me everything. I will love you even more than now. Tell me.'

He kissed my neck; his hands caressed my breasts. 'You love me, don't you?'

I nodded again. 'Yes, of course I love you, more than anyone in the world, and I don't want to lose you. You're brother, father, mother, sister, you're everything to me, the whole family that I never had.' Tears flooded my vision as I began to sob uncontrollably.

'Tell me', he whispered seductively.

'I can't tell you,' I cried. 'I promised not to tell. I'll betray another person if I tell. It will be impossible for you to understand. Don't force me to tell you, please let me have this one secret.'

'I **will** understand, and it won't make any difference to our relationship. I promise, I will love you just as much, maybe more. It will be a bond between us. Tell me, darling; tell me everything. You can trust me, I won't tell anyone.' His voice was cajoling, lulling me into submission. I tried to resist, but was hypnotized. 'Tell me darling', he said again kissing me fully on the lips, biting my nose playfully.

I tried to remember Patrick Boone's warning, but it became blurred, and faded out. I was mesmerized by Jigmai's voice or was he Harret? Who was he anyway? I lost my self and began to waver. Detective Rixen and the Great Magician from Bhutan suddenly merged into one character. He seized his opportunity.

The interrogation began. 'How did you meet?'

'We were playing cards at Dalmia's and he turned to me and said. 'Your man is a Pisces and he is very hard on you. He has nothing, so he's putting everything on you. He has possessed you, put a spell on you, and you can't have an equal relationship until you become empowered again.'

I looked at the love of my life. He seemed to accept the accusation. At least he did not deny it.

'Who was he?' he asked forcefully, suddenly agitated.
'A black man from Nigeria', I confessed.

The Great Magician looked shocked. 'A black man!' he exclaimed, as if seeing Patrick. 'A black magician! So he removed the spell for you. Tell me how he did that, darling. Did you have sex with him?'

'No, it wasn't sex, absolutely not. There was a shamanistic ritual, nothing more than that. I had to do it', I explained, 'I did it because I was in love with you and I thought what he said was true,' I sobbed. 'I did it for **you**!'

His face was a mask, impenetrable, as if frozen in deep contemplation.

'How many times did he do this ritual?'

'Three.'

'What else did he tell you?'

'He said if I ever told you, I would lose you.'

The spell was broken. Harret and Mrs Rixen vanished like ghosts before my eyes. I began to weep with despair. What had I done? Why had I told him? How did he get it out of me? Now everything was finished. 'Are we still going to get married? Do you still love me?' I asked in despair.

'Yes, darling, why not?' His voice was hard and impenetrable. 'I am happy you told me. 'What was his name?'

'That is something I am not saying,' I replied, drawing a boundary around myself. 'Don't even try to get it out of me. There is no need to know any more about this story. I've told you everything.'

I lay down on the bed exhausted. Jigmai arose quietly. He looked strangely calm and masterful. 'So, **this** is the meaning, this is the way it has to be,' he murmured to himself.

The next day he left for Manali, as planned, and I went back into retreat. His mother and sister had recently arrived from Bhutan and we agreed I should meet them before I went back to London.

Everything seemed to spring back into place as though nothing had happened. There was no thunderclap, no bolt of lightening. But the event was so shocking to both of us we never returned to the scene of the 'crime.' I never asked him to explain why he had used his powers to possess me, or indeed if he had even intentionally done so. Yet in retrospect, it was clear: this was the beginning of the decline, the almost invisible moment that marks change into an uncharted landscape.

Manali, 1984

A very pretty, elfin child, with an expression of mischievous curiosity came down the path to greet Jigmai and me as we got out of the taxi in Dhungri, the hillside above Manali bazaar. The wooden house where he had rented rooms was set in a forest of gigantic scotch pines, planted over a hundred years ago by an intrepid Scotsman known as Duff Dunbar.

'This is my sister, Yangchen', said Jigmai introducing me to the child, who looked no more than twelve. Yangchen looked at me briefly and grinned, then she took her brother's hand and they walked arm in arm onto the veranda of the house. An old crone wrapped in layers of Bhutanese cloth was sitting on a chair in the evening sun drinking home made brew.

'My mother,' said Jigmai, 'She's a little crazy. She was put in prison several times by the last king', he explained. 'She was my sister in my last life.' His mother grinned tipsily at me in recognition and offered me a glass. We sat together drinking in silent communication, broken occasionally by a volley of incoherent chatter in Bhutanese. From time to time she put her arms around me and sang a song with theatrical gestures, laughing and crying.

Half an hour later Yangchen emerged from the room bearing several cups and a teapot. First she poured her brother's into a fine china cup with a lid embossed with dragons and offered it to him, hands outstretched, palms graciously up. Her mother's was poured into another china cup with a saucer but without a lid; hers into a similar cup and saucer. Mine was poured into a plain, slightly chipped mug. I recognised this as the Tibetan culture of hierarchy: you are of lower caste than us, her tea ceremony proclaimed.

As night fell, I was led into the cold dark interior lit only by a naked ceiling bulb. Yangchen was squatting on the floor beside a primus stove, singing and very slowly peeling onions into the new red frying pan I'd brought from Sherabling. My water filter was on the table together with a portable typewriter. Jigmai put on the large heavy wool Canadian ski sweater I'd given him. He carried my bags up a narrow ladder into an attic where a bed had been prepared.

I climbed down the precarious ladder and sat next to Jigmai, who picked up a wooden flute and blasted the same shrill flat notes again and again. A small shrine on the window-sill displayed a photo of a very frail white, cotton clad yogi in the same posture as Milarepa, holding his hand to his ear: 'He is my father', said Jigmai, noticing my gaze. 'He was much older than my mother.'

It was eleven o'clock before a mountain of white rice, chili, potatoes and dal was heaped onto our plates. Jigmai said a short offering prayer in Tibetan and then they all rolled the food into little balls with their fingers and ate with tremendous gusto. I was offered the choice of chopsticks or a spoon, which I took gratefully. At midnight,

Yangchen walked her mother, singing tipsily, from the veranda to the spare bedroom which Jigmai had rented specifically for their visit. We left the unwashed dishes, pots, pans, and pressure cooker just as they were, on the dirt encrusted wooden floor. The rats would be having a midnight feast.

The days went by without any structure, discipline, or schedule. We got up when we wished; someone – Yangchen or I – carried the dirty dishes in a bucket to the local tap and washed them in cold water. By the time we had clean plates, it would be mid morning, and by the time we finished 'breakfast', it was within a few hours of tea. Dinner was always close to midnight, after hours of tortuous peeling and frying. In between Jigmai would play the flute or we would all go to the clubhouse, where he would show his mastery of ping-pong or billiards. Life was slower and more unstructured than I had ever experienced – a simple primitive existence.

It was clear from the moment I arrived, that Yangchen was the first lady, consulted like an oracle about every decision, however minor. She washed her brother's underwear, prepared his tea, made his bed, laid out his clothes, and followed his every footstep like a shadow.

One day we awoke in the late morning to the sound of Indian drums and flutes. Yangchen walked into our bedroom unexpectedly. 'There's a festival in Dhungri, hurry, come outside. I have a surprise for you.' We dressed quickly and went downstairs. On the veranda was a very beautiful young Tibetan girl, her dark hair gathered at the back with a pin, framing her refined features. Her movements were as soft and gracious as a princess.

Jigmai put out his hand to greet her. 'Ah ha, Thrinley Chodron', he said, 'how are you?' He shook her hand vigorously. I recognised the name. She was the sister of his best friend, Sey Rinpoche. Young as she was, she had the reputation of knowing her own mind, scorning the role of the Lama's wife trapped in rounds of tea-making.

She folded her hands at her heart before taking his outstretched hand. 'Very well, Rinpoche', she replied. 'I have just finished my college exams so I am having a summer holiday here in Manali'. She had the clipped sing-song accent of the convent school educated upper class elite. After a few minutes of pleasantries, I was introduced. 'This is Miss Norma Lee Vine', said Jigmai, 'she has been living at Sherabling and is a student of Tai Situ Rinpoche.' I could have been someone who had dropped in for the day.

'Let's go to the temple', said Yangchen buzzing excitedly. The two girls walked arm in arm with Jigmai at his sister's side. I walked uncertainly a few steps behind, unsure of my place. Hundreds of people had gathered at the temple, following a procession of musicians with drums, accompanying a statue inside a canopy. A loud-speaker was blasting out Hindi pop music.

There were many Tibetans in amongst the Indian families. Their gaze rested on Jigmai and Yangchen, to whom they smiled and bowed deferentially; and then they looked at Thrinley with the same look of respectful approval. She smiled back demurely, basking in their respect. They glanced briefly at me and turned away, unable to fathom if I was with this privileged group or not.

I knew that wearing Western clothes made me harder to read, but I had made a decision long ago not to wear Tibetan costume. The heavy ankle length tunic shaped like a sack, and defined at the waistline by long ties that crossed at the back into a wide pleat, reminded me of school uniforms. It obliterated the contours of the body, and smothered one's movements beneath its weighty folds. In the twilight zone of cultures I inhabited with Jigmai, I needed to hang onto my identity as a Western woman to keep my power. But today my power was seeping away.

Suddenly Jigmai turned to me. 'You should go back now and stay with mother. She is alone, we cannot leave her for long; she will just wander around and get drunk, maybe fall off the veranda. You know how she is.'

'I think that's Yangchen's job, not mine,' I replied brusquely.

He turned to Yangchen and they had a brief conversation. 'She wants to stay and enjoy with Thrinley; she hasn't had a friend to talk to since she came here. We won't be long, we will just have something to eat and walk Thrinley home, maybe a few hours. Go home and wait for me there.'

It was an embarrassing moment, which I was not equipped to handle with poise. I turned around and without saying goodbye, walked quickly away.

We sat together, mother and wife, as she called me, on the veranda, drinking tea. As the sun started to set, we drank the chang – Tibetan homemade beer – and when it was quite dark, we broke open the bottles of rum and made cocktails with apple juice and a squeeze of lemon. She looked at me kindly with eyes of compassion. We had no common language, but we understood each other deeply. She knew I was becoming more and more agitated as the afternoon faded into night. 'Where is he?' she seemed to be saying. 'Yes', I replied to her unspoken thought, 'he should be here by now. He's with another woman and I am full, from the tip of my toes to the top of my head', I said pointing to my body, 'with anger.' She put her arms around me and we laughed, drank and cried together. At ten o'clock we went into the house. I tried to prepare something to eat, but could only scramble eggs with some leftover spinach. At eleven o'clock, she fell asleep on the narrow sofa in the sitting room and I climbed the ladder to the attic.

At midnight Jigmai returned. I woke up from my fitful sleep. 'Where have you been? Why did you take so long?' I tried to ask calmly, but within seconds I was screaming. 'You said you were just going to walk her home, but you were away for nine hours! What were you doing? How dare you treat me like that?' I rose up from the bed and faced him. 'Who do you think I am, some peasant girl who is here to do your bidding?'

'We went to a restaurant,' Jigmai replied quietly.

'Really, how nice for you,' I spat the words ironically. 'I had to baby-sit for your mother while you went out to eat with your girlfriend!' I was shaking with resentment.

'What are you talking about?' Now he was shouting too.' I told you Guruji warned me about her family. She is not my girlfriend', his voice was rising, 'but she calls me her brother. I have known her family for many years. It was my duty to walk her home.'

'Yes, I know about your brother-sister relationships!' I let out all the pent up frustration of the last few weeks, my mounting anger, the humiliation I felt to the core of my womanhood. 'She's in love with you, I can see that; and you…you're just waiting your time to have her, to get her into bed and….'

I saw his hand swing round, coming towards me with great speed, and before I had time to utter another word it struck me on the head. The force of the blow was so great I spun round and landed on the floor. The shock stilled my mind making it crystal clear. There were no thoughts, no conflicting emotions. The whole episode vanished.

I got up, straightened my white lace nightdress and looked at him with perfect composure. 'That was really…. powerful. It's cleared my head. Let's go to sleep.' He took off his clothes cradling me in his arms as we relaxed into a deep, peaceful sleep.

In that moment of shock and clarity I knew something had happened, but it wasn't until later that I would be able to describe it as a blessing. At the heart of Tibetan Buddhism is the story of the great master Tilopa and his scholarly disciple, Naropa. Tilopa lived in a cave by a river catching fish, eating their entrails and bringing them to life again. Tilopa put Naropa through a series of tortuous challenges for twelve years. Naropa obeyed him with utter faith, but he was a scholar, and his conceptual mind was so strong he wasn't able to break through it. One day Tilopa picked up his shoe and slapped Naropa on the face. It shocked Naropa into recognising his own mind- the first step in becoming fully enlightened. Today that kind of behaviour would be called an abuse of power, and Tilopa could end up in court. We choose our reality and Naropa chose to submit himself to his Guru. Jigmai's blow cut through my pattern of jealousy, like scissors cutting the first link in an explosive chain reaction.

A month passed uneventfully. The sky was our television. At night we sat and watched the play of clouds changing colours swiftly as the sun set; and each elaborate pattern of stars that dressed up the naked sky.

And then it happened, the event that would mark the end of Harret Rixen, and of Jigmai too, and the beginning of Shabdrung Rinpoche. At mid-morning Jigmai rushed into the bedroom where I was sitting in meditation. 'Quickly, pack your bags, put everything away. Guruji is coming up the road. In ten minutes he will be here. Run into the forest and stay there until he leaves! He must not find you here!' Panic-stricken, Jigmai, Yangchen and I stuffed all my belongings into bags and hid them under the bed. It took only five minutes to obliterate all trace of my occupancy.

'Why is he coming?' I asked as I ran out the back door.
'He's coming with another Lama. I don't know exactly why. There was some talk of going to Zanskar this summer.'
'You should have told me.'
'It wasn't definite. I don't know myself. Now please go, run into the forest. I will send Yangchen to get you when it's safe to come out.'

I ran, stuffing some apples into my bag and taking a small cushion to sit on. I found the forest path, climbed up it for about five minutes until I was well concealed, and sat on the grass with my cushion beneath me. It was an ideal place to meditate, but my mind was racing. What did all this mean? If Jigmai went to Zangskar, he would be going as a Lama to his monasteries there. This was the major shift in his life he had been eagerly waiting for. I had been so submerged in the drama of this relationship I had let go of my greatest doubt, but now it reappeared: could Jigmai be married to a Western woman and be accepted by his people?

It was years since my first encounter with Guruji at Bijai Palace and yet nothing had shifted. I was still in hiding in the middle of a forest, my clothing stuffed under the bed that Jigmai and I slept in. I was still the hidden secret in his double life. Once again the humiliation was gnawing hungrily at my bones. I was still a beggar looking through the window, watching a royal feast. There was no place at the table for me

I imagined the scene: he would be presented with silk offering scarves, while they made three full-length prostrations, then they would offer presents. Yangchen would come out bearing a tray with china cups and an elaborate tea- pot embossed with dragons. She would pour the tea slowly into the cups and offer it gracefully with both hands, palms upwards: first her brother, followed by Guruji, the Lama, and her mother. I imagined her holding a mound of barley flour on a china plate in front of each of them, inviting them to take a pinch to throw into the air. They would all say 'Tashi Shok'- may all things be auspicious and flick the flour upwards. Then she would offer Bhutanese food – pieces of succulent pork with hot chillies.

How long would all this take? I looked at my watch. It was mid-day, the sun was still hot and I had already been there for an hour. I lay down on the rocks, helpless as a child locked in a closet. At three o'clock I heard my name as Yangchen came up the path calling me.

We walked into the house. Rice was scattered everywhere – they must have thrown it to bless the place – there were dirty china cups lying about where they had been left, with residue around the rims from the sticky butter tea. I went into the kitchen to make myself a cup of tea but it was full of plates with remnants of pork and chilli. I washed a fancy china cup and saucer and sat alone in a corner drinking tea.

'So, what happened?' I asked Jigmai when he entered the room. 'I was in the forest for four hours'. Then I couldn't help myself – 'that's quite a long time to be barred from your home, isn't it?'

'Guruji came with the head monk from my monastery in Zanskar. They have invited me to come in July and I have accepted. It will be a big trip – looks like one month going to all the Drukpa Kagyu monasteries. The monk said the people there have been waiting for me to come for the past twenty- five years. They are making all preparations.'

'That's wonderful' I replied sincerely. 'I am very happy for you; your life is changing direction. You will be a Lama now. That's good.'

I prepared to depart for Sherabling to pack up my house before going back to London. 'Mother says she loves you and wishes to see you again,' said Jigmai as his mother presented me with a beautifully woven embroidered purple Bhutanese belt. 'She said you are welcome to come and stay with her in Bhutan. She calls you my wife.' Yangchen smiled and embraced me briefly.

Still, Jigmai kept my hopes alive. 'I will let you know by the end of the year where and when we will be getting married,' he said. 'Wait for my letter.'

For months his voice echoed in my ear. 'I will let you know...Wait for my letter.'

Act Three

*Adepts are above good and evil only in their ecstatic realisation.
In their embodied condition they are as susceptible and liable
to moral considerations as the next man or woman.
Otherwise we must treat them on a par with the truly insane,
who are moral morons.*
(Holy Madness, Georg Feuerstein, p. 253)

CHAPTER 10

PEACE AND CONFLICT

Tai Situ wrote his signature on a letter typed on official Sherabling paper with the monastery letterhead in maroon and two deer on either side of the eight spoked dharma wheel. He stamped his seal under the signature, folded it neatly into an envelope and handed it to me. It was addressed to Elizabeth Kubler-Ross. In two brief paragraphs it introduced me as his student whom he was sending to hold discussions about a global Peace Conference. They had already met the year before, he told me, and he was impressed by her spirit and sincerity. At that meeting, he continued, the seeds had been sown of a global conference involving scientists, religious leaders, ex-military officers, artists, intellectuals, and VIP's of every shade and hue. 'Kubler-Ross has said she will ask Mrs Sadat[30] to be on the board of directors,' he added confidently. 'Since her husband's assassination, she has been working for peace.'

'Where is it going to be held, Rinpoche?' I asked, after reading the introduction quickly. 'I think in Hawaii' he replied, and added, 'then we can open it with an animal parade: all the animals walking on land and the dophins and sea creatures swimming beside them. Of course they will all have to be tame.' There was a tone of joyous excitement in his voice. 'It will be very beautiful,' he said,

[30] the wife of assassinated President Anwar Sadat

his wide-spaced eyes looking into the future. 'But maybe it will be more convenient to have it in San Francisco', he conceded realistically. Hawaii is a bit far for many people.'

I placed the envelope carefully into my bag. I had heard of Elizabeth Kubler-Ross, an eminent specialist in the emerging study of death and dying, and was honoured to have the letter of introduction. He promised to send me some funds to research the conference. I was deeply moved by his trust and vowed to use it carefully.

I asked his advice about having an operation to have a child. His expression changed instantly. He hesitated for a long time before answering. 'You have to get the best doctor. There is no threat to your life if you have this operation,' he added carefully. He looked concerned. 'Are you sure you are getting married?'

'Well, that's what he told me. He said it very clearly.'

'Well, if you get married, you must have children,' he reasoned thoughtfully. 'Wait until you are sure,' he cautioned.

'Here, take this.'He stretched out his hand and gave me a small clay image of Guru Rinpoche wrapped in a cloth. I bowed my head and placed the image on it for blessing.

He regarded me with an expression of deep compassion – what the Tibetans call loving- kindness – as I was leaving. I wouldn't see him again for at least another year, nor with the erratic phone lines at Sherabling, would I be able to call him. 'Send me letters, tell me everything about the meeting with Kubler-Ross,' he said.

I packed up my retreat house. I knew I was leaving Sherabling forever. If I married Jigmai, we woudn't be living here; if I didn't, I would have to resettle in the West. As it turned out, my timing was perfect for another reason. In October, Indira Gandhi was to be assassinated by her Sikh bodyguards and India would tighten her visa controls.

There would be a massive exodus of foreigners, some of whom had lived in India for more than twenty-five years. It was the end of an era.

But my sudden re-entry into the I'd left behind five years ago was purposeful. I was a dove flying into the big wide world, an emissary for peace.

London, June 1984

'Let's go to Louis', said Judy one Saturday afternoon in June as we were walking on Hampstead High Street. Her bouncing blonde hair and trademark candy pink lipstick made her unusually glamorous for a 'serious' Buddhist. 'I am sure you could do with a little gourmet pampering after all your deprivations in India', she said looking at my hollow cheeks. 'You look like you need an apple strudel with cream.'

I followed her into the genteel tearoom, decorated like a Viennese parlour, where the well-heeled of Hampstead indulged their fondness for delicate pastries. We took a table at the rear and I sat with my back to the door, placing my handbag on the floor. After an hour we called for the bill. My hand went down to reach for my bag. There was nothing there. I looked under the table and around the chairs. 'My bag….' I said to Judy

It was the first time in my life I'd had anything stolen; not even during five years in India had the smallest thing been taken from me. 'My passport', I said to Judy, 'my money, which fortunately is not much' – and then I remembered. The clay image of Guru Rinpoche that Tai Situ gave me before leaving, which I said I would keep with me always, was in the bag as well. 'That's the only thing I care about', I said to Judith. I felt bereft, as if I'd lost my protection. It felt as though my skin had been removed. We walked to the police station and filed a report, but nothing was ever returned.

I wrote a letter to Tai Situ telling him about the loss of the precious statue, which felt like an inauspicious sign. Eventually he sent a small plastic Taiwanese image of Guru Rinpoche, which I would wear around my neck for years until the plastic shield disintegrated. I also wrote about the theft to Jigmai. His reply was typed on the portable manual I had left him.

14th June 1984

> Dearest and precious Norma darling,
> Today I got your sweet and loving letter. Thanks for remembering me sweetheart. I was overjoyed to know about your safe journey to England, which means a lot to me. You lost the precious handbag which is of course a bad news, but never mind, be careful in future so you may not repeat it again. News about poor Judith is also not promising one. Dear give her my love and tell her not to worry too much, because this does not help at all. The money you sent to me from Delhi, I got it on 11/6/84. I never once thought it to be that difficult so dear I'm sorry for the trouble.
> Hey don't call yourself piece of poop or anything else similar to that, do you know why? Because you are my first love hence very special to me. Don't let yourself flow in the ocean of emotion, you won't get anything out of it except the immeasurable pain. Here I would like to add few lines of a poet in the name of my darling who refuses to understand me.
> "Oh but if I had the stars from the darkest night
> And the diamonds from the deepest ocean
> I'd forsake them all for your sweet kiss
> For that's all I'm wishin' to be ownin'"
> While I'm typing this letter I'm listening to John Lennon.

We will be eating soon. Weather has changed a lot since you left; it is much cooler than ever. Time seems to have speedened up its wings.
Sweet Danuta writes that she has waited for you to phone her and they are keeping an extra ticket for you for the Dylan concert.
Wish you to have a successful start. My mother sends you love and a big hug. Yangchen wishes you to have every success in life, which one can possess.
With love and blessings
Shabdrung Rinpoche
Manali India
PS- I think I will be in the west in 1985 so hope to see you then.

I read and re-read the letter many times. There was no doubt he loved me, no doubt he was coming to see me. The last line said nothing about marriage, but it seemed to indicate there was no change of plan – we would be married in 1985. Three weeks later on July 4th, an exact duplicate letter arrived with a neatly typed covering page.

Manali 4th July 84.

Dearest lovely Norma darling,
Few days ago I dropped few lines to you, but did not receive any answer. Maybe you have not got my letter, or you are too busy to reply. Anyway I am enclosing the copy of previous letter, so you may not miss anything. I been waiting for your letter, but now very soon I'm leaving for Zanskar.
Life over here is fine except that I miss you very much, although you will never understand it. I'm enjoying your red frying pan and water filter. Typewriter has proved to be of very important so thanks for it. I'm listening to music and about to eat dinner. It is 10 past 10pm....Tomorrow I'm going to Mandi to collect my money and do essential

shoppings for my coming trip. Mother sends her love to you.

With love and birdy kisses,
Ngawang Jigme

I wrote back, saying I was intending to see a doctor about the operation. I had a brief note just before he went to Zanskar:

Dear Norma,
Just a quick note to you. I'm leaving for Zangskar tomorrow the 15th July 1984.
I got your letter and I'm very fine. I'll write you in detail some other time. Hope you won't mind me being so short and brief.

With love,
N Jigmai
14/7/84

I read the letter quickly my heart in my mouth. But there was nothing to suggest any change. Jigmai and I were still together. I took out the scrap of paper with the name of the best surgeon in the field of microsurgery: Mr. Robert Winston[31], Hammersmith Hospital. I dialed the number, spoke to the receptionist and made the earliest possible appointment – in a month's time – with the grand master of microsurgery.

Mr Winston was sitting in a very ordinary NHS office at Hammersmith Hospital decorated with pictures of beaming mothers holding small infants, beside husbands standing proudly in their best suits. I noticed the formidable intelligence of his steady gaze, the permanent worry lines

---

31 And now twenty-five years later Lord Robert Winston is acclaimed and honoured internationally; a celebrity surgeon appearing on TV and literary festivals, whose authority is unquestioned.

on his forehead and the short bristly moustache, which gave him an air of authority.

His manner was brisk, like a general planning a military campaign. 'I've had a look at your x-rays, Miss Levine, and I have to tell you that the damage to your fallopian tubes is from several incidents of pelvic inflammatory disease, the first of which was about thirteen years ago and the last very recently. It is quite extensive. You see here,' he said pointing to a tiny dark line. 'These are the tubes. They are no bigger than a hair and very difficult to perform surgery on.' His voice was serious. 'You have only a small chance of conceiving even if the operation is successful.'

'How small?' I asked, perturbed.

'About five percent,' he said folding his fine hands with their short manicured fingernails neatly under his arms. He looked at me kindly but sternly, very much in control. I could understand why people made doctors into Gods. 'I would like to have the operation anyway. I know it will be successful,' I insisted.

'Operations are very serious,' he said gravely. 'You should think about it carefully. You're a healthy woman, there's nothing wrong with you, nothing threatening your life. You know,' he continued his deep voice low but emphatic, 'people can die under anesthetic. An operation like this will take four hours and it's not even necessary. In my opinion, it's not a chance worth taking. There are things in life other than having babies. It's not for everyone.'

I decided to take on God. 'I understand what you say, but I don't have to think about it. I want to do it, the sooner the better. I've been living in India for the last five years with a Tibetan Lama whom I'm going to marry. I know it's going to be all right,' I said confidently.

Mr. Winston gave me a penetrating look, the worry lines deepening in his forehead, and shrugged. 'Okay, it's up to you. I'm not recommending it, but if you want to go through with it, then call my receptionist and she'll book a time for you.' I stood up, thanked him and shook his hand.

It was September by the time I went into the Royal Masonic for the first operation of my life. I watched Mr. Winston putting on his gloves just before the anesthetist put the needle into my arm. 'Please do your hundred percent best.' I said.

'I am not God,' he replied. 'I can't make tissue that isn't there. I can only do the best that science can do.' I counted to ten and blacked out.

When I awoke I felt the stitches pulling in my belly and all the soreness of the incision, but the pain was not important. What I was feeling was worse than pain. It was as if I had entered a stark reality. The burden of karma is over now, a voice was saying, the whole thing is finished. It's not the beginning of a new chapter; it's the end of one. Was I having something similar to post natal depression? I wondered. The operation was pronounced 'successful'; but Mr. Winston warned me that my best chance of conceiving was within the next six months. 'Don't wait too long,' he said, smiling at me sceptically as I handed him a bottle of the smoothest saki as a token of gratitude.

After two weeks I had recovered, but the bleakness of depression continued. All my letters to Jigmai had no response; like putting a note into a bottle and throwing it out to sea. His trip to Zangskar was over; he was at home, but the link to him felt broken. I began to feel as though I was trying to grasp a phantom; the dynamic presence at the core of my life had gone.

It was in this hopeless state that I had to turn my attention to the peace conference, and contacted Kubler-Ross, the doyenne of dying. I attended one of her talks in

London and was surprised by her unremarkable appearance. She was a small, thin, grey-haired, chain-smoking woman in heavy walking shoes and a loose tweed skirt. But when we met after the talk I was surprised by her calmness. Her presence was so charged with radiant love, I immediately began to weep. Without saying a word, she held my hand and pressed into my palm a piece of paper with a date, plucked from her fiendishly busy schedule, for us to meet at her ranch in Virginia. I left, strangely comforted, as if the buddhas had sent an emissary to guide me.

I followed leads wherever they appeared. Joseph Rotblatt introduced me to the head of the Centre for Strategic Studies in London. He offered a small office from which to organise the conference and suggested I meet certain ex- military officers in the US now working actively for peace.

Warren Kenton, an eminent teacher of Kaballah, directed me to Keith Critchlow, who who sent me to the grande dame of poetry, Kathleen Raine. She received me at her salon near Kensington, and read aloud from her most recent volume like an ancient Greek muse. I wrote down everyone's ideas about the Peace Conference in a large notebook and turned the notes into letters, which I sent by registered post to Tai Situ.

By November, I had collected as much information in London as I could. I wrote draft after draft of the all-important proposal, defining the aim and purpose of the peace conference. I contemplated titles like Peace Within, Peace Without and struggled to encapsulate the core of our aims. The emphasis shifted all the time with each person I spoke to. I had to think more seriously than I ever had before, about the meaning of 'peace' and 'conference'. As for the subtitle, was the meeting global, or international? Was it a conference, a forum, or a colloquium?

I decided to leave London and work from the Black Mountains near Hay-on-Wye, at the home of my old friend, Maggie Russell. Maggie still maintained a close relationship with her Guru, Chogyam Trungpa Rinpoche, to whom she had been engaged many years before.

On November 11, my birthday, I sat on the sofa close to Maggie's phone, trying to conjure Jigmai to call me. I kept thinking of Maggie's conversation with Trungpa a few days ago. 'Rinpoche thinks that Shabdrung Rinpoche should leave India and come to live in the West,' she reported to me. 'It's not safe for him there.

The phone rang and I jumped to answer it. It wasn't Jigmai; it was Tai Situ. 'How are you?' he asked. He wasn't being polite, he was really asking. It was as though he had lifted the flood barriers and it all came pouring out. 'I had the operation,' I shouted down the phone, 'I went through everything, I got the best doctor, but he said I had only a five percent chance of conceiving. Still, I went through with it, but as soon as I woke up from the operation, I knew it was over. This relationship is now over,' I repeated. I heard my own voice, sharp with anger.

He didn't react to my anger; he didn't reproach me. Instead he spoke gently. 'How do you feel?' he asked. And suddenly a wave of relief spread over my body, as if the air had been let out of a tight balloon. 'Relieved,' I said, 'really relieved'. And I really was. Blindly trying to fulfill Joyce's vision had obsessed me and now I was free of it; and free also of some hellish black karma burdening my womb.

Calmer now, I told him the arrangements I'd made for the conference. He listened and approved. 'Before I do any more, I have to go to Canada to see my mother,' I said. There was a thoughtful pause. 'If you are not happy there, don't stay too long,' he advised.

When I put down the phone I wept for a long time. Jigmai did not call. I knew what I had blurted out was true: the relationship was over, but disengaging myself from the many-layered bonds of love, went far beyond a flash of intuition. It would have to go very deep, like extricating a mineshaft sunk into the core of the earth.

A few days later a neatly typed letter finally arrived.

Nov. 18, Sunday, Manali, India

Dear Norma,
I am sorry that I could not write to you promptly. I came back from my journey on Sept. 27. There was so many things to settle down and of course to settle my self back to old situation. I hope you understand what I mean. From your side I got three letters till today. I'm very happy to know about your health.
You did not wait to hear from me regarding your tube operation, so now what can I say.
I'm going to prepare for my trip to the west soon so hope to see you either in UK or in USA.
My poor mother remembers you a lot. She is sending her love to you. She will be going back to home very soon.
Manali is getting very cold in morning and evening. Rest is okay.

With love
Jigme

That was it: my intuition was confirmed. I took a piece of paper and wrote: 'Please get drunk and write me a love letter.' I found a £10 note in my purse, enclosed it in the letter and sent it.

****

Arctic winds were buffeting across the runway at Mirabelle airport in Montreal when I arrived to visit my mother in late November. After a few hours I understood what Tai had Situ had meant. The prodigal daughter was returning home after nine years, to a very frosty welcome, packed with layer after layer of icy resentment. The hopelessness of wanting her understanding for the extreme path I had taken was clear when I realised the suffering she had endured at my absence. After three days I moved out to stay with a friend.

'A letter has arrived from India', my mother reported on the phone. I saw Jigmai's unmistakeable handwriting on the envelope waiting for me on the hall table. With hands trembling, I opened it. It was a premature New Year's card sent in late November, with just a few lines written on it:

> Dear Norma,
> Life over here is getting ready to leap for a great change. But don't be sad my love, things don't happen the way one wishes all the time.
>
> With love,
> Jigmai

I stared in disbelief at the large bold slanted letters scrawled over the card. 'This is not the letter of a man to his fiancée', my mother said looking over my shoulder. It was true. There would be no marriage and no regrets either. It was the naked truth, as Jigmai used to say, laughing sardonically.

I touched the scar on my belly. There, reality cut into hopes, dreams, predictions, promises – and now lies? Were they lies or a paradigm shift, a new pattern in the kaleidoscope? They had all turned into a scar. I tore the card to shreds, put the pieces in a heap and lit them. Then I scattered the ashes in the cold Canadian wind.

As soon as Tai Situ's money arrived at my bank, I abandoned the frozen north; booked a flight for New York on People's Express and moved in with a friend in Manhattan for ten days, to make contacts for the conference. I felt like a figure from Dylan country: a complete unknown, with no direction and no home. Only the nobility of Tai Situ's vision and the warmth of his voice protected me from the void between skyscraper and pavement.

Elizabeth Kubler-Ross sat in a comfortable armchair in her large sitting room at her ranch in Virginia near a prominent Christmas tree hung with angels. Cards lined the mantelpiece six deep. We discussed her part in the conference: to lend her name, to invite famous guest speakers, like Shirley MacLaine and to act as advisor. This small, grey charismatic lady had her feet on the ground. 'You cannot organise a global conference without money,' she said firmly. 'You have to have funding, credit cards, phone cards and authority to make decisions. By the time it takes for a letter to reach Sherabling and return again, it will be one month. It's impossible to organise that way. We need to make decisions ourselves. Please send a letter to Tai Situ Rinpoche and tell him what I am saying.'

I wrote the letter dutifully, quoting Kubler-Ross, but never received a reply. The advice, as I found out later, was not well received. Tai Situ could not be written out of the decision of a conference he himself had initiated.

I continued to Washington to meet an important ex-general. He read Tai Situ's letter of introduction and looked hard at me. 'Are you willing to dedicate the next two years of your life to this dream, just to serve your teacher?' he asked bluntly. 'Yes,' I replied, with a defiant stare.

There was no end of organisations with ideas for a peace conference: the Institute for Integral Studies, Esselin, and the Maitreya Institute established by Situ Rinpoche, with whom I worked closely. There were those who thought Star Wars was the main global threat; there were lesbian activists who thought the problem was Men.

As the funds dwindled into a few hundred, I panicked at the thought of spending Tai Situ's money on myself and took a job cleaning houses in the Bay area. From international conference organiser to cleaning lady was another steep drop. I looked in the gilt bathroom mirror I was polishing and caught an expression in my eyes I had never seen before: fear. At nearly forty, I had no money, no career, no family, no nationality, and no husband. I was terrified at the thought of living a material life in the West again after five years of spiritual life in the East. And why was Jigmai not answering my letters? His silence was destroying my spirit.

Just as I was reaching the inevitable decision to leave San Francisco, a telegram slipped under my door. I opened it, trembling. 'MEET AT NIRULAS ON FIRST MARCH AT 11 AM. S N JIGME

I had one day to get to India; and with the time difference of twelve hours, half a day. I sent a telegram to a friend in Delhi to meet Jigmai in my place until I arrived. It never occurred to me to try to change the date. I was imprisoned inside a story. The only way out was to read the final chapter.

I booked a flight to Delhi with TWA arriving on March 2rd, filed all the peace conference documents into neat categories, and handed it over to Maitreya Institute. An hour later I arrived at the airport – to a scene of pandemonium.

The voice on the loudspeaker announced a twenty-four hour strike by TWA. I was put onto a Pan Am flight to Bombay instead with a connecting flight to Delhi. After a scrum at Bombay airport to board the Delhi flight, I arrived exhausted on the night of March 2 and immediately plunged into the last chapter of my story.

The waiters at Nirula's Hotel in Connaught Place shook their heads at my description of a short stout man with a deep voice called SN Jigmai; no one answering that description was seen yesterday, nor was there a message for me. My friend had turned up at the appointed time and place, but he had not been there. I took a room at Nirula's for the night, and began to write a diary to express my rage and grief.

It's 12:10 am, Monday March 4.

> "I slept a drugged sleep from 2pm till now, jet-lagged. I awoke to the knowledge that he may not want to meet me. He knows this is the showdown and may not have the courage to face it. There is a cancer inside me from keeping this all in for four years. Years of hope and fear, of service to 'a great man', of complete love, of craziness and fragile perfection. I feel like destroying the universe.
> Previously in moments of lucid despair like this, I would call on him, Shabdrung Ngawang Jigmai Rinpoche, to come to me. And he always did. Now there's no one there. He's not listening anymore. His inner ear is not turned to me. I've come halfway around the world to an empty space."
> "I know now that this relationship never ever had a chance to turn into marriage, that it was doomed from the start, and that Jigmai kept it going as long as he could knowing it would never be fulfilled. Why? I guess he loved me.
> There is nothing I could ever have done to make this work. Not any of the prayers, entreaties, pujas, sacrifices of my

body, nothing could ever have changed the outcome. Why then did I go on with it for years and years?

I have the strange feeling I've just given up. I know the outcome. I prepared the room for an honoured guest and waited in good faith, but he did not enter my house."

CHAPTER 11

THE SHABDRUNG'S FAMILIARS

March 8th, 1985, Manali.

I walked to the familiar door in Dhungri. For a second my heart sank. The place seemed vacated, just a heap of wood scraps. I turned around to see Yangchen looking at me with concern on her impish face. I opened my arms to hug her. Mother was sitting in a corner inside the room, pounding her stick and cackling for me to come over. I was so relieved I hugged them both.

'Where's Rinpoche?' I asked Yangchen.

'He went to Delhi today, plane from Kullu.'

He must have been boarding the plane as I was waiting for my baggage to arrive. We had passed like ships in the night. The inauspicious signs were fitting together like pieces of a ghoulish jigsaw.

'How long for?' I asked.

'Maybe ten days, maybe three days, not sure.' She shrugged her shoulders.

We relaxed on the veranda, drinking tea. I was surprised to find a door I had not seen before in the far corner. It opened into Jigmai's shrineroom, with a makeshift throne for him to receive guests and devotees. The shrine had two statues of the first Shabdrung, Ngawang Namgyal, and a statue of the Buddha in teaching posture. Several phurbas – ritual daggers used to destroy enemies – were standing on the left. With the sun streaming through the windows and the powerful smell of incense in the air, the room felt alive, as if the rituals it had seen were still happening.

I was looking at the first shrine room of the present Shabdrung and felt a torrent of conflicting emotions: love and longing, abandonment, betrayal. I have nurtured this precious being for four years, I was thinking, and now he will fulfil his destiny without me.

In the shrine room was a box full of letters; mostly mine. Every letter I had written over the past year had arrived, even an erotic letter describing my desire for him. Not a single one had been answered. Later, I found another inside the cupboard, the most forlorn of all. In it I described memories of our love-making, of my devotion and love for him, my small acts of kindness. Inside, folded neatly, was the £10 I had sent him and my last request: 'Please use this to get drunk and write a love letter to me.'

March 11

In the early morning I paced the forest path between the tall pines. As I reached the road I saw a taxi coming towards me. In it was a shape I knew. Jigmai! He looked straight ahead without turning his head. I gave a little cry of disbelief as the taxi continued. The driver stopped. I ran towards the car, opened the door and looked at Jigmai. He seemed barely to recognise me. 'May I accompany you?' I asked politely, as if he were a new acquaintance. He moved over reluctantly. 'Where are you staying?' he asked. 'At the Green Guest House', I replied, pointing to it from the road. 'I'll be there in two hours,' he said, sitting motionless as a stone.'Make it one', I replied. I got out and closed the door.

This was the exact opposite, I thought, to our meeting in Manali, when his taxi stopped at my feet after my extraordinary encounter with Patrick Boone Ikehi. It was as if the whole magic spell were spinning in reverse, rewinding into a curse.

When Jigmai arrived the drama started immediately.

'Why didn't you come to Delhi?' I asked.

'After I sent the telegram I realised you would not be able to get there, so I decided not to go.'

'And all my letters that you didn't answer?'

'Just lazy', he replied.

His manner was so casual it churned all my emotions. 'You sent me an urgent telegram to meet you in Delhi, and you didn't even bother to turn up?' I was screaming but I couldn't stop. 'You made me leave the work I was doing in San Francisco. I had the operation, remember, the one we agreed? I spent the last of my savings. Do you want to see the scar?' I pulled down my skirt and showed it to him. 'You knew I was having the operation in September. I told you before you went to Zangskar. Why didn't you tell me it was all over before you left?'

'I thought it would be worse to tell you before,' Jigmai replied simply.

'I spent a year in agony waiting for you, a year of loneliness, but you had promised…' I was sobbing now. 'I thought a bodhisattva could not lie, could not be cruel. I believed in that, I believed in **you**.' I stopped to catch my breath. Love and anger smothered me. I gasped for breath. 'And finally I had to come to you. Not you to me, but me to you. I came half way round the world because of your telegram!'

Now I was so exhausted I couldn't move.

'Let's lie down together.' He ignored my plea.

'Please,' I said. I can't sit here anymore like this with you. I'm going to explode.'

We lay stiffly like corpses in a coffin. When we touched, there was no sensation. We went through the motions of lovemaking, but his arms could not hold me, his mouth could not kiss me. It was as if we did not have physical bodies, but were ghosts imitating the gestures of love.

'Finally he spoke. 'I have something to tell you,' he said sitting up. 'Yes, of course I know that.' I replied 'That's why I came.' I felt on the edge of an abyss.

'I am tired of this cycle of suffering,' he began. 'I wish to give up worldly life. I will not marry.'

'You wish to become a monk?'

'Yes'

'You will not take another wife?'

'No, why should I want another wife?'

'I will not stop you, then. But you still owe me something. Otherwise the karma will continue and it will affect us both.'

'What do you want?'

It was a crucial moment, the moment I could have walked out of his life cleanly, with my dignity intact. I could have cut the ties fearlessly, like a dancing Vajra Yogini, free of attachment. But stripped of my own power, I was stuck in fear. The world no longer had a place for me. I needed to make my life again, from the beginning: food, clothing, and shelter; career, family, nationality. I needed something to present to the world.

I remembered an episode in the life story of Ngawang Namgyal, the first Shabdrung. 'I want us to marry for one year and try to have a baby. After that you can go, you are free.'

'A year is a long time. Anyway, I cannot marry.'

'Ngawang Namgyal married for a short time, until he had

produced a son; then he left his wife, took vows and became a monk.'

He looked at me curiously. 'You're very clever.'

'We had a commitment. I waited for you.' I looked at him for a sign of human warmth but he was as cold and still as a stone. My last illusions crumbled, like a bombed building. And all my resolution to respect his immense spiritual status suddenly made no sense at all.

I heard my shattered skeleton collapse onto the bed. 'There is something here I can't understand. Something more you have to tell me, but I'm tired now. I'll come tomorrow morning.'

At mid-day I climbed the stone steps. The crows were making so much noise overhead it stopped my thoughts. Crows were connected with the protector Mahakala and I began to wonder whether they were gathering purposefully around Jigmai's house.

'Aha, Norma,' Jigmai greeted me. 'Come in and have tea.' He made room for me to sit down. I looked into his eyes again but it was no use. 'The house is there', he said 'but the occupant is gone'.

He put on a woolen hat and went into the shrine room. 'Come in,' he said, when I opened the curtain. He was sitting on the throne reading a sacred text.

I pulled out a cushion and sat on the floor, cross-legged.

'I've given you my body and my mind for five years,' I said, fixing my gaze on him. 'I thought you were a bodhisattva, and that was the best offering. You often said I was no ordinary woman, that I was the one who brought you back to dharma. I would like my role in your life to be respected.'

After many more hours of talking, we reached our compromise.

He would come to England in June for three months and we would try to conceive a child. After that our sexual contact would end. And… he was prepared to give me money when he had some.

Thunder rolled in the mountains that night, lightning flashed across the sky while a few thick drops of rain fell. 'Even the weather is inauspicious,' I muttered. The Mona Lisa restaurant was closed. 'We settled for the Tourist Bungalow, and sat at a table next to a noisy Indian family. I looked at them and tears rolled uncontrollably down my cheeks.

'Pull yourself together', Jigmai said.

'I can't', I said, getting up. 'Please pay the bill and meet me in my room.'

When he arrived I was weeping with helplessness and loss. 'Do something for me,' I begged him, 'can't you see how I'm suffering?'

'I know', he relented, 'I can feel your pain. I'm also human'. He pressed his fingers to a place between my eyes and soon all torment vanished. My mind was calm and clear for the first time in over a year. 'We will sleep together tonight,' he said. I took a blanket and pillow from the guest-house and we climbed in the dark up the stone stairs cut into the mountainside.

He opened one of three doors off the upstairs veranda to reveal a single wooden bed covered by a thin mattress and a lumpy threadbare duvet. We took off our clothes leaving them in two heaps on the floor. It was like being invaded by a stranger. The strong intricate web woven from long nights of passionate, intense loving-making had broken. Later in the night, through my fragile, fretful sleep I sensed he had left the bed.

Then I felt a presence. Startled, I awoke to the sound of flapping outside the unlocked door. It seemed like a huge winged creature was trying to force its way into the room. 'Get out, get out,' I shouted automatically. Then I heard what sounded like a person with a bad leg walking on the veranda: a thump, then a dragging noise, then another thump, like a heavy step with the lame leg dragging behind it. I heard the flapping of huge wings and someone running. The door burst open as I bolted upright, staring into the darkness. There was nothing to see. The sounds continued for an immeasurable time. Exhausted, I fell back to sleep till the pale dawn light filtered through the cracks of the door.

I went outside to inspect the veranda. The door to the stairs that Yangchen bolted every night was unlocked. I looked into Jigmai's room; both he and Yangchen were asleep in their beds. The morning sun was shining through the scotch pines and creeping onto the veranda when at last Jigmai walked out of his room and came to sit beside me. 'How did you sleep?' I enquired.

'Not very well,' he replied. His face looked drained. 'I felt sick. I had pain in my stomach. Then my body started to shake and it felt like there was something dead inside me, like some part of me was dead. I never had this before'.

I stared numbly into the shadows of the forest.

Yangchen came onto the veranda, still in her nightdress, her long hair tangled in black thick skeins.

'There were lots of noises last night,' I said. 'It must have been the chickens that got loose. Some big roosters flew up to the veranda and tried to force their way into my room. They seemed very large, more like crows than roosters. Then I heard your mother coming up the stairs,' I continued. 'I guess she didn't have her walking stick, so her bad leg was dragging behind her.'

Jigmai and Yangchen stared at me. 'There aren't any roosters here,' said Jigmai. 'Mother did not leave her room last night,' said Yangchen. 'I also heard noises, but I thought it was a man running.'

I sat very still, remembering the biography of the first Shabdrung: the description of 'familiars' whom he commanded, and who were instrumental in defeating his enemies. 'I think they were your protectors,' I said to Jigmai after a long silence.

'Looks like that,' he replied.

'They're trying to get rid of me,' I said. 'Why? I served you for five years.'

Yangchen began talking to Jigmai in Bhutanese and he translated for me.

'I had a dream last night,' she said. I saw a figure, which felt like Guru Rinpoche. He was wearing a sword and his eyes were staring, bulging wrathfully. He looked at both of you making love and he said to Rinpoche, 'Are you a Lama or a worldly person?'

"A Lama", Rinpoche replied.

"We have been watching you for some time," the figure said, "and we have been very patient with you. You have not taken rebirth for **this**." 'He stared fiercely at you,' she said to Jigmai, 'and seemed about to strike you. "We will be patient no more," he warned and disappeared into the door of your shrine room.'

The meaning of Yangchen's dream was clear. Jigmai had to leave me to become a monk and a Lama. I drifted around in a daze, until I found myself back in my room at the Tourist Bungalow. I had experienced abandonment before, but never at such a primordial level. It felt like I was being expelled from the universe. A suicidal despair began to take over my mind. The protectors were working, but I had no protector.

I became aware of a gap in my circling thoughts, and of a deep silence in my mind. It was as if I were being guided to a new a level of consciousness and drifted into a half sleep. When I awoke and looked in the mirror my complexion looked fresh. I dressed purposefully, put a package of miso into my handbag and walked up the mountain to the cottage. Jigmai was lying down inside his room

'How do you feel?' I asked.

'Not very well.' He sat up and drank black tea; then I offered him the package to turn into a hot, nourishing drink. He waited until Yangchen left the room and we were alone.

'How do you feel?' he asked.

'Better now,' I replied. 'I have something important to tell you. I lay down to sleep for a while, and when I awoke I understood something. I remembered that you are the Shabdrung Rinpoche and that it is a mistake to be attached to you as a man. I had so much suffering from this attachment. That's why you were feeling ill. But I don't want to hurt you; I want to help you instead.'

It was a moment of clarity, one I would struggle to maintain over the coming days and months.

Jigmai listened attentively. 'How would you like to help?'

'I'm not sure. Tell me about Zanskar. You haven't said anything about it.'

His eyes lit up with joy. 'The people had been waiting for me for twenty-five years. Thousands came to receive my blessing. I spent four hours just giving blessings after an initiation. Everywhere the people were weeping to see me, and I also wept.

'Then suddenly I knew who I was. My lineage blood woke up. I visited a Naropa cave and felt I had to return there to meditate. In one place there was no rain for a very long time and no crops. After my visit, the rain fell. In another place I was asked to change the course of a river. After making prayers and offerings, I told the people what to do. Then the river changed its course. It flowed the opposite way.

'Before this I was never sure if the protectors were with me or against me. Then I knew they were with me and would continue to help me.'

'But the most special thing,' he continued, 'was the death of Guruji. A few days before he died, he announced that he would die. He was not showing any signs of illness. He called me to him and asked, "Is there anything you can do to help me?"

I said, "You know more about these things than I do. You have studied and practiced more than me."

'Guruji laughed; then he said seriously. "You see the devotion of these people towards you? It's your responsibility to help them. It is my dying wish that you should become a monk and help these people."

"I will do my best," I promised.

'Then Guruji sat in meditation posture and passed away. The area around his heart was warm for several days. His fingers were still supple. There was no stiffness in his body. And a rainbow around the sun remained for seven days.'

'Guruji was a siddha?' I asked amazed. 'We didn't know it when he was alive. It seemed like he was an angry revengeful person, threatening to kill me, spitting at you, putting the CID onto me. We thought he was just a mad old monk who was trying to keep us from being together.'

'All these things only show at death,' Jigmai said. 'Now I feel he is more powerful in death than when he was alive. I feel him all the time. Look at me. My mind turned from worldly ways to dharma.' There was a long silence. 'The

Buddha had to leave his wife and child to become the Buddha; I also have to leave you to serve all sentient beings.'

I looked at him measuring his words. His face was radiant, glistening as if he had been anointed with oil. I thought of the clumsy, panting Man Singh with his blue turban and over-bearing manner, the more sophisticated elegant Harret Rixen in a canvas hat carrying an attaché case, and S.N.Jigmai who was waiting for his moment to go onstage. These people were gone. The tremendous energy was there but now the container could hold it. I looked at his sensual, volatile mouth changing constantly – smiling, playing, teasing, manipulating; listened to the beautiful well- modulated voice, and felt his charm. He was detached yet available to all. There were no crazy passions to throw him off course.

This quality of radiant equanimity made him irresistible to me; at the same time my heart ached for his exquisite touch, the perfect fit of our bodies together in union, the fine clear scent of his skin, the immense power of his sexuality, so finely tuned to mine. I would never find it again; I knew that. We had both created this kind of ecstatic and agonising love.

I saw him writing on an envelope and looked at it when he left the room: 'Today is a day of great importance in my life. A great understanding is there between us. Hope it continues in future life.'

I moved my belongings to the room next to Jigmai's. The strange noises in the night never returned.

One morning the house erupted. Jigmai and Mother were out-shouting each other. Jigmai grabbed Mother by the arm, pushed her into a chair and slapped her face several times. Mother then packed her things. 'You can damn well do what you like,' Jigmai said. 'I will not stop you.' She hobbled off to the bazaar followed by her servant loaded with her belongings wrapped in old rags. She was determined to get on the bus and go to Bhutan.

'Please, go and get her back,' I pleaded.

'No,' he replied. 'Let her karma overtake her, let her die in the streets, or on the bus. She's a stupid woman,' he said, with disgust.

'But she's your mother.'

'So what!'

'She gave birth to you. Look', I begged him, 'she's in an old, sick body. Nobody is taking care of her. She's dirty, there's no toilet; she doesn't always get meals. She has no one to speak to, and she's been here for a whole year! No wonder she wants to go home.'

'It's not my fault,' Jigmai said defensively. 'I've sent telegrams for them to come and get her but no one replies.'

Finally, he relented. He went to the bazaar and brought her back, promising to take her to the Bhutanese border in ten days.

All my doubts about Jigmai returned. How could he be so heartless towards his own mother? Or was he, like his ancestor Drukpa Kunley, the divine madman of Bhutan, humiliating her publicly to clear her of negative karmas? Or could it be that holiness can reside in the frailest of vessels?

On the morning of their departure, I sat forlorn on the veranda, while waves of abandonment crashed over me, washing away my good resolutions like matchsticks. A tall, thin English woman with large, hollow eyes walked haltingly along the path. We looked into each other's eyes and recognised something. 'Do you see that woman?' I asked Jigmai. 'She is haunted by some tragedy. She has the eyes of a ghost. Her body isn't there anymore. You've done the same to me. I'm a ghost now, haunted by memories.

My life is gone. When the Buddha left his wife, he left her with a child and a palace and all the means to support her life. You are leaving me with nothing. Please give me your blessing.'

Tears flowed down my cheeks and wet my tangled hair. Jigmai's heart was at last moved. 'I will do something for you. I promise we will see each other again.'

It was time to leave. We all climbed into a taxi and drove to the bus stand. Some Tibetan women got into the bus, followed by a few Bhutanese girls. They gasped when they recognised Shabdrung Rinpoche, and bowed their heads. I offered Mother some fruit for her journey, quite sure I would never see her again. I kissed Yangchen on the cheek and bowed to Rinpoche. He called me over to him. 'Darling,' he said in a low but distinct voice, 'I gave you my fresh cock. The girls in Bhutan would die for that.' I stood there speechless. 'Don't forget it,' he added.

I was still too caught up in human attachment, and my Western ethics to understand what he meant, from his position, literally a world away: that I had been the receptacle for a great blessing, bestowed by a Tantric master. Through our love union, he had planted the seeds of enlightenment. I am not sure what I believe, even now. But decades later, the seeds did grow.

When I got back to the house, I went into the shrine room, locked the door behind me, and sat praying at the feet of Guru Rinpoche. For the first time Guru Rinpoche felt truly real to me, as if he were in the same room.'Why is this happening?' I asked him directly. 'Please release me from this nightmare. *Om Ah Hung Vajra Guru Pema Siddhi Hung*.' I said his mantra thousands of times, lying on the mattress until dark 'Please hear my prayers. I loved the man you've taken from me. Let me have something to sustain my life. Let all be auspicious. Help me.'

I packed my bags and went to Sherabling. When I arrived in the late morning, the sound of large Tibetan horns was blasting from the temple. I entered, as I had done so many times before, and sat watching Tai Situpa perform the Red Crown ceremony, in which he becomes the Buddha Maitreya and bestows the blessing of Maitreya on devotees. I had always been moved by the power of this ritual, but now I watched it like a spectator. I was beside myself, crumpled with shock and grief.

In the afternoon I waited outside Tai Situ's door. After an hour I was ushered into his room. I prostrated mechanically three times, jerking up and down like a marionette, and pulled a cushion as close to him as I could get. 'What happened?' he asked with concern. The tightness had built up around my heart and I couldn't speak. He waited calmly.

'He said he would not marry me, that he has to become a monk and serve his people. He promised his Guruji before he died. Guruji had the death of a siddha in Zangskar, sat up in meditation, rainbows everywhere...'

'Do you believe him?' Tai Situ asked me. 'Do you believe he's going to be a monk?'

'I don't know. That's what he said.'

Tai Situ looked sceptical.

'Then he performed some miracles,' I continued. 'He changed the course of the water so that it flowed in the opposite direction. Then he said he knew the protectors were with him. "So," he said to me, "now I have to leave you. Just as the Buddha left his wife to serve all sentient beings so I have to leave you."

'But you are a sentient being,' Tai Situ said.

'Yes, but nobody cares about me. Even his protectors came to kick me out. One night we tried to make love, but it was as if we were both ghosts. There was nothing there anymore. Then I heard strange sounds, like a huge bird

trying to get into my door, and frightening thumping sounds. Where is the compassion for me?' I started to cry.
'Those are his **worldly** protectors,' Tai Situ said firmly.
'What does that mean?'
'They aren't enlightened. They are not wisdom protectors. He has **worldly** protectors because of his lineage. It happened that way. They are like the mafia.'

'What have I done wrong? I asked. 'My life is in ruins.' I sobbed with exhaustion.
'I am sorry. I couldn't see the future,' Tai Situ admitted.
'Does anyone?' I asked warily.
'Yes, some Lamas do. Karmapa does,' he said.
'If this can happen to someone who has offered everything for five years to a great bodhisattva, then I don't believe in the dharma any more,' I said.

Then Tai Situ focused on me very forcefully and with great strength of intent like an empowerment said simply. 'I want you to know that I could never do what he has done to you. Never. But you have learned a lot. That is very good.'
'I've lost everything', I replied. 'I am sick, my heart is broken, I put all my money into building this house, I have nothing left. No career, no money, no family, no country. Everything is gone. I don't call that good. I call that unbearable suffering.'
'You've learned a lot,' he repeated.
'A lot about what?'
'The dharma,' said Tai Situ.

Years later I understood the meaning of his words. It was the eye of the needle: it was as impossible for a rich man to enter the kingdom of heaven as to go through the eye of a needle. In spiritual life you have to lose everything before you can win.

CHAPTER 12

UNFINISHED BUSINESS

London, 1985

I stood in the queue marked Foreigners and looked at the immigration officers in their cubicles. Some were Sikh; some were white. One of the Britishers, as Jigmai called them, beckoned me over. He had a no-nonsense, tight-faced look. I handed him my Canadian passport covered with page after page of six months UK tourist visas. 'What is your permanent address?' he asked thumbing the pages quickly. 'I've been living in India for the last five years', I replied. 'Before that I was in Wales, in Hay-on-Wye,' I added, hoping he had good memories of climbing there; or combing the bookshops. He glanced at my long layered Indian skirt, sandals, dangly earrings and long curly hair. It was 1985 but I was clearly not in style with Dynasty shoulder pads, big hair, large clip-on earrings and killer heels.

'How are you paying for your visit here?'

I took out Maggie's letter of invitation and handed it to him.

'How much money do you have on you?'

'Right now just £100, but my mother in Canada is sending money for me.'

'Go through the gate on the left and wait there. You're being detained for questioning.' He snapped my passport shut and handed it back to me.

I sat down next to an African woman in exotic tribal dress with a necklace of long eyeteeth. Near her was a thin, sad-faced Indian couple in Punjabi dress. Suddenly I was on the losing side. In the last five years of the Thatcher regime, EU was in, Commonwealth out. Everyone in the room seemed to be from a Commonwealth country and looked distressed, or bored. As I waited my turn I learned some people had been there overnight.

After an hour I was escorted to a smaller room with a desk where an Immigration officer interrogated me. I had to answer questions about my income, about the last job I'd had. I began to nod off; it was after midnight, according to my body clock. I heard a voice telling me of my right to lie down on a couch if I couldn't answer more questions and my right to go to a canteen for food and drink. 'Have a cup of coffee, then come back here,' the officer suggested. 'I really want to get through this as quickly as possible,' I said. I don't want to stay overnight.'
'We'll decide that,' he said. At six o'clock in the evening, nine hours after landing, I was freed to report within one week to the Home Office in Cardiff.

My case for remaining in the UK now began in earnest. Lady Betjeman, the ex-mayor of Hay, John Pugh, ex-diplomat to the Seychelles gave me an impeccable character references. Even my MP took up the case in a parliamentary memo. A year later the Immigration Service turned down my application for a business visa and informed me that deportation was the next stage.

I was desperate but helpless, my brain running at top speed. There was no answer. The phone rang. It was a Russian Princess I had met, an MBE, Legion d'Honneur and philanthropist, with friends in high places. 'Norma', she said, 'You were right about that dreadful man. He is a con-man. (I had warned her about someone I'd known in India who was about to enter her life.). 'You were the only person who helped me. Is there anything I can do for you?' 'Do you mean it?' I asked. 'Of course I mean it, darling,' she replied.

'I'm about to be deported,' I said panic stricken. 'Do you know anyone in the Home Office?'
'Don't worry, darling', she said. 'I know the Immigration Minister, but I think it's better to write to the Home Secretary.' Three weeks later I was granted 'indefinite leave to remain.'

At least now I could begin to fit the pieces of my strange life together. It began with Joyce and her vision of the future. When I told her what had happened, she looked thoughtful. 'When I first saw you, the possibility of marriage was there, very clearly. But at a certain point the entire menu changed and you were not on it anymore.' The future was not fixed, I realised. It was no more than clusters of possibilities that assembled and disintegrated like dustclouds, according to myriad conditions. Not even Tai Situ could have seen what would happen.

I met a Sufi healer and asked if she could heal my broken heart. She helped me gently onto her couch like a wounded animal, and covered my body in a white blanket. Her hands felt like gossamer as she lightly touched my feet. When she looked down at me with a look of deep compassion, I saw the face of the goddess Tara. I began to weep from deep within, a place I had never reached during all the struggles with Jigmai. The tears came like a tidal wave of anguish. 'Your heart has been broken,' she said as she held her delicate hands over my heart. 'I don't know who this man is who has broken your heart, but he delivered a terrible crushing blow to your spirit.'

Maggie once again gave me shelter from the storm at Old House, her home in the Black Mountains. Letters from Jigmai arrived frequently describing the difficulties in leaving India and getting permission to enter the UK; but he was determined to come, he assured me, and was making every effort to keep his promise to me. I was confused by his tone, as if we had had only a minor quarrel, not the brutal end, or near end, of our lives together. "Dearest Norma Darling", he wrote on May 13th/85, and described the latest position on the travel plans "for which I'm committed to some dear one." He signed it, "With all my love".

Within a few days he wrote again; on June 29th he confirmed his intention, though soon afterwards, he told me, his papers still had not arrived and his mother was in poor health. He had waited in Delhi for ten days to get his visa but failed. He had even tried to phone but Maggie answered; he regretted he could not speak to me or even leave a message… "Please do not have any grudges against me. I have done my best."

I lost confidence in plans of all kinds, in all promises about the future; in everything. The more I thought of being with Jigmai, of trying to conceive, then perhaps bringing up our child alone, the less certain I became.

I wondered whether it was better to tell him not to come, or to let the other events of his trip happen. He was scheduled to meet Danuta in Denmark, Graham in London, and a photographer who had accompanied him to Zanskar. While I was still thinking it over, he phoned to announce his arrival.

I looked at the short stout figure pushing a trolley through Arrivals at Heathrow. He was dressed like a tourist, and giggling uncontrollably as he tried to guide the trolley wheels around the corner. 'Hallo,' he said, grinning. He took off his spectacles and mopped his brow. 'There was a Siddarji[32] at the immigration desk', he said 'and I couldn't believe that I was in England, so I said to him in Hindi, "Am I in England, or back in India?" And he didn't answer me, because he didn't speak Hindi. So I started to laugh, and then he laughed too.'

'Welcome to Britain,' I said 'land of Shakespeare wallah. May I give you a lift somewhere?'

We got into the maroon Morris I'd recently bought for £80. Jigmai complimented me on my 'new car'. We stopped in a pub for lunch, and continued to Old House, which I was renting from Maggie – who had moved to Canada to be with Chogyam Trungpa.

I showed Jigmai into his own bedroom up a small flight of stairs near where I was sleeping, and watched him unpack. Out came a five-kilo sack of red Manali rice, a large packet of red-hot chillies, hard Tibetan cheese from Ladakh, to fry with the chillies and a variety of exotic spices. 'I thought I should bring my own food,' he explained, as I laughed with disbelief, 'just in case I can't enjoy the food in your country.'

He carried his emergency supplies into the kitchen and prepared a meal, eating it with undisguised gusto. Then he lay on the sofa. 'Where are you sleeping, Norma?' he asked. 'I have my own little bedroom here, next to the sitting room,' I said pointing to the archway that led into a small space with a bed and table. He pulled me to him. 'Come and lie with me here.'

---

32 Sikh man

'Actually, I have something to tell you.'
'You can tell me later, after we have made love.'
'My heart was pounding but I plunged in. 'No I can't. I've thought about everything that's happened between us, and I can't go through with it. I can't trust you. So how can I have your baby? Who knows, you may not even recognise your own child. You may say it's not yours. I feel I'd be getting into another trap and I can't bear it. That's it. I can't say it more clearly than that.'

He sat up quite calm. 'Why didn't you tell me before?'
'I was trying to work out whether it was better to tell you, or to let you have this trip for all the other reasons; then suddenly you came.'
He got up and walked slowly to the long rectangular dining table. Jigmai looked thoughtful. 'It seems that Guruji is controlling my life even more than he did when he was alive.'

That brought back all the confusions that always surrounded Jigmai for me. 'You think this has happened so that you won't get involved with me? That it's Guruji's interference?'
'I think so. He has had so much effect on me since he died. So now our agreement is finished. I am free. Good, very good.'
'I was so desperate I was pleading with you to give me something.... That's over now,' I replied.

There was a loud knock. At the door stood Will, one of my oldest friends, wearing a well-worn hiking jacket and a wool Afghani cap on his balding head. His skin was pink and glowing, fresh from the outdoors. 'May I come in?' he asked politely. I nodded. I had invited him to meet 'a friend' who was staying with me, following Jigmai's instructions not to tell anyone who he was.

Will took off his heavy walking boots and tiptoed into the room. When he saw Jigmai he stopped in wonder and his face lit up. 'Rinpoche,' he smiled, 'I am honoured to meet you.' Jigmai looked at me and burst into laughter. 'I didn't tell him anything,' I said quietly to Iigmai..

They sat on the sofa together while I went into the kitchen to make tea. When I came out they were both dozing. Jigmai woke up, said something in Bhutanese, and turned to Will. 'You don't remember, do you?'
Will replied, 'no Rinpoche, I don't remember anything.'
They sounded like old friends.

We all drank tea slowly, and drove to Hay-on-Wye. Jigmai was animated, enjoying the warmth of his new family. We started looking into all the bookshops; but Jigmai was more interested in the traditional haberdashery, a shop called Galsworthy's, the country gentleman's outfitters. We watched while he tried on hats, looking at himself carefully in the mirror to measure the effect. He selected a fine trilby made – as he found out later to his horror – of pigskin. 'Let me buy this for you,' I said, remembering Mohan Singh's turbans, and Harret Rixen's collection of brimmed hats.

It was five o'clock and the shopkeepers were beginning to close for the day. 'Would you like a drink, Rinpoche?' Will asked. We sat down at a small table with a view of the famous clocktower of Hay. I excused myself, promising to pick them up at nine o'clock.

I returned to find Jigmai and Will sitting at a table with an empty bottle of Pernod. Will was resting on the table but he staggered to his feet while Jigmai looked on. It was clear that they had both had a great deal of alcohol, though Jigmai seemed unaffected. We got into the car, and I drove back up the narrow mountain road. As soon as I could, I went to bed, leaving two old friends sitting at the dining room table with a full bottle of whisky.

Through the thin partition wall I heard the sound of a large amount of liquid being poured into a glass, and Jigmai's voice saying, 'Drink it'. 'I can't, Rinpoche, I'll be ill', said Will shakily. 'Drink it,' Jigmai commanded in a deep voice. There was a long silence. I could hear the gulping of liquid and the sound of a glass rolling across the table. I heard Jigmai say, 'If I want this to be water, it is water, if I want it to be alcohol, it is alcohol. It's all mind', and he laughed. The last sounds before falling asleep were his footsteps on the stairs going up to his room.

When I got up in the morning there was an empty pint glass on the table, an empty whisky bottle and Will asleep on the sofa. His face looked radiantly peaceful. When he told me what had happened, it was clear he had experienced an important meditative state – the essence of mind free of limitations. He described how the alcohol seemed to become nectar in his body, and his mind filled with bliss. He could never be the same again, he said. He had taken the leap of faith knowing he had met his spiritual master.

****

Danuta clapped her hands with excitement as we approached her door. She held out a white silk offering scarf to Jigmai and seized his hand, her eyes glistening with joy. Her life had changed radically from the lone, questing spirit we had known in India. She was studying to become a nurse and bringing up a child. But in spite of the financial strain, she prepared food and drink in bountiful quantities.

She showed us to our room on the first floor of her small house. The double bed had been carefully prepared with cushions and a large decorative spread. I looked around for an alternative sleeping arrangement and saw a small sofa in the corner of the entranceway. I could curl up and sleep there without affecting Danuta's arrangement. We sat sipping vodka and eating a Danish smorgasbord of cheese, fish, and exotic pastes.

It was a fine clear day, perfect for a stroll outside. Standing on the street outside a newsagent I told Danuta some of the recent events. She looked at me with passionate intensity. 'Norma, can't you see he still loves you? I know he loves you, I can see it.' 'But he broke our relationship', I explained to Danuta. 'I think he had to. There wasn't any choice. His life is moving in another direction. Everything is finished now. This is just an attempt to make a different ending, one we can both live with; instead of the grotesque one we had in India.' Jigmai re-emerged from the newsagent a few minutes later carrying a magazine.

When we returned to the house, we continued drinking. The nightmare of our broken love began to haunt me as it would for many years. Jigmai kept on drinking, downing one glass after another while I wept bitter tears of betrayal. By the evening we had become locked into a downwards spiral, and no one could rescue us. The atmosphere was charged with a sullen, torpid energy like the quiet intensity before an electrical storm.

I went upstairs, put on a nightdress and prepared to sleep on the small sofa. Jigmai was lying on the bed, turning the pages of the magazine he had bought that afternoon. 'Norma, come here,' he called. I went over to him, and saw that the magazine was hardcore pornography. I was thrown back into mental turmoil: the old confusions between Jigmai the master and Jigmai the man. I looked at the picture he showed me and recoiled in disgust. Jigmai held me by the arm. 'I want you now,' he said. I jumped off the bed and ran to the entranceway. He came after me, grabbed my arm and tried to push me down onto the sofa. 'No', I shouted. 'No! You can't force me. That's rape!'

Outraged, I pushed him away so hard that his glasses fell off and crashed to the floor. He picked them up in disbelief. One lens was broken. Without his glasses he was almost blind. He started to bellow like a caged bull as I raced downstairs running from room to room like a trapped animal, trying to find a way out. Now Danuta appeared and pleaded with him. Desperate to get away, I ran out into the street in my nightdress. Through the lamplight of the open window I saw Danuta still trying to calm him. Then I found another door and slipped into her room. 'Don't tell him I'm here,' I begged when she came in. 'Please.' All night I could hear Jigmai crying in pain for his lost love. 'Norma, Norma, where is my Norma? I want Norma.' All I wanted to do was get away.

In the morning Danuta and I led Jigmai by the hand to an optician's, where he picked out the most expensive glasses in the shop. I paid the price gladly, eager to prevent the karma of causing harm to a tenth level bodhisattva – just in case.

As soon as I could I was on a plane back to London, leaving Jigmai with Danuta in Denmark. Later when we said our final goodbyes at Heathrow, we embraced: I looked at him and saw the love that was still there, for both of us. Uncontrollable tears flowed down my face. In the letter he sent soon after arriving in Delhi, I had the proof of love I had longed for – too late.

Wed 20 Nov

My dearest darling Norma,
I am going to reveal whole story which took place in my life just after saying goodbye to you at the airport. The most painful thing was to say goodbye to you. I don't know why, but I was deeply moved by your love and tears. I could very clearly see that those tears were shed from the depth of heart and the sign of true love. I very much respect your feelings and the love that you possess for me in your heart. As you know darling, I may not say it again but whatsoever I am writing now is the voice of heart which is very soft and delicate as any delicate and a kind person can possess in the world yet you know the other side of heart. Well darling, by the time it reaches to you it may not have any meaning to you but I feel that no matter what you feel but I should open my heart and tell you how I felt and how even now when I'm writing. And I'm also aware of it that I may lost in the depth of ocean. But my promise to meet you in Delhi is still very strong and I will give it a practical shape. You don't know how much I loved you and even now I love you very much. ....
I did not feel very good after leaving aircraft. I just missed England. Maybe I missed English friends and my lovely darling Norma... I am longing for you darling. For the first time I felt how difficult it would be to stay without you. I also felt how right you were when you said I can't stay without company....
I went to Nirula's. Everything strucked as a shock to me, the way the waiters move, the way people look. Ah! Everything seems to be sick and so slow, it is like watching slow motion TV. People are out of shape and ugly. But the greatest thing is the air and its taste. Ha! Wonderful. It really takes care of you. I did not like the Indians, the only thing I liked was the air and India itself. But some how now I feel may be I may one day stay in West. Somehow I like your company very much, but unfortunatrely things are not very certain in my life yet. But I'm sure in few days

time I should be able to know more clearly, more certain, more stable more to the direction of my goal. It seems to me that suddenly I have made up my mind to struggle in life honestly. I think I was never been honest with my life. I deceived and played with my life a lot, now I should sincerely compensate it. I'm guilty to my soul. Even all these feelings I'm not upset – depressed but I'm gaining new strength and a sense of happiness in my mind and body. I think I benefited myself a lot by visiting West...It also seems I got a lot more to do than I'm doing. Still my heart is longing for you as I started the letter. ....Love seems to be mysterious to me, and even more the power of it. But it is a shame I could not give you more than admitting myself being in love with you though you got my love which no woman would get so easily. **As long as the power of your love stays in my heart I won't involve with another woman. I shall wait for your love to die before I involve with another woman. These lines may give you a chance to measure my love.** As I am a man of pride I will try to keep this place difficult to reach. Sex means not a great deal to me. Character means a lot to me. I don't look around to be supported, but I try to give support, so my love, never feel yourself lonely. I would be there to help you but don't expect a lot since I haven't got much to give. So my love may stay young and we may meet in the holy land of India. I hope you may enjoy reading this letter....Do not show it to someone else but keep it close to your heart.
Fare well my love and hope to see you soon.

With love and best wishes,
Jigmai
21/11/85

On December 31 he wrote to say he had gone to Assam to see his family. Again he spoke of love.

> I loved you and tried to be loyal and honest as I could. Please convey my good wishes to Will and tell him I remember him.... I also feel that still we can share certain thoughts and feelings. I have a great faith in you and consider you as my very understanding friend. ...Wish you happy New Year, with love, Jigmai

A few days later, on January 2, 1986, came another long letter.

2 January 86 Manali

> Dearest Norma,
> I have decided to write you one elaborate letter so that we may not have any misunderstanding. I never liked to have any misunderstanding between us, but there was some and that was very unfortunate. As I have mentioned in my previous letter, why I could not reply your letter promptly. Just to make it more clear what happened to me when I reached in Delhi. I suddenly felt very lonely, and the same feeling was there although I was in Manali for short time before I left for Assam. The friends looked very incapable of filling the absence of my left friends, like you and some other ones. The most sad thing was that I could not share my feelings, thoughts, secrets and no one to whom I could trust. While I was in England and Denmark I never felt so much need of my family as I felt when I was back to India. Although lot of my followers were in Delhi on their way to Bodh Gaya, nothing seems to be able to budge certain things.
> But everything went in vain because even after waiting for 15 days I could not see any of them. I was very desperate to see my father and sister, but no one tried hard to make it happen. I was very handicapped because of political

reasons. Somehow my lone consolation was seing my brother Karma. They have shared the land and property among themselves, even my sister got her equal share from the parents. I was given nothing because I was not there at that time. So now I am homeless, landless and familyless. Actually my all responsibilities towards the home is finished, yet still I feel that I should look after my parents though they have not given me anything but I think I should give them whatsoever I can. I also want to keep my sister with me, but certain things are not clear yet. It looks like my relation with the youngest one (brother) is finished and with Karma also the strings are not so strong, so it comes to my sister only. But she can stay with me only if she wants to be a nice girl and protects the pride of ancient forefathers. ...I hope you are not bored with all this because I consider you as my best friend and so I trust you that you would keep everything with yourself. I wanted to share the feelings.

It is indeed a very sad thing to hear your rottonning financial situation. I can never imagine you are having problems even to buy your food...I can see your position very clearly and yet I can't do anything. Since you are my love, even before you asked me, I was thinking to see the ways that I could help you, financially if necessary. But you have asked me suddenly for Rs 30,000 that you may need in India. I do not know what happens at that time when you may be in India. At present I am definitely not in a position to gather so much money since I already had spent a lot. Anyway you can have Rs 10,000 when you come to India that is a promise, for the rest 20,000 I will try my best if I can raise that amount but please don't count on me for that. I sincerely want to help you as much as I can but without the money it is quite useless to proclaim anything, but believe me if I have the money I will never hesitate to help you. I think you can also have some faith in me.

As I used to talk to you about money, nothing has happened so far. I do not know whether something would ever happen. In case if my chance I happen to get some money then I would make you my business partner or I become your partner. It is also a pity that both of us are trying to stand on our feet at the same time. I was planning to buy a small piece of land where I could build my house. …
I still adore you and the memories of being together in the past. Everything seems to be like a sweet dream. As you know dreams are dreams and one has to wake from dreams sooner or later. Please do not hesitate to write me or to open your heart. You may also ask me anything I am capable to give you.

With love,
Jigmai

As he said – 'dreams are dreams and one has to wake from dreams sooner or later.' I was still in the half dream of early morning, living with a splintered reality. Neither of us had fully awakened yet.

CHAPTER 13

CRAZY LOVE

I will never forget you
Even if I wish to be
I can't somehow.
I will always keep you
In the depth of my heart
Unknown and unheard by
The cruel people of world
(SN Jigmai, January 2, 1986, Manali)

Delhi, October 1988.

I opened the door from the street onto the stairs that led into Nirula's restaurant. Breakfast at Nirula's was a treat I gave myself on landing in Delhi where I had been coming for the past two years on business. On the last occasion Jigmai had met me as promised, and delivered 15,000 rupees (about £500) to help me start my business.

Our communication had been sporadic. One letter from him in April '86 said, "I'm spending my time more or less the same way. Nothing much has happened so far but still I'm hopeful." The next one in July informed me he had bought a piece of land in Manali, and he expected the house to be completed in November.

"So you can see, I am also getting established in my life slowly but steadily. I invite you to stay with us in case you happen to be around Kullu Valleys in future."

Another letter dated 12th January 87 reported that nothing was happening in his life: "I am sitting on the same chair where I been sitting for ages." He was spending most of his time playing billiards. "Even so I am very satisfied man now more than ever before."

In July '88 he said he would be visiting Europe next year, and if I was interested to meet him in England, "please let me know". (I wasn't and we didn't.) Svend was staying with him, he said, tending the flower garden.

As soon as I walked into Nirula's famous buffet, I saw Jigmai sitting at one of the tables, together with Sven. Surprised, I walked over to their table. 'I told you she was going to come in just now,' I heard Jigmai say quietly to Sven.

'Hello'. They moved over to make room for me but it seemed I had arrived at the wrong moment. 'I have some monks coming from Bhutan,' Jigmai told me; 'I have to go and pick them up. Perhaps we could meet tonight.' 'Okay', I replied, 'let's meet here at 8 o'clock in the Chinese room.'

I went on with my breakfast as though nothing had happened. It was all so dream-like: there was no point in trying to work out meanings.

At exactly eight o'clock, we walked together through the red lacquered door of the Chinese room. I noticed a plump white porcelain Buddha, image of prosperity, laughing in a corner beside a trickling waterfall. We sat down at a table and began ordering.

'How is your life?' asked Jigmai.

'Not easy!' I replied. I told him about the gruesome year battling the Home Office. 'Since then I've been trying to set up my business, earn my living, live a normal life. I managed to buy a house last year. But settling into the West has been very hard.' My heart felt leaden.

'And your practice?'

'Sometimes I do it, sometimes not. I don't have the same beliefs, the same trust and faith anymore.' The tears gathered in my eyes as I faced its truth for the first time.

'And your mother and family?'

'My mother was supposed to give me the money my father left in his will, but she made it very complicated tying it up in all kind of trusts. So that wasn't easy either.' I suddenly had the impression he was sucking everything out of me, and it made me feel uneasy.

'What about you? I see you're not a monk.'

'Ah, yes, that's a little difficult also. I am still deciding about it. There are many things to consider.'

'I see. Go on. You don't seem to be saying much about yourself.'

'Everything is same, same as before.'

'Your sister is still with you?'

'Yes, I am trying to keep her with me, but she is growing up her own way.'

'And your mother?'

'Ah, she made a recovery, very unexpected. She still remembers you.'

We sat in an awkward silence. I felt drained. 'Let's go,' I said. 'I'd like to get back to my room. I'm jet lagged, I need to sleep.'

'Yes, you must take rest', he agreed. He paid the bill, and offered to drop me off at my hotel in a taxi. As I got out of the taxi I said, 'I'm sorry we cannot be good friends.'

'At least we're not bad friends,' he said, laughing. 'I don't think we're friends at all,' I replied. 'I don't want to meet again.' I went to my room and cried.

The next morning, while finishing breakfast at Nirula's, Jigmai walked in, followed by Sven. They came to my table and sat down as I moved over hesitantly. 'Looks like we are meeting again,' Jigmai said. 'Yes', I replied 'but I can't stay long. I have an appointment and the traffic is bad.' I looked at my watch, put money on the table, excused myself with a polite smile and left. I tried to block out all thoughts of Jigmai as the rickshaw spun and whizzed like a mosquito through the cars, bullock carts and trucks that cram every centimetre of the road to Old Delhi.

Three days later it was time to leave Delhi and go to Sherabling. Unusually, I decided to fly to Kullu and take a taxi from there. The plane was a twelve-seater winged insect that proudly proclaimed on its fragile body, 'We are no flight of fancy'. An hour later I was at Kullu airport, walking down the tarmac into the small airport lobby no larger than a sitting room. I picked up my bags and went to search for a trolley.

Positioned prominently next to his trolley was Jigmai! I stared at him in disbelief. He had not been on the same airplane, so how could he be here now, picking up his baggage? 'How did you get here?' I asked. 'You weren't on my plane.'

'There was a plane at two o'clock,' he replied, 'but it was late departing, so it arrived before yours.' He looked pleased, but I was shaken. I was determined to ignore the bizarre coincidence and get to Sherabling.

A large chaotic group of passengers formed around the taxi-drivers. I asked one driver to take me to Sherabling, but when he worked out the distance and time, he refused, as did every driver in the airport. Each driver walked out the door with another passenger, until I was left standing alone in the room.

Jigmai was still there, watching the drama with interest. He came over and said, 'It looks like you'll be coming back to Manali with me tonight.'I was silent for a moment, but it was no use. 'Yes,' I said. 'It looks like that's meant to happen.'

We sat together in the back seat of his car. Shortly after leaving Kullu, there was a road sign marked 'DETOUR'. 'There's been a landslide after the monsoon,' Jigmai explained, 'so we have to take the old long road into Manali.Now it takes more than two hours' 'Why do you think we've been meeting like this?' I asked him. 'There must be a reason.'

'Yes,' he replied. 'It doesn't happen otherwise.'

'What do you think is the reason?' I persisted.

'Let's see.' He turned to me, and started to talk very clearly and honestly as if forced suddenly from within. 'I realize I've treated you very badly,' he started, 'and it has upset you a lot. I was not honest with you.'

'You seemed to be playing with me. You were cruel for some reason I couldn't understand, even after everything was over. Why?'

'Because I am still in love with you', he said. 'And I don't know what to do about it.'

His confession touched me deeply. I understood for the first time how he too, was confused by his double existence as Lama and ordinary man: that we were both victims of the same conflict and now we were locked into each other's hearts in a way that neither of us had ever experienced.

'I'm still in pain too,' I said. 'I loved you so much that the whole world stopped when we were together. It's been impossible to find my life again. I'm only half a person now, a shadow looking for a body. I believed so much in you. The shock of your sudden change nearly killed me.'

It was six o'clock when we pulled up in front of his new house. It sat on a slope of land with the mountains behind, overlooking a scattering of other new houses. I realised that he was not building a house, but a monastery, with a residence for himself. Some young monks greeted us. They left my bags downstairs, outside the door to a small, dark, unused room with a single bed.

Immediately we entered I felt the cold from the damp cement. The house was still unfinished, but the kitchen was already streaked with soot from the wood fires. Upstairs was drier, cleaner and brightly painted– his shrineroom, his bedroom, and his sister's room.

I put my bags inside the spare room; and joined him in the private reception room off his bedroom. He had changed into the comfortable tracksuit I remembered, putting on the ski sweater I'd left him. A monk brought tea and biscuits. Jigmai fished into the stack of cassette tapes and put on Bonnie Rait. The tug of beautiful old memories was pulling at my heart as we drank a glass of Old Monk rum. 'I'll never forget when we were in Goa and we listened to Bonnie Rait, and you said, "Bonnie Rait!" You were jumping up and down on the bed, you were so happy.'

'Until we broke up,'he said reflectively, 'everything was half-half. You did some things, I did some things, but it was a tie, no one winning; no one losing. Love all. Afterwards when we broke up, it got very crazy. It went somewhere else.'

'Somewhere unfamiliar and dark,' I said. 'Something separated us. It wasn't us that did it; it was other forces.'
'You are establishing your new life, and so am I, but love is still there and it doesn't leave,' Jigmai said. 'I don't know what to do with it; that's why I hurt you', he repeated. 'I can't bear the pain.'

My crumpled dead heart stirred. It was as close to an apology as he would make. I looked at him and saw how much he needed a companion in his life. 'I don't know what you achieved by it', I said. 'You're still not a monk, and I don't think you can be a monk. You need the kind of companionship I gave you.'

'Yes, looks like you're right.'

I opened up all the anguish I'd held so tightly in my heart.

'I never really told you about the operation. I didn't tell you what it was like to stay in a room where no one visited me, while the other women's husbands brought flowers every day. I wanted to wear your ring around my neck in the operating theatre for good luck; I argued with the nurses, and in the end they let me keep it beside the bed. You know that silly ring you gave me once? The one that looked like it came out of a crackerjack box?'

'Yes, I remember'. He smiled.

'It wasn't worth anything, but you gave it to me and it meant love to me.' I downed the glass of rum and cried until my neck was wet. 'I still don't understand how you could abandon the woman you loved. I went from one healer to another. One said my heart had been broken. I even went to a medium who channeled Guru Rinpoche.'

'Did it help you?' he asked.

'Yes, but the belief in love went out of my life and I've been carrying a lead bullet in my heart.'

I looked at my watch. It was two o'clock in the morning. I was exhausted but relieved that we could talk at last from our hearts. It was clear why it wasn't possible to make a life together. Love wasn't enough. Our new separate lives had to go ahead, however crippled both might be. Now at last the bullet was removed; my wounded heart could heal.

****

It was 6 am, six months after I'd seen Jigmai for the last time. The bright light of late spring was coming through the skylight of my attic bedroom in Hay-on-Wye. I had just awakened from a dream. Suddenly the phone rang. I picked it up, and heard the unmistakable voice of Jigmai, gruff and peremptory. He didn't say hello, just: 'What do you want me to do with your sleeping bag?' I was missing a sleeping bag which had been in the back of his car, but when asked, he denied it was there.

'Why did you keep it?' I asked him back.

'I didn't use it.'

'That's not the point. Why did you keep it?' I repeated.

But he too only repeated, 'What do you want me to do with it?'

There was a pause.

'Leave it at Sikkim House and I'll pick it up when I go there.'

And without saying goodbye, I calmly put the phone down. Perhaps he still wanted to keep a piece of me, I thought. I never heard his voice again.

When I next went to Delhi, I asked the manager of Sikkim House if someone had left a sleeping bag for me, but no one had. They let me search all the shelves and compartments to make sure. Perhaps Jigmai had kept it after all – or burned it, to purge our crazy love.

There were no more letters after that, no more inexplicable synchronous meetings. The years went by. My business, based on my Buddhist knowledge, flourished. I was asked to write a book about Buddhism, and did. I called it ***Blessing Power of the Buddhas***. Strangely, it glowed with inspiration from a deep bond with Guru Rinpoche. Something was coming back to me, in fits and starts, a splutter, then a burst. The light was returning.

The final intimate rupture with Jigmai – indeed all the painful episodes, and the beautiful ones too – would never leave my memory. They remained frozen deep inside me, like an ancient city with byzantine pathways intact at the bottom of a winter lake.

The disturbance that had haunted me from the beginning never really went away: how could this bizarre story of crazy love happen with an enlightened being?

Years later during an interview with the great Lama, Mingyur Rinpoche, I finally dared to dive into the dark waters of my deepest doubts. Jigmai was supposed to be at the highest stage of the spiritual path, a tenth level bodhisattva. Bodhi means blossomed or enlightened, sattva means heroic mind. At the first level a bodhisattva is already enlightened but through the strength of his compassion, he vows to return, to help all beings out of their suffering. As the Dalai Lama[33] has written, at the tenth level, the bodhisattva generates such powerful wisdom that it removes all the imprints formed by past delusions, culminating in the attainment of full omniscience, or Buddhahood.

So now I wanted to ask Mingyur Rinpoche, was it possible for a tenth level bodhisattva to be psychologically disturbed, if he had been murdered in a previous lifetime?

Looking at Mingyur Rinpoche's face was like looking into a pool of water so clear you could see right to the depths.

'No, it's not possible,' he answered without hesitation. 'There are two kinds of karma.[34] One is uncontrolled karma; the other is, you still have karma, but you have control.

---

33 Who Am I? The Dalai Lama

34 Karma: the law of cause and result

Uncontrolled karma ceases at the first bodhisattva level. They still have karma but they can control it. They have to be reborn in the human realms but they can choose the circumstances of their rebirth.'

'From the bodhisattva's point of view', he continued, 'they don't have a real physical body. It's not real flesh and blood. Other people see it as that, but they themselves don't. They have a mental body or illusory body. It is a kind of body; it is not only mind. But it is not like an ordinary human body. Not karmic body.'

I thought of Jigmai's rages, his crazy mood swings. Was Mingyur Rinpoche saying he had permission to behave like that because he was free of the gross physical body? 'If such a person shows a lot of negative emotions, is it crazy wisdom or disturbed mind?' I persisted.

'If he is a bodhisattva,' Mingyur Rinpoche said clearly, 'there's no disturbance; the meaning will appear. But there are many different ways.' He suddenly thought of a way of explaining this. 'The bodhisattva himself is like the moon and ordinary beings are like the lake. If the lake moves, the reflection moves, if the lake is clear, the reflection is clear. If the lake is cloudy, then the reflection is also cloudy. Sometimes the reflection is round, sometimes it's triangular; sometimes it is only half…'

'How I see him is just a reflection of my own disturbances rather than how he actually is?' I asked.

'It is an interdependent manifestation.'

My rational faculty dissolved as my mind calmed momentarily and I saw clearly to the bottom of the pool. It was an interaction. It was my own karmic patterns interacting with Jigmai's turbulent history that had made this whole story of crazy love happen.

I looked at Mingyur Rinpoche's face. It was radiant and clear as a full moon. I knew that he was coming from wisdom mind, telling the truth *as it is*. But my awareness could hold onto this wisdom for only a moment before the reasoning mind took over. Thoughts could never get there; it was beyond concept.

This epiphany would light up my mind and deepen in the years to come.

****

I organised pilgrimages to remote parts of Tibet, and worked with all my heart for the lineage of the Karmapas. In 1992, eleven years after the 16th Karmapa had passed away, the 17th Karmapa was enthroned at his monastery in Tibet. I traveled to Tibet to watch the ceremony. There was no mistaking the eight year old nomad boy seated on the throne: he possessed the same spiritual dignity as his predecessor.

When I met the 17th Karmapa six years later in India, he said 'Thank you'. It had a startling and immediate effect. I looked at his face and now understood the perfection of beauty expressed in the Buddha's form. His eyes shaped like lotus petals opened my heart and devotion flowed into it, like rain filling a cracked riverbed. The frozen labyrinths of my crazy love with Jigmai with its hidden blessings, and all the uncertainties that haunted me about the Buddhist path ever since, began at last, to melt.

****

Jigmai married Thrinley Chodron in 1998. I heard the news in 2000 passing through Manali on the way to Ladakh, high in the Himalayas. I thought perhaps he had met his consort. Taking a consort was sometimes prescribed for Lamas to lengthen their lifespan.

I continued my journey up into the high mountains, happy to leave the valley behind.

In April 2003 an email arrived from Danuta:

> His Holiness Ngawang Namgyal Shabdrung Rinpoche passed away last Saturday.
>
> Let us pray together that He will return to us very soon, and that we will accumulate enough merit to be worthy of serving Him and being helped on our path to Buddhahood.
>
> With my love,
>
> Danuta

I felt a sad wave of relief passing through my body. I knew Thrinley and I would meet and exchange stories. It was inevitable. Then I could salvage the missing piece of my own story and everything would fall into place.

Act Four

One of the first signs of a saint will be the fact that other people do not know what to make of him. (Thomas Merton, New Seeds of Contemplation, p. 103)

CHAPTER 14

A MEETING BY THE BODHI TREE

Bodh Gaya December 2003

'Norma!' I heard my name called from the direction of the sacred bodhi tree, where the Buddha was enlightened. A small figure in a brown Tibetan tunic and pale silk blouse was sitting on the grass to the side of the stupa, flanked by two young girls with the distinctive high cheekbones and long hair of Bhutanese aristocracy. A thin ray of sun filtered through the clouds. It took a few moments for the clock to roll back. 'Thrinley,' I cried, and ran over to her. The lovely clear face of the girl I had last seen in the Himalayas ten years ago, before her marriage to the Shabdrung Rinpoche had changed. Tears came into my eyes as we embraced, gazing at each other. Her once glowing skin was dull, her eyes were heavy, her forehead creased with anxiety. There was no radiance. I sensed a disturbance right away.

'I am so happy to see you,' I said overcoming my shock. 'Since Shabdrung Rinpoche died you've been very much on my mind. I knew we would meet, because we had to talk. I wanted to see how your marriage to him had affected you. He left an indelible mark on me.'

We stood holding hands, two women of exactly the same height and build, fine-boned, small-breasted, slim. Her hair was long and black with a slight wave, unlike the typically straight glossy hair of Tibetan women. I looked down at her hand. It was small with tapering fingers very similar to mine. We could have been cast from the same mould, one Eastern, one Western, although I was older by fifteen years.

'How did he die?' I asked.

'Cancer.'

'I heard throat.'

'No. Nasal passages, from the eyes; it was going into the brain.'

'His eyes were always his weak point,' I said, remembering the thick spectacles he took off only to sleep.

'Yes, he often said it.'

'When did he die?'

'April 5th.'

She looked more closely at me. 'You have not grown older. You look well. I wanted to meet you for a long time,' she said. 'I always said to Rinpoche I would like to see you again. But he said, "Why? She would only kill you."

I was taken aback by the swift thrust of sudden combat. I had intuited they would marry the first time I saw them together in Manali, but the jealousy had evaporated instantly, and I never felt it again.

'He broke his commitment to me because he was not supposed to marry.' I replied boldly. 'He told me he had to become a monk. We had loved each other very deeply so it wasn't easy to let go, but I hoped it was for the benefit of the dharma. When I heard he had married you, I wished the same thing. I hoped you were his consort. But now it looks like he broke his promise to me. He betrayed me,' I said, looking at her closely.

'Betrayed you? Ha ha,' she laughed in mockery. She turned to the two Bhutanese girls like a queen to her ladies in waiting. Her slim neck tilted upwards, showing her high cheekbones and the fine straight line of her nose.

'It's true, Thrinley,' I said. Did you know Guruji?'

'Yes, of course,' she replied. 'He was Rinpoche's teacher and a very learned Lama.'

'When Guruji was dying in Zanskar,' I explained, 'he called Rinpoche to him and said, "Promise that you will become a monk and serve your people." Rinpoche said that he had to do what his Guruji wished. So, just as the Buddha had renounced his wife and kingdom, he had to leave me. I told him if he was breaking his commitment with me, and causing so much suffering, then he must keep his promise and become a monk. If he married, I was sure there would be dire consequences. Now do you understand?'

'I also told him once he should become a monk,' she murmured, 'but he got angry and said I am not the person to tell him what to do.'

'He never told you about his promise to Guruji?'

'No. Maybe he was lying to you to get out of the marriage,' she retorted sharply.

'I don't think so,' I said firmly. 'Guruji wanted him to be a monk, I am sure of it. I thought marrying you would either make or break both of you,' I continued. 'Either he would take you as his tantric consort and use it to transform you both, or it would not work. Otherwise, I truly felt sorry for you.'

'I was also afraid of his possessiveness', she confided. 'Even my family was against marrying him. But he wanted to marry me so much. He said I was his inspiration.'

He had said the same to me, but now was not the time to say so. I wanted her real feelings, not the socially acceptable story. 'I think you were his salvation,' I said. 'But I heard it was you who went after him.'

'Let that be, whatever people say, let it be' she shrugged. 'I will tell you how it was.'

'I had known the Shabdrung all my life, but it was many years later, in Delhi before we started to meet alone. One evening it was late and his sister told me to sleep in the spare bed in his room. I said to him, "I don't want you to touch me," and he didn't. Before long he was sending his car around to get me, and he even predicted the exact day I would be able to get my US visa. One day he gave me the keys to his flat and told me I could stay there any time. The flat was dirty and I cleaned it up. I saw his clothes lying around. He was a very high Lama and there was no one to do his washing. So I washed them. You know Danuta?' she asked.

I nodded. How could I ever forget Danuta with her pale skin and gaunt cheekbones? 'Was she still obsessed with Shabdrung?'

'Yes, she was very attached to him. She called up from Europe and was shocked to find a woman answering the phone. She was obviously jealous. So I had a jealous wife and a jealous husband without even being married!'

'He tried to discourage me from going to the US although he knew it would be good for me. "Good for you but not for me", he said. "Why don't you stay in India and we will get married?" I said, "No, I must go." He drove me to the airport and told me to call him when I arrived. I liked that; he was taking care of me. I felt I had a father again.'

'So we called each other from the US', she continued. 'He called me, I called him, it was mutual. 'We courted for three years, seeing each other occasionally. Once, someone introduced me to a nice, very good-looking American. I was impressed, but somehow, as I told my friends, I was already hooked, booked and cooked.' She laughed with delight.

'So we got married' she said proudly. 'We had a big wedding in San Francisco. You must have heard about it.'

I shook my head and looked away.

'I have the video' she said. 'I'll show you.'

Photos of Jigmai's wedding – the wedding of the man who had left me to become a monk! Was she trying to make me jealous? Did she need to demolish his past to secure first place in his life?

'I was a virgin,' she said earnestly. 'I gave myself to him only after we were married, never before. And he respected me for it. So I said to him, "I will give myself to you but I will do it in my own time."

I was fascinated to hear how she had hooked him. 'Smart move,' I said. But I bet it didn't stop his jealousy.'

'No! He would call me and accuse me of having a man in my room,' she said in a burst of emotion. It was so insulting. He made me feel like…a common woman, a prostitute.'

'Did you ever try smiling and saying hello to another man in his presence?' I asked.

'Yes, he wouldn't allow that either. I was accused of betrayal, even with monks. He wouldn't even allow me to go to see my own Guru.' She bit her lip.

'All my friends in San Francisco said, "don't marry that man," she blurted out. "Are you sure you want to marry him?" they said. "You will lose yourself; you won't be able to do anything. You'll just be his servant". They were right. I had to wash his clothes, cook his food, and make his tea.'

It came pouring out now. 'From early morning till late at night I had to serve him. I was his secretary, his housekeeper, and his administrator. He was also mean with money. He made me bring him receipts for everything

I spent in the bazaar. I fought with him. "I won't spend your money," I said. "Take mine, I don't care about it." As soon as I did that he was sweet and generous, he gave me money and didn't check again.'

'With me he was always mean', I replied. He made me pay for my own dinner and often ordered me to pay for his. "Carry my bags," he would say, when we were walking to catch a bus. Once he woke me up to tell me to go and close a dripping tap. He even hit me on two occasions. Once I hit him back.' I waited for her reaction.

'He hit everyone,' she said flatly. 'He was very good at that.'

She paused. 'Once he hid me from the Indian Intelligence Bureau', she confided. 'He didn't want them to know he had married.'

'He hid me from Guruji' I said. 'I had to leave the house for four hours and run into the forest. I tried to run away several times, but he wouldn't let me go.'

'I wanted to run away too,' she said, looking down. I almost did, a year after we were married. Then I thought about the consequences of leaving him: that I would lose my name, and be without a husband so I decided to submit. I accepted him as my Guru, and it became much easier.'

'How long did it take?' I asked.

'After one year of marriage I submitted, but I didn't have a life. I never saw my family although we lived one kilometre away. I could see them for only ten minutes at a time. He would send a car to pick me up. I had no friends either. I had to be there entirely for him, to devote myself to him. That's what he wanted, and that's what I did,' she said emphatically.

'You know,' she said leaning towards me, 'once I even said to Rinpoche,"This is what you must have done to Norma as well. She told me about it. Now I know what she meant." He didn't let anyone or anything into my life. No Lamas came to see us, none of my friends, none of my family. He didn't let me grow. It would have benefited him as well.' Her voice came in waves of emotion.

Then she paused, and quietened. 'But I'm happy I did it. He said I would have plenty of time afterwards for myself, and he was right. It was good I did it, because we had only five years together. I have no regrets, no guilt. I gave everything, like my mother gave to my father.'

'We were together for five years too,' I said quietly.

She looked surprised. 'So long?'

'Yes, and almost as much time breaking up, because we kept meeting unexpectedly, as if we still had karma to work through. He got me; he could get any woman he wanted,' I said.

She looked at me in silent recognition. 'He knew how to capture a woman sexually. His sexual energy was extraordinary. How was he with you?' I asked.

'Not so much, but yes,' she said measuring her reply. 'He was very good in sex. You taught him well.'

'I didn't need to teach him.' I countered her haughty remark quickly. 'We were in love and it is love that makes love.' I decided to come to the point. 'Did you also have tantric sex?'

'He was a great tantric master,' she replied with perfect propriety, evading the question.

'Yes, he could perform tantric sex,' I retorted, trying to probe deeper, 'but he only did it when it suited him for his own personal reasons, not for liberation.'

She agreed, 'Everything had to be for him, his way, his time. No one else existed. Once he kept hundreds of Bhutanese waiting outside for hours in the cold and dark. "Let them come in," I said. "No," he said, "let them wait. They should suffer." He was angry with the Bhutanese for his situation. He felt betrayed by everyone, by his family, by Bhutan…'

'…by the Lamas and the dharma,' I added. 'He hated so many Lamas.'

'Yes, they all betrayed him. There was some psychological disturbance,' she said sadly. 'He was very unhappy.'

I remembered the teaching from Mingyur Rinpoche about the moon on the water.

'He was so powerful,' she said, her eyes glowing with admiration. 'Did you ever meet anyone with such power?'

'But where was the compassion?' I asked. It seemed she had forgotten the main quality of a Buddha. 'I seldom saw compassion, did you?'

'Not much,' she admitted. At the end I did, but many times I wondered about it.'

'I wonder if he just took it out on women.' I mused.

'It was a very confusing manifestation,' she said. 'I used to say to him he was the most egotistical person I had ever met. You have heard of Shakya Shri?'

I nodded.

'He was a great 19th century mahasiddha[35]. When he meditated his seat would levitate into the air and his body became transparent. You could put a candle in front of him and see it the other side. My father was his grandson', she said matter of factly. 'You know Dilgo Khyentse?'

'Of course,' I replied, 'he was very famous, particularly for the powers he showed at his death. I believe he was also your Guru. But Shabdrung felt a particular resentment towards him because he was the Guru to the Bhutanese royal family.'

---

[35] a yogi having great miraculous powers

'Yes. Rinpoche used to taunt me' – her voice lowered in imitation – "How did Dilgo Khyentse die, tell me about it. Who is Shakya Shri?" 'Then you know how he laughed – Ha Ha Ha. "You will see when I die", he would say. He was very confident about it. And in the end he showed me he was a buddha,' she said.

'The buddha who possessed women?' I laughed impulsively, teasing her.

'...who came back to torture women,' she nodded. 'You see, I understand. I also suffered with him. I don't know what it meant in your case. Maybe some strange karmic connection that had to be purified. But for me it was a great teaching, a great purification. I don't think a Western woman could be with him.'

I was stung by her remark but said nothing. I knew I had given from the depths of my heart but I couldn't interrupt the flow. I needed to know about his death. 'Was he prepared for death?' I asked.

'Death was somehow there for him his whole life,' she replied.

'Tell me how he died. Did he sit up in meditation?'

'Yes, he did everything; consciousness transference, everything. One day I will tell you.'

'It was so confusing,' I said. 'He seemed very worldly. He proposed marriage to me practically the first time we met.'

'He always denied that;' she said. 'I asked him many times. "Some strange karma," he used to say, "I don't understand it myself." 'He never wanted to talk about you. I always wanted to meet you and talk to you but it couldn't have happened until he died. I would like to write his life story.'

'I want to write a book about our relationship. It was so extraordinary,' I said slowly. Things out of this world happened. But I don't think anybody could write an ordinary biography about him. He had no kingdom, no court, and no real disciples.'

'No,' she said thoughtfully. 'The only story of the Shabdrung is what he left with us, the marks he left on us. That is his life story. Before he died,' she recalled, 'Rinpoche said, "Whoever has met me, whoever has known me, will never be able to forget me. I will leave a mark on their lives. And after I go they will meet and talk about me. And each of them will have a different story to tell."

I turned to her. 'Now, tell me how he died. I need to know.

'I will tell you,' she said, 'but not now. 'We'll meet again, I am sure of it.'

Thrinley and I continued to meet, unplanned, every day for six days. On the seventh day, I was sitting on my wooden board at the stupa when I saw her approaching. I got up to embrace her. She looked pale in a soft mauve scarf and silk jacket. 'I want to talk to you today,' she said.

The sun was struggling to clear the fog as we walked through the bazaar to my guest-house. In my room the calm was so profound it felt like entering a state of meditation. I made tea, handed the cup to Thrinley, and sat down quietly.

'I'm listening', I said.

CHAPTER 15

DEATH

THE WIFE'S STORY

Thrinley sat cross-legged on the bed and began. 'Before Rinpoche went to Tawang Monastery,[36] we had a very tearful parting. He didn't want to leave me and I didn't want to leave him. The monks must have thought we were behaving like newlyweds. I remember he looked at himself in the mirror and said, "This body is getting so fat and ugly now I think I should change it." I started to cry and asked, 'What do you mean?' He made fun of me. "You're not a little baby; don't cry. Just joking."

'When he came back from Tawang his eyes were very bad. He had double vision and he couldn't move around well, so he stopped exercising. He got very fat. We went to many opticians, changed his glasses many times but it didn't make any difference. Then he got a small lump under his jaw, and he thought the lump was connected with his eyes. We found the name of a specialist hospital in Vellore in South India and decided to go there for tests. Before we went we did a big puja[37] for him at Pedong. At the end of it I sang the dakini song and made offerings, as beautifully as I could. As I was singing, I saw his throne rise

---

[36] in Arunachal Pradesh, NE India

[37] ritual ceremony

into the air with him on it. I was crying so much I could hardly go on. I knew it was a sign. "You should know what it means," he said. "You are khandro[38] – ha ha, ha".

'Then he showed me all his personal things and how to take care of them. He showed me his special phurba[39] and what to do with it. It was a phurba belonging to the first Shabdrung, Ngawang Namgyal.

I was crying all the time. "You're a practitioner," he kept saying, "now is the time you must practice."

'In the hospital we had a very good doctor who had been trained in the UK. He diagnosed it as a very serious cancer behind the eyes in the nasal passages. They started Rinpoche on a program of radiation and chemotherapy. He used to take the pills and laugh. He looked very well, he didn't lose his hair, he lost weight and his face was radiant.

'We were very close during that time. The six months in hospital when he was dying was the happiest time we had together. Before that there were always so many Bhutanese people coming and we were always running here and there. In the hospital there was only Yangchen, and Danuta. We had paid for her ticket to come over, but she spoiled everything. Rinpoche didn't want to think about death and Danuta kept saying, 'Rinpoche, you are dying'. He didn't want to hear it. We were playing games, watching World Cup cricket. "We are here now in the present. Let's enjoy it." Finally we told her to go back. Then we had our only time alone together.

'I slept by his side in the room; I bathed him, took him to the toilet, and checked his urine.

---

[38] dakini or highly evolved spiritual woman

[39] ritual dagger used to subdue enemies

'The doctors told me he had only two months to live. They left it to me to tell him myself. "Two months," he said, "ha ha ha. Let's enjoy them. Turn on the television." He was a warrior.'

'Yes, that's what I felt' I said. 'He was not a Lama, radiating loving kindness and compassion. He was a warrior, fearless and aggressive.'

'There were tankhas[40] in the room of the first Shabdrung Rinpoche and the Medicine Buddha', Thrinley continued. 'He began to do pujas, recite prayers and rest his mind in meditation. One day he couldn't eat the dinner and the next day he vomited up everything, even the medicine. He began to get weak. Then at five in the evening he sat up in the vajra position[41] and went into meditation. One hour, two hours; I left him alone. He was breathing, his pulse was there but his mind was deep in meditation. The doctors tried to bring him out of it but they couldn't.

'At about 10 o'clock at night the doctors called a meeting. What was this strange state? Was it the result of the chemotherapy? They began to consult other doctors and to look in books. They called his name. They touched him, but he didn't respond to anything. I heard him say 'Heeg,' then again 'Heeg,' and a third time, 'Heeg.' He was doing the phowa[42]. At about 5 in the morning he came out of it and we laid him down.

'Some time after that he became conscious. "Come and sit near me, Thrinley Chodron, and say all your prayers. Hold my hand. I feel something has changed in

40 religious paintings on cloth, framed with brocade

41 legs crossed with feet resting on the thighs

42 consciousness transference- a yogic practice in which one ejects the consciousness out of the body

my brain, something I haven't experienced before." I sat beside him saying my prayers.

'When the doctors came they put him on a drip and took him into intensive care where they put him on a respirator and to many other machines. It was a big room with about ten people, all on life support machines.

'Then there was a huge clap of thunder; and a bolt of lightening, and rain began to fall heavily. There hadn't been rain for some years in that place. I went outside and looked at the sky. The clouds and lightening formed a picture and I saw dakinis; perhaps this was a vision I don't know. I passed out. I knew it meant the dakinis were coming to get Rinpoche. The monks caught me and brought me into the room. The machines showed that Rinpoche was improving. They took away the respirator and left him with just a face-mask. They said it would be a risk to remove it; it might cause his heart to go. He wanted to say something to me, but I couldn't take the risk, so they left it on.

'Then I poured my heart out to him. I told him my feelings for him, that he was a great Lama; that I realized he was my Guru. I was crying, and then I looked at him. Two huge teardrops were rolling down his cheeks. Suddenly I remembered the phurba and brought it to him. He held my hand while I put it on his head, and he guided my hand to place it on each of the chakras.

'Soon after that he died. He was lying down on his right side, the same as the Buddha. We took him to our apartment and sat him up in meditation. His face was radiant and peaceful. The monks came and offered white scarves to him. There was a perfume coming from his body. The doctors came and said, "Tomorrow will be very hot, the body will start to smell, we must enbalm him." But we insisted he could not be moved, or anything done to his body. Nothing was done but the next day there was still a perfume coming from his body. The doctors were amazed.

'We wanted to take his body back to his monastery at Pedong; to do that we had to have a certificate of enbalment from the hospital. We had to argue for a long time with the doctor, but finally she said she would make one for us. So we got him onto the plane in a coffin. There were many people and cars waiting for us at the airport.

'In Bhutan there had been an earthquake two days before Rinpoche died and many people heard the sound of the conch shell and other music. When we got to Pedong they again sat him in meditation for the forty-nine days puja. All of Bhutan was there to pay their respects. The kudung[43] will be open for only one more time before they put it into a stupa. I will let you know when that time is.'

I had never heard of even the greatest yogis sitting up in meditative absorption for twelve hours before death. We were both crying. 'We are sisters,' she said. 'Who else is there who can know this whole story?'
Shanti' she said looking at me. 'You know 'shanti'?
I nodded. 'It means peace,'she said. 'It opens the heart.'

****

THE DOCTORS STORY

Vellore, 2003

Dr Subharshani John, head of the cancer ward, sat in her swivel chair in the office of the radiation department at the Christian Medical Hospital in Vellore. Her gold

---

43 enclosure where the body sits in after death meditation

earrings bobbed as she spoke, her red saree staying neatly in place on her broad shoulders.

I braced myself to make the compulsory introduction. 'I was the first wife of the Shabdrung Rinpoche who died here last April,' I said. I met his wife recently and she told me about his death. She said that many things happened that were not ordinary events.'

The doctor looked startled. 'What do you mean?'

'She said he sat up in meditation for a period of twelve hours before he went into intensive care, and nobody could shake him out of it,' I replied.

The doctor shook her head. 'There was a period when he was not responding, and he sat up, and stayed sitting up for awhile; but it was for a short time, certainly not twelve hours,' she said.

'Were you checking at night?' I asked.

'Yes, we do blood pressure checks every few hours on a patient like that,' she explained. 'No one reported that he was sitting up at any point, which they would have to do. It was about 7 pm when we first saw he was unconscious, but his wife said to leave him, that he was sometimes like that when he was meditating. Medically he was unconscious, and lying down. In the morning she was very concerned, "I want an MRI done for him right now," the doctor said imitating Thrinley's haughty tone. I couldn't help but smile. 'The MRI showed some change in the brain, which could have been cancer. We can't be sure because there was no autopsy. After that time, around 7 pm, he never regained consciousness, and never spoke again.' I began to feel concerned about the discrepancies between her reportage and Thrinley's story of miracles.

'Was his wife there at the moment he died?' I asked.

'I am not sure,' Dr John said. 'She was in and out of the intensive care unit. No one can stay all the time in intensive care with a patient. He died of secondary causes, of infection, pneumonia in the lungs.'

'How did he respond when you told him he had only two months to live?'

The doctor looked indignant. 'We never told him that. It's never so clear. It was the other woman, the nurse, who said that.'

'Danuta', I said quietly.

'Yes. She predicted his death, you could say, though there were no signs. You see, he was responding very well to the treatment. He refused the chemotherapy, it didn't agree with him and he didn't want to take it, so he stopped after a few doses. But the radiation therapy was working well. After treatment, he was in good condition, and he even went on holiday to Kerala with his wife.'

'Was there anything unusual about him at all?' I asked as a last hope. Dr John relaxed a bit and smiled.'There was one thing. We didn't know how important he was politically or spiritually in his country. We had no idea, because he didn't act like a VIP. He was very natural, making jokes, laughing, and talking to everyone. His spirits were very good.'

It was difficult to hide my disappointment. I had hoped for a confirmation of miracles, not reports of cheerful behaviour.

I tried again. 'After he died,' I said, 'and they took him back to India, his wife told me that his body did not deteriorate, even though it was not enbalmed. She said there was a perfume coming from it.'

The doctor's smile disappeared. 'But he was enbalmed' she said. 'He could never have left here and travelled without being enbalmed.'

'His wife said that you wanted to enbalm him, but she wouldn't let it be done. Finally because they needed a certificate to travel on the plane, you kindly gave her one anyway.'

'Impossible', Dr John retorted. 'I guarantee you: if an enbalment certificate was issued from this hospital, an enbalment was done.' She had called in another doctor, who had also attended the Shabdrung. They had agreed on every point. Now both nodded their heads forcefully.

'Was there anything unusual about his death?' I asked one more time. 'Anything hard to explain from a medical viewpoint?'

'No, nothing.'

In desperation I asked. 'Was there a thunderstorm around that time?'

'I don't remember anything like that,' Dr John said. 'But it's possible. Thunderstorms do sometimes occur at that time of year.'

'Was there any other doctor in attendance at that time?' I asked, finally.

'Yes. Dr Thomas Samuel, but he left some time ago. I can give you his email.'

I left the hospital feeling empty. How could the stories be so different? Were the doctors afraid to talk about anything unusual for fear it would attract unwanted attention. Perhaps an enbalnment had never been done and the certificate issued anyway. Or was Thrinley simply exaggerating?

Only later did I realize that the unusual thing I'd been seeking was right there in Dr John's words. Being outgoing, caring and happy when you're about to die is hardly a usual condition.

I emailed Dr Samuel immediately, explaining who I was and asking three main questions. 'I would greatly appreciate your help in this matter,' I wrote.

Dear Ms Levine,
Greetings from Padhar Hospital. I would be glad to answer your queries to the best of my knowledge and my memories of Mr.Rimpoche.You posted three questions

Ques 1. Would you be able to tell me if he sat up in a meditative trance for a lengthy period of time (12 hours is what his wife said) before going into intensive care?

Ans: 1 When I was called to see him in the middle of night he appeared to be in deep sleep, his vital signs were stable but he was not responding to any of our stimuli. For a brief moment he sat up on his bed, still appearing to be in deep sleep. He was also briefly seen by one of our General Medicine consultants and was shifted to intensive care the same morning. I cannot comment on whether it was 12 hours.

Ques 2 Did you see him after he died when he was moved to another area? His wife claims that although he had not been enbalmed, his body did not deteriorate during that 3 day period but that there was a perfume coming from it. Can you corroborate any of this? In particular, do you know if the body was enbalmed or not, and when the enbalming was performed?

Ans: 2 After his death his body was taken away to their home in Vellore, apparently for some ritual. When it was brought back, only formalin was injected, without any organ removal, and subsequenlty left in deep freeze. It was again taken to their place of residence (don't remember after how many hours). Dr.John and I visited the home where his body was kept before they left. There were numerous things like chocolates, flowers, etc kept near him, so cannot comment where the fragrance came from.

Ques 3 Do you remember a thunderstorm during this period?

Ans: 3 I am sorry I do not remember any thunder storm. I hope I have answered most of your queries.

Dr. Thomas Samuel

Kathmandu February 2003

It was Tibetan New Year in Kathmandu when Thrinley and I met again. We sat in the kitchen of a friend's home, drinking tea and eating the hard pretzel-shaped biscuits that seem to overflow from every metal container in Tibetan homes at New Year. Thrinley was wearing a silk brocade Tibetan tunic and a soft silk blouse, as befitted the wife of a Lama. 'I have completed all the ceremonies for Rinpoche, as I promised him before he died' she said. 'He could not have picked a better wife.' 'Yes,' I said, and added, 'but it would have been better if he had not married at all. I think he would still be alive.' She stared at me, too shocked to reply.

'I have to tell you' I said carefully, 'I went to Vellore on my way to Trivandrum.'Did you speak to the doctors?' she asked impatiently. 'Yes.' I spoke as objectively as I could, like a journalist filing a report. 'I spoke to Dr John. I tried to find out if she could corroborate any of the miracles you told me about; particularly that Rinpoche sat up in meditation for twelve hours. But both she and another doctor denied it. They said he sat up very briefly, but that there was no period of twelve hours when he was sitting up. They were quite firm about this.'

'Dr John wasn't there all the time;' Thrinley retorted. 'There was a Dr Samuel.'I replied in the same objective tone, that I had contacted Dr Samuel by email, and told her what he had said: that 'Mr Rinpoche' had sat up for a brief moment but he could say nothing about twelve hours.

There had been a discrepancy between the two doctors' testimony about the enbalnment certificate, however, I continued. Dr John insisted he could not have had a certificate without being embalmed – though, I added, that may have been to protect her – but Dr Samuel said only that he had been injected with formalin. 'Still no one could confirm anything miraculous,' I said. 'They didn't even notice the thunderstorm.'

Thrinley listened in amazement. 'But they were so inspired by his death they said they would write down everything for me! I didn't insist at the time because I was still in shock. Why would I lie?' she asked with utter candour. 'Perhaps you're not lying.' I said diplomatically. 'Maybe it's your cultural reality.' She looked bewildered. 'You should talk to Sonam Dorje', she said at length. He's the Shabdrung's head monk and he was there. He can tell you what he saw.'

THE MONK'S TALE

Bodh Gaya, December 2004

Sonam Dorje looked the picture of a perfect monk: neat and pleasant, intelligent and methodical. We sat in the sun on the lawn beside the Shabdrung's residence, while he recalled the last hours of his master's life. His devotion to the Shabdrung was clear, but his account was precise and unemotional.

At eight o'clock one night Rinpoche refused to take his medicine or open his mouth to eat. He was staring straight ahead and not speaking. Many doctors came, but they couldn't make him respond. 'For a couple of hours in the middle of the night, he was going like this,' Sonam Dorje teetered on his chair, 'then he would sit upright again,' he said. 'He had his faculties, because he kept falling down, then sitting up again. Both he and Thrinley tried to make him lie down, shouting, "Please, Rinpoche, sleep, you are tired." Sometimes he slept, and again he would sit up. 'Afterwards we realised we had made a great mistake because we forced him to lie down and we regretted it,' he said.

Finally they all went to sleep. Around four or five o'clock in the morning a nurse came and told them Rinpoche shouldn't sleep too much. When they tried to wake him up, he was unconscious. He was taken into intensive care where they did an MRI scan. At first they couldn't find anything. Finally the doctor told them that the cancer cells had reached the brain. That night, the fourth of April, the doctor reported that the patient was improving. 'Rinpoche opened his eyes and looked at me; then he closed his eyes,' said Sonam Dorje. But within a very short time they had to reconnect the tubes. The doctors said, "He will not live long. If you want to inform anybody, do so now." In the late afternoon a black cloud came and there was a very heavy storm.

The Khenpo from Bhutan arrived around nine o'clock at night, together with friends, family and sponsors. They all went inside the ICU and offered white scarves. Rinpoche was lying down, one hand tied to the bed so that he couldn't get up. After about ten minutes, he died. 'He was just waiting for Khenpo', Sonam Dorje said. The doctor told them they could take the body out of the hospital to their house, an unusual permission.

Next morning the District Officer from Vellore came. He used to come almost every week to see Rinpoche, because there were very strict orders from the External Affairs Ministry of the Indian Government to watch over him. He offered flowers and told them they had to do the enbalnment according to Indian law. But when it came to incisions, they were adamant. They refused to allow his body to be cut open. It was agreed that the doctor would give a formalin injection only, and then they could take the body. 'The doctor told us this medicine will only last one or two days, so you will have a very big problem on the way because of the smell. We said, "We are taking the risk; if anything happens we are responsible." Sonam Dorje accompanied the body to the operating theatre. In front of my eyes they put in some injection.

'When we were taking his body from Vellore to the airport at Chennai, for the whole journey there was a rainbow around the sun. It started at 11 or 12 o'clock, and our flight was at one o'clock. Even in Bhutan people could see it,' said the head monk. 'When we reached Calcutta we stayed in a guesthouse. Some Bhutanese doctors came and spent the night with Rinpoche's body. In the morning they told us they had heard the sound of very beautiful music. They asked if we had been doing a puja, but we hadn't. "But we heard the sounds of instruments!" they said. 'These unusual things happened many times in Rinpoche's life.'

'When we got him to his monastery at Pedong, we took him out of the coffin, gave him a bath, and put him in the sitting position. We started doing our puja. One day, two days three days – his body did not smell. We felt his chest and it was very warm. To this day there are three or four people checking his body almost every month. We just clean him gently; sometimes in the summer – because Pedong is very damp- there is mould, but there is no rotting, no smell. He remains inside his residence. It's not airtight, but it's as if it were airtight. He is still sitting upright; even now his head is not dropping. There is no support. We just sat him in meditation position, and he stayed there. This is very unusual. There is no medicine that can preserve a body like this. His face is painted gold, but his body is shrivelling. We will build a proper stupa for him and move him there. Then it will be possible to have an audience with him.'

After all the conflicting stories of Jigmai's death, this was the miracle that convinced me. I remembered the biography of the first Shabdrung, Ngawang Namgyal: the mystery surrounding the length of his supreme death meditation – this was the same mystery.

The head monk was continuing his narrative. 'When we reached Pedong there was a big clap of thunder. Everybody heard, and understood. "Thundering dragon," I remembered Jigmai saying. "That's what Bhutan means."

I understood too. It was a sign: the land of Bhutan was bearing witness to the passing of its spiritual king.

Act Five

We are such stuff
As dreams are made on, and our little life
Is rounded with a sleep.
(Shakespeare, The Tempest)

CHAPTER 16

REINCARNATION

Bodh Gaya, December 28, 2004

Basant, the manager of the Shabdrung's travel agency in Delhi, drank in my bittersweet memories of Jigmai's wild youth like nectar. 'You had what I wish I'd had,' he said to me wistfully. He couldn't know, of course, how the drops of blood splattering the LOVE letter Jigmai had sent at the start of our relationship were prophetic of what it would become – a painful rupture etched in blood.

A few days after hearing the story of the Shabdrung's death from Sonam Dorje, Basant and I met unexpectedly in Bodh Gaya. As we were talking, two monks from the Shabdrung's Institute walked in, came straight to Basant and started talking in eager hushed tones. I excused myself and went to my hotel next door.

Within half an hour Basant came to my room. His eyes were glowing as he looked intensely at me. I thought I heard his heart thumping. Then he spoke. 'The reincarnation of our Rinpoche, the Shabdrung, is arriving tomorrow morning, very early. They had to get him out of Bhutan before we could speak.'

My mind reeled. Could it be true? Could the great Shabdrung and the man who had caused me so much joy and anguish, be back in the world? 'But how has he managed to incarnate so quickly?' I cried. 'It isn't possible.

Jigmai died only one year and eight months ago. How old is the child?' 'One year and one month,' said Basant proudly. 'But that's not even enough time to be in the womb for nine months!'I said. 'Maybe he emanated before he died,' Basant said mysteriously.

I had heard about Tibetan masters whose powers were so great they could project an aspect of their consciousness into a womb even before their own death. Could Jigmai have done that? 'Ask Sonam Dorje tomorrow,' said Basant. 'He can give you all the details.'

I sat stunned, letting the hum of excitement surround me. I couldn't digest this new twist in the story. It was hard enough to accept that Jigmai had transformed into the Shabdrung at his death. I didn't realise I would have to accept his return as well.

That night I had a clear dream. I was sorting through Jigmai's love letters when I noticed something strange. A big dried up turd lay amongst the letters. I felt confused, wondering what to do with it, when Jigmai appeared. He looked at the turd, picked it up and threw it away. 'Aha', I thought, 'that's what to do with it.' I awoke feeling relieved and grateful

At eight o'clock next morning, I arrived at the Institute. 'Who recognised the child as the incarnation of the Shabdrung?' I asked Sonam Dorje. 'Karmapa', he replied immediately. 'He wrote everything down and our oracle drew a map to show where he was.' I was silent. Karmapa didn't make mistakes. 'And how old is the child?' I asked. 'One year and one month.' He saw my puzzled expression and confirmed Basant's explanation. 'Shabdrung must have emanated while he was still alive, in hospital,' he said.

We were shown into the Shabdrung's quarters, a bare room with a bed and carpets. A small child with bright eyes and milk white skin was propped up beside his mother, a young woman who seemed to be in a state of grace. A gentle looking man was standing nearby in Bhutanese dress: clearly the father. A Danish nun went in first and offered her scarf. The child received it in silence.

I was next. I placed my scarf on the table and looked him in the eye. Instantly he stopped being a child. He looked back at me with an intense, direct stare, which he held for a significant time. Then he threw his ball eagerly at me. It fell on the floor. I picked it up and placed it in his lap. He threw it again. I picked it up again, put it back in his lap and looked at him. He stared penetratingly at me for a very long moment. I met his gaze and smiled. With the others who came after me, he turned into a small baby, squirming and crying. 'You are the one he recognised,' they all said excitedly, as we gathered outside the room.

I began to look at the drama unfolding round me as though watching the last act of a play when all the characters assemble for the finale. First the two lovers in their new forms: one older and wiser, the other reincarned as a young baby but remembering his past life. And now I saw Yangchen, the sister, come to join the cast.

Her face was the same as that of the mischievous young girl I remembered so many years ago. We hugged with joy. 'You look the same,' she said as she introduced me to her husband, a young man in Bhutanese dress called Sherpa Dorje. Her two sons were standing beside her. One, who was dressed as a monk, had been recognised as a reincarnate lama.

Sonam Dorje then took us on a tour of the temple. I gazed around from the marble floor to the high vaulted ceilings. Since I'd last been there, the shrine room had been exquisitely decorated, lavished with intricate sculpting, and painted. 'It must have been difficult for

Rinpoche to achieve all this, when he wasn't a monk,' I remarked. 'He tried to become one several times,' Sonam Dorje replied. 'He went to the Dalai Lama and asked for ordination, but the Dalai Lama told him he had to have a special one for his lineage, which he could only get from the head Lama in Bhutan. We invited the Je Khenpo in '92 and '93. Both times the government of Bhutan objected. After that I think Rinpoche lost hope.'

Once again my image of Jigmai shifted. 'You think he sincerely wanted to become a monk?' I asked. Sonam Dorje reflected for a moment. "Yes. After we started the monastery project he changed. Before, he never used to bother about spiritual things; he always used to go to the clubhouse to play snooker, ping-pong, or football. It's sad', he said thoughtfully. 'I wish you had seen it. Rinpoche had changed.'

As he spoke he ushered us into another room. There, alone on a sofa, bundled in Bhutanese cloth, was Jigmai's old mother, looking only slightly more wizened than when we had last met, twenty years before. I sat down beside her and held her hand, hoping she would recognize me, in spite of her mental deterioration. We had shared laughter, tears, midnight meals and countless bottles of old monk rum. Finally she spoke. 'She tells me you had some meals together,' said Sonam Dorje.

Outside the residence, devotees continued to arrive. The overhanging branch of a willow gave partial shade from the bright midday sun. 'Now, tell me how the Shabdrung was recognised,' I requested Sonam Dorje. He called the abbot of the monastery, the Khenpo, who took us to a private room upstairs. I looked at the many pictures on the wall of the Shabdrung, and became intrigued by two of them. In one he was radiant and vigorous; in the other he looked twenty years older, although they were taken only three years apart.

The Khenpo described the search for the Shabdrung in such detail I became completely absorbed in the drama. I could barely contain my excitement when he produced the documents showing the clues like a treasure hunt and how they unravelled into the discovery of a child with the outline of a dragon on his back. The full story cannot be disclosed at this time, but the Karmapa confirmed unequivocally that he had indeed recognised the Shabdrung.

CHAPTER 17

SACRED LOVE

I took a motor rickshaw to the Institute early the next afternoon. The baby Shabdrung was in the arms of an adoring monk on the pathway to the garden, where several chairs had been placed in the sun. I asked the monk, 'Does Rinpoche give blessing?' He said something in Bhutanese to the child, who immediately stretched out his tiny hand and tapped me perfectly on the front of my head. He pulled out some petals from the flower he was holding in his hands and placed them delicately on my head. I held out my prayer beads and he touched them, rolling them momentarily with his fingers. I felt the same relief and certainty as I had when waking from my dream.

Sonam Dorje sat beside me in the sun. 'This morning we went to Karmapa for the hair-cutting ceremony, purification, and name-giving,' he said. Karma Mipham Jigdrel Ngawang Namgyal: Fearless Ngawang Namgyal was the name given by Karmapa to the 10th Shabdrung.

'What level was the Shabdrung?' I asked suddenly, moved by the blessing I had just received from a one-year old child. 'Tenth level. Same as Karmapa and the Dalai Lama. There are only a few.' 'Of course I knew that is what he was supposed to be,' I replied. 'But his behaviour was so radically unconventional. He didn't want to be a Lama. He wouldn't let us call him Rinpoche; he didn't want to teach the dharma. I wanted the dharma, the Lama and tantric teachings. But he didn't. He wanted a worldly relationship. "Call me Jigmai," he said. So I did. I gave him what he wanted.'

'That **is** dharma', said Sonam Dorje looking at me firmly.

'I knew Rinpoche at the period where he had very little spiritual guidance; almost none,' I said, 'and many of his actions were extremely shocking to me. Some people said he was a crazy yogi.'

'He was a great yogi,' Sonam Dorje said. 'The buddhas come in different forms. Their buddha nature is beyond our imagination. He was like that.'

'Very often I thought he was acting from confusion, not from compassion and wisdom,' I confessed.

'I stayed with him for 13 years,' Sonam Dorje replied. 'I found him very compassionate and generous. With a real dharma practitioner, the most important thing is not the action but the motivation. He used to scold me, sometimes beat me. But that was to help me. I have learned many things being with him.'

What had I learned? I wondered. At the very beginning I had felt that Jigmai was a character looking for an author. I had become one of his authors. I had created a solid personality for a man who was in reality a chimera, appearing as an ordinary worldly man. Like the lover who comes at night and leaves before dawn, so that the princess never sees his face, I had never seen his human face, because he didn't have one. He was a mirror reflecting my own face. Our story was really my story. I could see the primitive figures on the rim of the Wheel of Life craving and grasping like mechanical toys, and it all made sense: Mingyur Rinpoche's long-ago analogy of the moon reflected on water.

For twenty-three years I'd been trying to understand that story. Now at last I knew. The lesson that Jigmai had taught me was that attachment is pain. It wasn't about tantric sex or bliss, showers of flowers or magnificent rainbows. It was about the fact that the cause of suffering is desire, and the cause of desire is grasping and craving. In all my longing to attain higher states of meditation, I'd forgotten the first and most basic Buddhist truth. Attachment is suffering.

A monk came and invited us upstairs to have tea with the Khenpo. He was in an expansive mood and probed me gently about my relationship with the Shabdrung. Finally I told him we frequently made love 'in the ordinary way'. He looked at me with interest. 'You may have felt that, but Rinpoche may not. They may do the same as ordinary people, but in reality they have that power to control their energy. For someone like that, it is not necessary to show tantric female and male sex. If our Rinpoche did that, it is of great benefit for you.'

'Well he did - many times.'

We all laughed. 'That is a priceless thing. I'm not saying this about every Lama but with Shabdrung, yes.'

I decided to tell all and go for the punch-line. He said, "Darling, you got my fresh cock, the girls in Bhutan would die for that."

The Khenpo exploded with laughter. 'You are one of the luckiest people in the world', he said and paused. 'Why did you not marry?' I told him our story briefly and at the end, for the first time, I was smiling.

Then I remembered something else. 'At the very beginning, he sent me a letter with the word LOVE written in his own blood, so that I would never forget his love for me. There were large splotches of blood all around it too,' I said, remembering the page. 'You still have that letter?' the Khenpo asked excitedly.'Yes,' I replied. 'I keep it in a drawer.''Take it out, and frame it in a gold case,' he said. 'And please' – his voice filled with devotion- 'please, when you die, leave it to us in your will. It's a sacred relic.' I promised I would.

And finally I understood: Jigmai had given me the sacred love I was looking for from the start. It had been with me all the time. 'You have suffered a lot but you have received a great blessing,' the Khenpo confirmed.

****

When the time came to leave Bodh Gaya, I wanted to make a final offering to the young Shabdrung. I picked out a garland of marigolds, like the ones worn at Indian weddings and offered at Hindu temples. Then a young boy appeared in front of me selling white lotus flowers. By mid-day they had begun to wilt, but I picked the freshest, and jumped into a rickshaw. It was the third day the new incarnation had been in Bodh Gaya and large groups of Tibetans and Bhutanese were queuing to receive blessing from him. I sat beside his mother on the lawn admiring the dazzling white radiance of her skin. 'Did you have any dreams or signs when you were pregnant?' I asked. 'The night before Rinpoche was born,' she replied simply, 'I dreamt I saw a child with milk white skin sitting next to Guru Rinpoche.'

Sherpa Dorje, Yangchen's husband, joined us. The huge influx of visitors, he said, had tired the young Rinpoche and he was sleeping. While we waited he spoke, measuring his words carefully about the Shabdrung's marriage, as if he wanted me to know something. 'We asked the oracle in Bhutan whether Shabdrung should marry. The oracle said 'no', but Shabdrung was defiant. He said, "It's too late now." But he told me he was not happy, that he was very frustrated.' I remembered Basant telling me how quickly Shabrung had aged after his marriage and recalled the photos I had seen yesterday. I sat pondering this latest clue. The oracle confirmed the importance of Guruji's dying wish, and my own intuition. Jigmai was not meant to marry Thrinley, or me; he was not meant to marry anyone.

A picture came into my mind of him sitting in the sun outside Scenic Cottage in Manali, absorbed in a chess game. And now the last pieces of the puzzle fell into place: Jigmai's whole life was a game of chess with the King of Bhutan: when he sought ordination, the King blocked it because as a monk he would be a greater threat to the throne. So finally Jigmai married, losing his last chance to take back Bhutan. And when, in 1987, the King had challenged him to prove he was the true incarnation of Ngawang Namgyal there was only one way left: he had to die. He always said the true proof of a Lama's greatness was his mastery over death. He looked at the chessboard, and made his move. A new incarnation could start afresh. Jigmai picked his successor, and chose his time to die. Checkmate.

I sat in the sun feeling the lightness of being wholly in the present. Everything seemed bathed in stillness, resting undisturbed, just as it was. Jigmai had left behind so many stories, distinct but blending like the colours of a rainbow, and just as insubstantial. Thrinley, Sonam Dorje, Will, Danuta, and I … we each had a different story to tell.

A monk came and told me the young Shabdrung had awakened. I entered his room and bowing, placed the garland of marigolds around his neck. It seemed to irritate him; he pulled it off. I was left with the white lotus, the perfect flower that grows from mud, as enlightenment grows from ignorance. As I looked into the fresh young face of the child, I knew what to do. I knelt down before him, as he held out both hands to receive the white lotus.

EPILOGUE

"All composed things are like a dream,
a phantom, a drop of dew, a flash of lightning.
That is how to meditate on them,
That is how to observe them." (The Buddha)

The body of the Shabdrung, though clinically dead for three years, was sitting upright without any support in the meditation posture, his head tilting to the right. There was still flesh on his face; his beard was black. I had come thousands of miles to his monastery in Kalimpong on the Indian side of the border with Bhutan to see this phenomenon for myself. It defied all the terms used to describe a dead body. It was not a corpse, mummy or skeleton; nor was it any of the words to describe a representation: not an effigy, waxworks, or statue. It was a body in suspended animation between life and death.

I stared long and hard at the face trying to recognise Jigmai while Sonam Dorje stood beside me explaining the transformation. The eyes, which were mostly water, had dried up so they had put herbs inside the sockets and painted them. The lips were also painted with herbs, in a soft pink colour. Although he had died with a smiling face, his lips were now drooping because the doctors had to extract some teeth during radiation. His hair was mostly black underneath the brocade blue cap and his beard had not changed at all. Nor had his nails hardened. The skin around the chest area was almost like normal skin, he said.

You could pinch it, and he didn't know whether he was imagining it or not but it felt warm. The skin on the arms, legs and stomach was drying and hardening; in some places it pinched into pleats. For the first year he had been flexible, now the joints were hardening.

The body was now called Machen – Great Mother. He was adorned with a blue brocade cap, his face was painted gold, and a gold silk cloth covered a white slip over his naked body.

The decorated enclosure had an outer shrine with water bowls and offerings in front of a glass window. The top of the outer ceremonial box was covered in gauze allowing the air to circulate; only the lower part was wood. The inner sanctum where the Machen was sitting on a platform inside a niche also had a shelf displaying shrine bowls and offerings wrapped in silver paper. There were three statues of the first Shabdrung Ngawang Namgyal: one large and two smaller ones and a photo of the Shabdrung before he died. Behind these representations sat the extraordinary display of the Machen in meditation. I noticed a facial resemblance between all of them, almost like a family likeness. Small Buddha tankhas hung in a row across the upper part of the inner sanctum where no one, except seven appointed monks who had been with him during and after his death, was allowed to enter.

I asked permission to put my head inside the inner chamber where he was sitting and sniffed keenly to pick up a smell. There was something quite distinct – a fresh clear fragrance, though no incense was burning. A phrase usually used ironically flashed through my mind. 'The odour of sanctity.' It was as if life had stopped but the process of death had not taken over.

'It shows that there is no death,' said Sonam Dorje, 'no big boundary between death and life. This is beyond our explanation. It shows the actual truth of Buddhism. There is no birth, no death.'

I remembered the Buddha's words in the Prajnaparamita, the Sutra on Transcendent Wisdom:

> All things are empty:
> Nothing is born, nothing dies,
> nothing is pure, nothing is stained,
> nothing increases and nothing decreases. ...
>
> There is no ignorance,
> and no end to ignorance.
> There is no old age and death,
> and no end to old age and death.
> There is no suffering, no cause of suffering,
> no end to suffering, no path to follow.
>
> There is no attainment of wisdom,
> and no wisdom to attain.
> The Bodhisattvas rely on the Perfection of Wisdom,
> and so with no delusions,
> they feel no fear,
> and have Nirvana here and now. ...
>
> The Perfection of Wisdom is the greatest mantra.
> It is the clearest mantra,
> the highest mantra,
> the mantra that removes all suffering.

This is truth that cannot be doubted.
Say it so:

> Gaté,
> gaté,
> paragaté,
> parasamgaté.
> Bodhi!
> Svaha!

Which means...

Gone,
gone,
gone over,
gone fully over.
Awakened!
So be it!

I sat looking at the inner sanctum, enclosed by a curtain on each side, through the outer front window. The plastic flowers and twinkling lights that flashed on and off highlighting the face, reminded me of a carnival. Soon all thoughts and associations disappeared, and I felt a fine presence, a sense of deep peace.

I began to talk in a low voice to someone I called Jigmai, although the face I was staring was beyond name and identity with just a subtle part of existence remaining.

'Do you know I am here?' I asked. I travelled for three days to see you one last time before you disappear from sight and become a legend. When you were alive, I never recognized you. I thought you were wild and crazy. We had a big drama together: history, romance, comedy, tragedy, and now transcendence. All vanished, like a dream. Do you remember the letter you gave me with LOVE written in blood from your own hand? I've had it all these years but now I've taken it out of my drawer and framed it. Eternal love.'

'At last I can see you're really the Shabdrung. Your death proves it beyond a doubt. You had the same death as Ngawang Namgyal. It's sad you could not show your greatness during your life, but the people whose lives you touched will never forget you.'

The Bhutanese came and went, offering scarves, prostrating, and like me, watching the Machen, mesmerised. A monk came in carrying a tray of food which he placed on the shrine as he would every day four times a day – serving the Machen breakfast, lunch, tea, and dinner. The Chamberlain conducted a brief ritual chant each time food was offered, banging his large drum and ringing his bell at the final service. Then the Cook removed the tray and offered it to the assembled Bhutanese as blessing. I held my hand out to receive the rice and dark tea.

A young Bhutanese girl came to me and asked, 'Did you know the Shabdrung?' 'Yes,' I replied. I was his intimate companion for many years.' I hesitated. 'I was the woman he loved.' She came closer and looked at me her eyes glowing. 'You are very lucky,' she whispered, touching my hand. I nodded and held her gaze for a moment. There had been no ring binding us, just the power of love. How wonderful!

At 5:30 I was still sitting on the floor beside the Machen when the Chamberlain came in to empty the water bowls and close the shrine for the day. He took a white offering scarf and tilted it towards the Machen as if to catch a ray of light from the body, then he put it around my neck. He closed the curtains on either side of the box, drew the one in front, and turned off the twinkling lights like a stage manager closing a miniature theatre. The neither-death-nor-life display that had no explanation, no accompanying name-tag, disappeared from sight. In one week, the day of the Buddha's birth, enlightenment and parinirvana, it would be moved into a memorial stupa where it would sit forever.

Acknowledgments

I would like to acknowledge with deepest gratitude the people who made invaluable editing comments:

Shri Dharmakirti, Carole Angier, Mick Brown, Jessica Woollard.

And those who provided invaluable information: Sonam Dorje, and the Khenpo of Druk Ngawang Thubten Choling, Khandro Thrinley Chodron, and Dr. Subarshani John.

Most of all I wish to acknowledge the blessing and guidance of His Holiness the 17th Gyalwang Karmapa, Ogyen Trinley Dorje.